Janner's Practical Guide to
The Employment Act, 1980
— industrial relations and
employment law

COMMON LAW
EQUITY
CASE REPORTS
STATUTES 1800-1980
PRECEDENTS
JANNER'S EMPLOYMENT ACT
toki

GREVILLE JANNER

Janner's Practical Guide to *The Employment Act, 1980*
— industrial relations and employment law

Illustrations by Tobi

BUSINESS BOOKS
London Melbourne Sydney Auckland Johannesburg

Business Books Ltd
An imprint of the Hutchinson Publishing Group
24 Highbury Crescent, London N5 1RX

Hutchinson Group (Australia) Pty Ltd
30–32 Cremorne Street, Richmond South, Victoria 3121
PO Box 151, Broadway, New South Wales 2007

Hutchinson Group (NZ) Ltd
32–34 View Road, PO Box 40–086, Glenfield, Auckland 10

Hutchinson Group (SA) (Pty) Ltd
PO Box 337, Bergvlei 2012, South Africa

First published 1980
Reprinted 1981

© GREVILLE JANNER, 1980

Photoset in 11 on 12 point Times

Printed in Great Britain by The Anchor Press Ltd
and bound by Wm Brendon & Son Ltd,
both of Tiptree, Essex

British Library Cataloguing in Publication Data
Janner, Greville
   Janner's practical guide to the Employment
Act, 1980.
   1. Great Britain. Laws, statutes, etc.
     (Individual titles). Employment Act 1980
   2. Labour laws and legislation — Great Britain
   I. Practical guide to the Employment Act 1980
   344'.41'011   KD3004.5/

ISBN 0 09 142990 0

For
Marianne and Victor Keats

OTHER BOOKS BY GREVILLE JANNER, QC, MP
(EWAN MITCHELL) INCLUDE:

Janner's Compendium of Employment Law
Janner's Employment Forms
Janner's Product Liability
The Employer's and Personnel Manager's Handbook of Draft Letters of Employment Law
The Employer's Guide to the Law on Health, Safety and Welfare at Work
The Director's and Company Secretary's Handbook of Draft Legal Letters
The Director's and Company Secretary's Handbook of Draft Contract Letters
The Caterer's Lawyer and Restaurateur's Legal Guide
The Retailer's Lawyer
The Sales Executive's Lawyer and Businessman's Guide to the Laws of Buying and Selling
The Business and Professional Man's Lawyer
The Businessman's Guide to Letter-writing and to the Law on Letters
The Businessman's Guide to Speech-making and to the Laws and Conduct of Meetings
The Director's Lawyer and Company Secretary's Legal Guide
The Lawyer and His World
Farming and the Law
You and the Law
Your Property and the Law and Investor's Legal Guide
Coping with Crime — the businessman's guide to dealing with stealing, spying, fraud, false trade descriptions and other common commercial crimes
The Businessman's Legal Lexicon
The Employer's Lawyer
The Businessman's Guide to Travel
The Businessman's Guide to Commercial Conduct and the Law
The Transport Manager's Lawyer and Transport Operator's Legal Guide
RAC Motorist's Lawyer

Contents

Introduction   xi

Part One   Individual rights and protection

Chapter 1 Introduction   3
          2 Appointment and dismissal — introduction   5
          3 When is an employee 'dismissed'?   7
          4 Unfair and wrongful 'dismissal'   10
          5 'Misconduct' — and summary dismissal   14
          6 Remedies for wrongful dismissal   16
          7 When is a dismissal 'constructive'?   18
          8 Unfair dismissal — the new rules   20
          9 The burden of proof — a summary   24
         10 Fixed-term contracts   26
         11 Written reasons   28
         12 Redundancies   30
         13 Maternity rights, old and new   34
         14 Maternity notices   38
         15 Guarantee pay   40
         16 Discrimination   42

Part Two   Trade union, collective and corporate rights

Chapter 17 Introduction   49
          18 The background   52
          19 Industrial relations law — a quick guide   54

20	Laws, regulations and codes	57
21	'Independent' trade unions	59
22	When is a union 'recognised'?	61
23	Recognition procedures	63
24	Fair wages and 'recognised' and 'comparable' terms	67
25	Collective bargaining, disclosure of information and worker participation	69
26	Secret ballots and union procedures	72
27	Time off work — and union elections	75
28	Union membership agreements and closed shops	80
29	Closed shops — the new rules	83
30	Future closed shops	86
31	Dismissing the 'free rider'	88
32	Picketing — in law and in practice	91
33	Picketing and secondary action — the new rules	94
34	Trade union immunities — and further legislation?	98
35	'Unreasonable exclusion or expulsion'	100
36	Indemnities from unions	105
37	Trade unions, courts and lawyers	108
38	All the best — from ACAS	111
39	Conciliation and arbitration	115
40	EEC industrial relations law	118
41	A martyr's charter?	120

Part Three   Appendices

Appendix	1	*The Employment Act, 1980* — a summary	127
	2	*The Employment Act, 1980*	135
	3	Extracts from *The Trade Union and Labour Relations Act, 1974* (as amended)	166
	4	Extracts from *The Employment Protection Act, 1975*	178
	5	Extracts from *The Employment Protection (Consolidation) Act, 1978* (as amended)	186

Contents ix

6	Extracts from *The Companies Act, 1980*	220
7	Extracts from ACAS Code of Practice: *Disciplinary Practice and Procedures in Employment*	223
8	Extracts from ACAS Code of Practice: *Disclosure of Information to Trade Unions for Collective Bargaining Purposes*	227
9	Extracts from ACAS Code of Practice: *Time Off for Trade Union Duties and Activities*	231
10	'TUC disputes, principles and procedures' — a summary	237
11	New employment forms	238
12	Help! — where to get advice	241
13	Draft Code of Practice on Picketing	243
14	Draft Code of Practice on the Closed Shop	258

Index 277

The final Codes of Practice on Picketing and the Closed Shop are now reproduced in appendices 13 and 14 (replacing the Draft Codes in the first printing of this book). Elsewhere in the text please read Final Code instead of Draft Code and ignore the comments under 'Commencement dates' p. xv. Pages affected are: ix, xv, 58, 87, 94, 276 and 277.

Introduction

In law as in life, you cannot always judge impact by size. *The Employment Act, 1980*, is cunningly contrived, politically powerful and potentially devastating in its industrial effects. The fact that it is only a fraction of the length of the Industrial Relations Act should deceive no one. Every manager must appreciate its impact and understand not only what it says but also what it means — for management and especially for those trade unions with which he deals. He must not only appreciate the legal meaning of its words but also and especially how he can cope with its effects.

The personnel or industrial relations executive or manager must also slot this new Parliamentary emanation into his own perspective among the plethora of recent statutes and court decisions. Most of these have descended upon us since 1971. Some affect the individual employee's protection at law; others the rights and remedies of workers' organisations; some both. Some affect the executive or manager as an employer's representative; some provide him with the protection that he may need more than those whose working lives he controls. They may be protected by the strong arm of the trade union; he is not.

Either way, it is not enough to know what the law says that you may do to your employees. You must also consider the industrial relations implications of exercising your powers. Failure to take those implications fully into account may be a prelude to industrial catastrophe.

For instance: under the new Act, you become entitled to seek an indemnity from a trade union which induces you to dismiss an employee who lawfully opts out of a closed shop, by calling or threatening industrial action. Exercise that right and two results are likely. First: you will win your case and probably receive your indemnity. Second: you will also win the undying enmity of that union — which may refuse to obey the Court's order.

What will you do then? Will you go back to the Court and seek to have the order enforced? Will you try to have the money removed from the union's bank account? If so, then will the union not exercise the power which it still holds, to grind your business to a lurching halt?

Or take the law on picketing. Theoretically, the new Act strengthens the hand of the police and of the employer in preventing secondary picketing and blacking. But should *you* make use of your new power? Will the Government seek to prod the police into taking action? Or would the use of the new power make matters worse?

Trade union leaders have described the new Act as a 'martyr's charter'. They say that the exercise of the new powers on (for instance) picketing, provides an open invitation to those who wish to flout the law and who hope to be imprisoned as a result. Are they right?

It is not enough, then, for you to know what the law says. You must also consider in each case how it is likely to operate. In any industrial situation you must look to the powers given to you and to the likely industrial results of their exercise. You must anxiously examine the options open to you, before you decide how to act — or, indeed, whether it may not be wiser neither to act nor to react.

So this book has a double purpose. It is designed to explain in detail the meaning of the new law, in the context of the old. And it also seeks to explain the practical implications of that law, for the practical executive or manager who must cope with its effect.

It is comparatively easy to outline the law and to explain its meaning. Legal jargon, after all, is a form of shorthand through which experts express ideas in a form comprehensible to them. Every trade or profession uses jargon. Legal shorthand is just more complicated and more hideous than most. But to put the words into plain English and to explain their meaning requires the combined art of lawyer and writer.

The major problem comes when you try to analyse how the

Introduction xiii

new rules are likely to operate in practice. If you act in a particular way how will the unions react? Is a particular new rule likely to bring industrial peace, or to create havoc? Will a new Section live in theory but die in practice? The old (and by common consent, unsatisfactory) rules on the recognition of trade unions have been abolished. They are not replaced. So what will happen?

Theoretically, new 'approved' closed shops may lawfully arise, where enough employees secretly vote in their favour. But are the restrictions not in fact so great that 'union membership agreements' (as they are properly called) are more likely to be informal than formal, and if so then will they be effective?

If an employee 'genuinely' objects on grounds of 'conscience or other deeply held personal conviction' to belonging to 'any trade union whatsoever or to a particular trade union', he may opt out of a closed-shop arrangement. If he does so and if the union objects, what happens then? Do you make use of the powers given to you by the new Act? Or do you co-operate with the union as best you can and take the legal consequences?

These are the questions of practical people, deeply involved in industrial relations. Their answer requires not merely legal knowledge but also industrial relations experience — and often, political shrewdness and a touch of prophetic vision. In each case, the law may be a matter of explainable fact; preparation and how to cope with it is strictly a matter of opinion.

In this book, I shall don my QC's wig and do my best to explain the *meaning* of the rules, new and old — with special emphasis on the 1980 Act. As to the *effect* of the law and the way of handling it, I shall give you the benefit of my well considered bias. To be a lawyer (in the eyes of the public) is bad enough; to be a politician is worse; to be a lawyer politician is the ultimate in wickedness — unless, of course, you happen to need his help. At that stage, the combination of legal knowledge and political cunning may provide your sole hope of industrial salvation.

So I make no apology whatever for adding to the bleak legal explanation the dimension of political assessment and colour. Whether or not you agree with my views is a matter for you — this is a free country and you are entitled to be wrong! What does matter, though, is that you should regard the law — and particularly that area of law which deals with industrial and personnel relations — as providing a weapon which (like any other) must be used with discretion and with discrimination. It provides a background to your work; a framework for your relations with your workforce, individually and collectively; a basis for your own rights and remedies and those of the people who work for and with you; a creation of Parliament and of the Courts, which — like all other human effort — is not only fallible but certain to fail if operated otherwise than with common sense and with uncommon care and understanding.

I hope, then, that this book will be both readable and read; that it will provide a lucid explanation of industrial relations law in general and of the new Act in particular, in a form that is tolerably bearable and bearably tolerable. The fact that I believe that so many of the provisions in the new Act are misguided no more frees me from the duty of explaining them than it can protect you from the need to cope with them.

I hope that this book will also help you to keep out of trouble and (especially) away from courts and tribunals. Where trouble cannot be avoided, then I hope that it will keep it to a minimum. At worst, you should at least recognise your mistakes after you have committed them. It should also help you to know when to go to a lawyer, before it is too late for him to help you.

To a large extent, this book supplements my *Compendium of Employment Law*. Whilst providing a complete analysis and explanation of the new law and while putting it into the context of existing employment protection rules, both individual and collective, it does not cover the same breadth as the *Compendium*. Nor, of course, does it more than touch on the area dealt with in my *Employer's Guide to the Law on Health and Safety at Work*. As to the precedents contained in my *Employment Forms*, these remain largely unchanged, but that book now includes a 'Stop Press' setting out any alterations in the text. Additional forms made necessary by the new Act are included as Appendix 10 to this book, as well as in the Supplement to my *Employment Forms*.

* * *

In preparing this book both for reading and for reference, I

Introduction xv

have been greatly helped by many people. My especial thanks to Rt Hon. Harold Walker, MP; to Prof. Peter Wallington of Lancaster University; to Mr Paul Secher, LLB and to Miss Kathy McLeod, LLB; to my son, Mr Daniel Janner, BA (Cantab.), Barrister; to my wife; to Mr David Roth and to my secretaries, Mrs Pat Garner and Mrs Margaret Lancaster. Each has contributed to the usefulness and accuracy of this work. The opinions and any errors are my own.

Finally: I have greatly appreciated the perennial courtesy and kindness that I have received from Rt Hon. Jim Prior, MP, Patrick Mayhew, QC, MP, and Jim Lester, MP — the three Ministers at the Department of Employment. In true Parliamentary tradition, they have been patiently helpful to a colleague who so often dissents from so many of their views.

August 1980 GREVILLE JANNER

Commencement dates

The Act received the Royal Assent on 1 August 1980. By 1 October all its sections will be in effect, other than 19(a) — repeal of the press charter provisions in section 1A of the 1974 Act.

The Employment Secretary has already prepared draft codes (included as Appendices 13 and 14). Consultations will be completed by 10 October and codes in final form are expected to be laid before Parliament and approved during the two-week session beginning 27 October — and to come into force by the end of the year, at the latest.

The most urgent procedures requiring immediate attention concern maternity leave (section 11) — and readers' attention is specially drawn to my draft form (Appendix 11).

Note Details of both public and in-company lectures by the author, on employment, industrial relations, boardroom law and health and safety may be obtained from Mr Paul Secher, JS Associates, 230 Grand Buildings, Trafalgar Square, London WC2 (Telephone: 01 839 6985).

'You'll find me an easy manager to work for – as long as you obey the rules – !'

Part One
INDIVIDUAL RIGHTS AND PROTECTION

Chapter 1

Introduction

The Employment Act, 1980 (which I shall from now on refer to as 'the 1980 Act') is designed to change two balances.

First: the Government believes that the scales are tipped too far in favour of the individual employee. So a number of personal rights are curtailed. Changes include the following:
1   The unfair dismissal rules are amended:
    a   An employer is no longer required to prove that a dismissal was 'fair'.
    b   An employee may 'contract out' of his unfair dismissal and redundancy protection if he has a fixed-term contract for one year, instead of the previous two years.
    c   The minimum two weeks' pay (at a maximum of £120 per week) for an employee who was dismissed 'unfairly', but suffered no actual loss, is abolished.
2   The rules on maternity pay and maternity leave are tightened up by the introduction of new and more complicated procedures.

In Part 1 of this book, I shall outline the basic rules on appointment and dismissal and put the changes into their proper context.

Second: the 1980 Act reduces the protection of unions and of their officers and makes important changes in union procedures. Some of these alterations also affect individual rights. For instance, the rules that prevent unions from enforcing closed shops at the same time give employees the right to opt out of union membership. These rules are conveniently considered in Part 2 of the book, along with remaining changes in trade union law — again in the context of the existing rules.

It is unfortunate that the law, like life, cannot be fitted conveniently into neat compartments. Personal and corporate rights, remedies, responsibilities and restrictions spill over, one into the other. Still: Parliament has consolidated the bulk of an employee's personal protection into *The Employment Protection (Consolidation) Act, 1978* ('the 1978 Act'). And an Act consolidating trade union and corporate law (by definition, without making any changes in it) is expected in 1981. So in following the great divide created by the legislature, I hope that the explanation of its efforts to regulate the world of industrial relations will be reasonably clear.

Chapter 2

Appointment and dismissal — introduction

A contract is a legally binding agreement between two or more parties. The most important contracts in our working lives are the ones that provide our jobs. An employee works under a 'contract of employment', which is simply a contract of a particular kind. It is a legally binding agreement between his employer and himself under which he agrees to provide specified work or service in return for pay and other benefits.

A contract is made when the employee is taken on. The appointment or hiring is the creation of the contract of employment.

The main terms of an employment contract may be agreed orally or in writing but should in any event be put in writing within 13 weeks of the start of the employment. Written particulars of any variation must be supplied to the employee within four weeks of the change. These rules are now contained in the 1978 Act. The better the parties know their rights, the less likely it is that they will end up battling over wrongs, in courts or tribunals.

The 1980 Act makes no changes in the law on appointment. Nor are the required written particulars altered.

The 1980 Act has combined with other Government action to reduce an employee's protection when his employent is terminated. When he is 'dismissed', his employers put an end to his contract. If they do so lawfully — giving him his proper notice or pay in lieu — then he will have no claim for 'wrongful' dismissal. If the dismissal is 'fair' — or if the employee is not qualified for protection, either because he comes outside the rules or because the business itself is small — then he cannot successfully claim compensation for 'unfair dismissal'. For either right, the employee must prove that he was 'dismissed'. To get damages for 'wrongful dismissal' he must also prove that he did not get his proper notice or pay in lieu. To succeed in a claim for an 'unfair dismissal' remedy, he must show that he is qualified; his employer must then prove the reasons for the dismissal; and the tribunal will decide whether or not the dismissal was 'fair', holding the scales of justice level and looking at all the circumstances of the case.

If the dismissal is 'unfair', then the tribunal retains its right to order reinstatement or re-engagement; and compensatory, basic and additional awards are still available. The basis for the awards and their amounts have changed.

So to put the rules into proper context, we now examine in outline the dismissal rules and then consider the changes in detail.

Chapter 3

When is an employee 'dismissed'?

An employee cannot succeed in a claim for compensation (or for any other remedy) for unfair dismissal unless he was *dismissed* unfairly. He cannot get damages for wrongful dismissal unless he was *dismissed* without his proper notice or pay in lieu. Nor can he be awarded redundancy pay, unless he was *dismissed* as redundant.

So when is an employee 'dismissed' in law? And when does he leave voluntarily?

Some years ago, an excellent employer decided to close down a section of his business. He called in all the employees who worked there and said: 'I don't know when — but we are going to have to make you all redundant before long. Jobs in this district are hard to get, so we suggest that you start looking now.'

A manager found a new job; left the company; and claimed his redundancy pay. Unfortunately for him, both the industrial tribunal concerned and the appeal court held that he had jumped the gun. He left before he was actually dismissed. To receive a warning of impending dismissal is not the same as to be sacked.

A secretary rowed with her boss who said: 'If this happens again, you will be sacked'. She walked out — and claimed that she had been dismissed unfairly. An industrial tribunal held that she had not been 'dismissed' at all.

In another hilarious case, a manager told an employee to 'fuck off' — which he promptly did, straight round to the local employment exchange, where he obtained and filled in a form claiming compensation for unfair dismissal. The case was reported in a national newspaper as follows: 'The chairman of a Midlands tribunal, a white-haired lady, said: "Nowadays, when you tell someone to fuck off, that is not a dismissal but merely a request that he leave the room. . ."!' No dismissal — no claim.

In another case, the manager told his employee to 'fuck off' three times in a morning. 'I could see I wasn't wanted', the employee said. He was awarded £1,822 compensation. Presumably liability depends on the frequency and tone of voice . . . and on all the other circumstances of the case.

A Mr Woolf was told that he would shortly be made redundant and that he was required to stay on until his notice expired. After negotiations, he left his employment three months early and claimed a redundancy payment. The tribunal and the appeal court both held that the employer had terminated the employment and the employee had only asked to substitute an earlier date for dismissal. On the facts of that case, the employee had not put an end to the arrangement on a basis which the employer had accepted.

Early in 1977, a supervisor called Vaughan, who knew that the unit in which he worked was about to be closed down, found himself other work. He claimed his redundancy pay. As he had not received formal notice from his employers, he lost the £1,284 to which he would otherwise have been entitled.

'As a result of doing what a decent man would do', said the Judge at the Employment Appeal Tribunal, 'in strict law he put himself on the wrong side of the fence'. Perhaps (the Judge continued) the employers would like to consider whether their 'moral obligations' did not 'transcend their strict obligations of law' and whether, in the circumstances they would not make a redundancy payment voluntarily.

Of course, there is nothing to prevent a voluntary payment — except that the Redundancy Fund will only grant a rebate (now of 41 per cent) where the payment is required by law and not merely by morality or by the power of negotiation.

The result of all these cases, from the employer's viewpoint, then? No 'dismissal' means no protection for his employee against unfair or wrongful dismissal or against redundancy. If the employee jumps the legal gun, so much the worse for him.

Be warned, though: if you apply pressures on an employee to leave without a formal sacking, that may amount to a 'constructive' dismissal. You must not by your wrongful behaviour 'repudiate' (or smash) the contract of employment, and force your employee out of his job. The borderline between voluntary departure and constructive dismissal is often narrow.

As for the employee who wishes to retain his rights in law, he should be careful not to leave before he is dismissed — actually or constructively. If he does receive his notice and he wishes to leave before it expires, he should take advice. If he follows the procedures set out in the 1978 Act (replacing *The Redundancy Payments Act, 1965*), he can leave his post but retain his legal position.

Finally: if you get involved in this sort of common situation and you regard your case (personally or on behalf of your company or firm) as borderline, take advice — before you take the plunge. Once the employee is pushed out or leaves voluntarily (as the case may be), the deed is done — forever.

Chapter 4

Unfair and wrongful 'dismissal'

Who owns a man's job? 'In the old days', said a judge, 'it was the employer. A man talked about "his job" but it did not belong to him in any real sense. Today, though, a man has what amounts to a property in his job.'

Most businessmen are tenants of their property and have a 'property' in their premises, so that even if they are given proper notice, the chances are that the law (thanks to *The Landlord and Tenant Act, 1954*) will allow them to remain*. Equally your employees now have a similar right to retain the work that enables them to pay the rent or the mortgage instalments which keep roofs above their heads.

Today, the employee's protection is divided into two main categories. First, if he does not receive his proper notice or pay in lieu, then he is 'wrongfully' dismissed. He has a claim for damages in a civil court — generally up to £2,000 in the County Court; over £2,000 in the High Court. Second, he may claim compensation for 'unfair dismissal' from an industrial tribunal.

Most businessmen must understand the rules from two viewpoints. They are employers of others, anxious to obey the law and not to involve their companies or firms in the payment of damages or compensation. Equally, they are themselves usually employees — however mighty. If they are to be dismissed, they need to know how to ensure that the dismissal was 'wrongful' or 'unfair', or both.

The old law on 'wrongful' dismissal has not changed. If an employee has behaved so scandalously as to 'repudiate' his

---

*They must, of course, serve appropriate counter-notices, to protect their positions.

contract of service — if he has stolen or committed some other terrible misdeed, or if he has been guilty of a series of minor misdemeanours, adding up in due course to a major one — then he may be summarily dismissed. Otherwise he is entitled to his proper notice or pay in lieu.

An employee should get agreed notice; in the absence of agreement, reasonable notice; and in any event, not less than the statutory minimum. To find the agreed notice, you look at an employee's contract of service or at the written particulars with which he should have been supplied to comply with the 1978 Act.

Reasonable notice may be very high. In the case of a senior employee of some 30 years' standing and with professional qualifications, the Court of Appeal recently said that 'reasonable' notice would be between six and twelve months.

The statutory minimum periods are: after four weeks' service, seven days' notice; after two years, two weeks; after three years, three weeks; after four years, four weeks; and so on up to a maximum of twelve weeks after twelve years.

Dismiss an employee who has not earned the summary sack and fail to give him his proper notice and he is entitled to damages for 'wrongful' dismissal, even if he has only been with you a very short time. An executive who had a fixed minimum period of three months' employment was wrongfully dismissed after only a few weeks. He was awarded £1,200. He could not have obtained compensation for unfair dismissal, of course, because he had not been continuously employed for the minimum 52-week period.

Damages for wrongful dismissal are usually easily assessed. They are: the remuneration (including bonus or commission) which the employee would have earned during the period of notice; plus accrued holiday pay, and compensation for lost benefits — pension rights, use of company car or canteen and the like. Once the employer has stepped over the borderline and dismissed 'wrongfully', the employee is entitled to his damages, in full. The employer cannot get the damages reduced by saying: 'The man contributed to his own dismissal because of his misconduct'. Either he was dismissed 'wrongfully' or lawfully.

Still, the dismissed employee's security *was* confined to his period of notice or pay in lieu or (where appropriate) to the equivalent damages. He had to mitigate his loss by finding other work to reduce that loss, if he was wrongfully dismissed. And even if he never got another job . . . even if his status was totally destroyed . . . the law could not help him. It is that unfair situation which the *unfair* dismissal rules have largely altered.

To come under the benevolent wing of the unfair dismissal protection, an employee must have been continuously on the books for at least 52 weeks (as defined), except in those cases where he claims he was sacked because his employers deprived him of his right to belong to an independent trade union or (more likely) not to belong to a non-independent union, or on the ground of race or sex discrimination. In those cases, there is no minimum time limit.

Again, a claimant must have been continuously employed for a normal working week of 16 hours or more (or 8 hours after five years' continuous service). As in the case of redundancy pay, the part-timer who normally works for less than 16 (or 8) hours is excluded.

Pensioners are also out. While there is no lower age limit for unfair dismissal (no one under 20 can get redundancy pay — he must be employed two years after reaching the age of 18) the upper limit is the normal retirement age for the business or national pension age, whichever is the later.

The 1980 Act has introduced another exception to the one-year qualification rule. Employees of small firms, i.e. where the number of employees together with employees of any associated company does not exceed 20, normally have to wait two years before they gain any unfair dismissal rights.

Full-timers of one year's standing and under retirement age are, in general, now entitled not to be dismissed 'unfairly'.

Once an employee has shown that he was 'dismissed' — and that he did not leave voluntarily — then it is up to the employer to show the 'reason' for the dismissal. Reasons include: the employee's conduct; redundancy; lack of 'qualification' or capability; absence of sufficient technical qualifications; and any other 'substantial reason'.

The next question? Whether the employer acted 'fairly' in treating the reason as sufficient to warrant dismissal. This is determined after consideration of all the circumstances of the case. These include the size and administrative resources of the employer's undertaking.

Initial statistics after the increase in the qualifying period for protection from 26 to 52 weeks showed a reduction of 26 per cent in applications. But it seems that the number is starting to rise.

The potential award to a successful applicant has gone up to £16,090 — £6,250 compensation (as before); £3,600 basic award (now the maximum forfeited redundancy pay); and £6,240 additional award, where an employer unreasonably refuses to carry out an order for reinstatement or re-engagement of a dismissed employee.

Additional awards are very rare. But the number and amounts of compensatory and basic awards are increasing. However, the 1980 Act abolishes the minimum entitlement to two weeks' pay under the basic award. It also empowers tribunals to reduce the basic award in cases where the employee has unreasonably refused an offer of reinstatement. Industrial tribunals now also have the discretion to reduce the award on the grounds of the employee's conduct before the dismissal where this would not come under the heading of fault which contributed to the dismissal.

Still: over 72 per cent of claims heard by industrial tribunals are dismissed — and awards to successful employees average out at under £600 apiece.

So much for the belief that industrial tribunals are weighted in favour of employees. Applicants are generally less articulate than their managers; they have trouble in getting evidence — usually available only from former colleagues, still in the job and anxious not to follow them into the wilderness; and some cases are just bad.

Chapter 5
'Misconduct' — and summary dismissal

When are you entitled to dismiss an employee summarily?

Mr Pepper was employed by Major Webb as his head gardener. One dread Saturday, he reacted to a lawful order by stating the following: 'I couldn't care less about your bloody greenhouse and your sodding garden'. So saying, he walked off. Major Webb sacked him on the spot.

Mr Pepper sued for damages for wrongful dismissal, alleging that 'one act of temper, one insolent outburst, did not merit so severe a punishment'. The County Court judge agreed with him. After all, just as we must all endure occasional afflictions of the body, so employers must put up with sporadic outbursts of minor contract-breaking. But Major Webb was a fighting man. He appealed.

'What will justify an instant dismissal?', queried Lord Justice Harman, delivering the first judgment. The answer? 'Something done by the employee which impliedly or expressly is a repudiation of the fundamental terms of the contract.' One major act of contract-breaking will do. If your assistant is dishonest or your cleaner sets light to the office or factory or shop, instant dismissal is justified. The contract of service is destroyed. But even minor acts of misbehaviour — slovenliness, discourtesy or petty negligence, for instance — will justify the summary sack, if they become habitual or persistent.

What of Mr Pepper? He 'did not care a hoot' about looking after the garden or greenhouse. Therefore, said the judge, he had no lawful complaint if he was summarily dismissed.

Anyway, the judge added, 'this was the last straw'. The man had been acting unsatisfactorily for some months. He had previously behaved with 'dumb insolence'. Now he had disobeyed a reasonable request from his employer. He had reacted with insolence instead of obedience. He was rightly sacked.

Lord Justice Karminski said this: 'In my view, the essential question here is whether the employer was justified in his summary dismissal of the gardener on the ground of wilful disobedience of a lawful and reasonable order. . . . It has long been a part of our law that a servant repudiates the contract of service if he wilfully disobeys a lawful order.'

In a later case, the court emphasised that where there is an isolated act of this sort it will be wrong to dismiss an employee without notice or pay in lieu, unless there has been a past history of disobedience. So be careful to consider each case on its own facts.

Note: if you decide to give notice or pay in lieu to an employee whom you believe that you could dismiss summarily, write a letter to him emphasising that you are paying him 'without prejudice' to your view that he had forfeited his rights because of his conduct. Your generosity will not then be used against you in any 'unfair' dismissal claim.

Chapter 6

Remedies for wrongful dismissal

Damages for breach of contract are normally designed to compensate. Their object is to put the innocent party in the same position, financially at least, as he would have been had the contract been honoured by the other party. If you dismiss summarily, without just cause, you (on behalf of your company or firm or yourself, as the case may be) repudiate the contract of service. Hence, the business becomes liable to pay damages. *Prima facie*, the amount of the employer's loss is the amount of wages in lieu of notice that he should have received (see Chapter 8 for his additional remedies for unfair dismissal, i.e. where the employer has acted unreasonably).

If the rules ended there, all would be reasonably simple. But they do not. There is a standard principle of contract law that a person who suffers as a result of a breach must do what he can to 'mitigate his damage'. He must, that is, keep it as low as he reasonably can. If you are convicted of a crime, your lawyer will make a 'plea in mitigation', begging the court to keep down the sentence. Where there is a breach of contract, the sufferer must do what he can to keep his loss to a minimum.

Suppose that your company puts in an order for goods. Delivery is not received. The company cannot take no action, do nothing and sue for any loss of profit which it suffers as a result, even if the whole plant has to close down. It must seek to mitigate its loss by getting the goods elsewhere. If it has to pay more, then its 'damage' will be the difference between the price which it would have paid, had the contract been honoured, and the price which it had to pay as a result of the breach. Equally, if it manages to get the same goods at the same price, it will have suffered no loss, so no damages will be recoverable. If it manages to get in the material for an even lower price, it will have made a profit. And that will not only be a piece of good fortune for the company but also for the contract breaker.

Or suppose that you book rooms in some splendid seaside hotel for a sales conference. For some reason the conference is called off. Your company has broken its contract with the hotel and is liable to pay damages. But the hotel cannot simply leave the rooms empty and charge your company. It must do what it can to rent the rooms to others. If it fails, then you will be unlucky. If it succeeds the hotel will have mitigated its damage and have suffered no loss.

Now apply these rules to the employee summarily dismissed. He must seek other employment, as soon as he can. He must do his best to get another job. If he tries, but fails, then his damage will be the full amount of the wages in lieu which he should have received. If he succeeds, then any wages that he manages to earn during the period of notice together with unemployment pay received, employment expenses saved and tax and stoppages unendured will be deducted from the wages in lieu in ascertaining his damages. If he gets another job, either at the same salary and right away, or at a higher salary, he will have suffered no loss, will not be entitled to any compensation and will get no damages from the contract-breaking employers.

'If I dismiss without justification, can I pay wages in lieu of compensation right away?'

You can.

'But if I wait until after the period of notice has expired, there's an excellent chance that the person will get less?'

There is.

'If he has managed to get some other work, the wages received will be deductible from the wages in lieu — so the company may have to pay little or nothing?'

Correct.

'And if he got no further work, we'll only have to pay him the lot if he can show that he did not relax and have a holiday at our expense — that he really tried to get back into harness?'

Yes. If you want to be nasty, you may dismiss summarily when you have no just cause for doing so, and then sit back and hope for the best. You will probably save your company some money. Equally, you are unlikely to contribute to good industrial relations. And if the dismissal was 'unfair', watch out for trouble from the tribunals.

Chapter 7

When is a dismissal 'constructive'?

An employee who wants his unfair dismissal remedies must first show that he was 'dismissed' (see Chapter 2).

Usually, the employer agrees that he has dismissed . . . sacked . . . discharged . . . fired. . . . But where the employee walks out . . . resigns . . . the next question is: was he dismissed 'constructively'? Was he forced out of his job? Or did he 'terminate his contract . . . in circumstances such that he was entitled to terminate it without notice by reason of the employer's conduct'?

Just as the wife who is pushed out of the matrimonial home may still be deserted 'constructively', even though she physically leaves, so the employee who is shoved out of his employment may be 'dismissed' in law, even if he actually terminated the arrangement — provided that he was entitled to do so.

Which begs the question, of course: when is an employee entitled to terminate his contract because of his employer's conduct?

Not long ago, the Court of Appeal held that an employee was only entitled to terminate the contract 'by reason of the employer's conduct' if the employer had done something so dreadful as to amount to a 'repudiation'. It was not enough that the employer had behaved unreasonably. He must have smashed the contract — behaved in a way that an ordinary, reasonable employee would have said: 'I could not be expected to stay on'.

Then the Employment Appeal Tribunal 'distinguished' this decision. Being bound by the rules laid down by the Court of Appeal, it said, in effect: 'That's not really what the judges meant. . . . The true meaning of the decision was that if the employer behaved sufficiently unreasonably, the employee might leave'.

The latest in the series was *Western Excavating (ECC) Limited* v. *Sharp*. Back swung the pendulum. The claimant had asked for three hours off work to play cards for a team. His request was refused. But he went anyway and was dismissed. The employers' disciplinary panel substituted five days' suspension without pay for the dismissal, which left Mr Sharp in financial difficulties. He asked for an advance on his accrued holiday pay, but this was refused, as was a request for a loan of £40. He left and brought a claim for unfair dismissal.

'The rival tests' as to what constitutes constructive dismissal, said the redoubtable Lord Denning, are 'the contract test and the unreasonableness test'. Under the former, if the employer was guilty of conduct which was a significant breach, going to the root of the contract of employment, or which showed that he no longer intends to be bound by one or more of its essential terms, then the employee is entitled to treat himself as discharged from any further performance; and if he did so, the employee was constructively dismissed.

'Under the unreasonableness test, the employer conducted himself or his affairs so unreasonably that the employee was justified in leaving.'

In Lord Denning's opinion, the contract test is the right one. The test of 'unreasonable conduct', he said, 'is too indefinite by far'. It had led to findings of constructive dismissal on the most whimsical grounds. The contract test is more certain and can well be understood by intelligent laymen, under the guidance of a legally qualified chairman. Mr Sharp had not been 'dismissed'.

Lord Justice Lawton agreed. 'Sensible persons', he said, 'have no difficulty in recognising conduct which operates to bring a contract of employment to an end. . . . Persistent and unwanted amorous advances by an employer to a female member of his staff would, for example, clearly be such conduct'.

Chapter 8

Unfair dismissal — the new rules

Unless an employee can show that he was dismissed on the grounds of discrimination (sex, race or trade union), he must now wait twelve months (instead of the previous six) before he becomes qualified for unfair dismissal protection. If he then brings his case before a tribunal, the burden of proving fairness no longer rests on the employer. The tribunal must look at all the facts and circumstances and decide whether or not the dismissal was fair. Unlike most other criminal or civil cases, where the scales are tipped in favour of the accused or the defendant (respectively), here they are held level.

What effect, then, are these changes likely to have on an employee's chances of winning an unfair dismissal claim? How is the executive or manager likely to be affected in his official capacity — or, if he himself needs to bring a claim, what will happen to his chances? To answer these questions, we must look at the realities and at the statistics.

If an employee brings an unfair dismissal claim, a conciliation officer will call on him and on his employer within a matter of weeks. He will try to bring about a settlement.

Some employers believe that conciliation officers 'lean' too heavily on them. Then they point out, for instance, not only the hazards of industrial tribunal litigation and the risks of losing a case, but also the undoubted cost of winning one.

When considering whether or not to fight a case, you must consider all the factors. First: will you need to employ a lawyer or have you someone sufficiently knowledgeable and articulate to do the job for you? If so, then you may well be better off on your own.

A 1978 sample showed that where applicants were

represented by lawyers, they were successful in approximately 35 per cent of cases, when represented by their trade union the success rate was about 20 per cent. Self represented applicants were successful in about 28 per cent of cases. Naturally, no one knows how much worse the represented applicants would have fared, had they appeared in person in what is essentially an informal forum. My view: unless you have no one who can clearly speak out for you or unless the stakes are high or the legal issues intricate, do the job yourself. You will save money and your prospects of success should not be much lower.

Second: how much will it cost you to prepare and to copy any relevant documents? This amount is likely to be much smaller than the cost of employing a lawyer.

Third: how much time will the contest take. How many people will have to be interviewed? How many statements must you take? How many witnesses will be needed at court and for how long? Will the case finish in one day or may it be adjourned, either part heard or perhaps because there was not even time to begin it?

Add up all these factors and you will probably emerge with a cost of somewhere between £500 and £5,000 for *winning* a case. So conciliation officers are right to point to the advantages of a settlement.

Equally, the ACAS men will tell the employee of the chances of losing even a case which looks like a dead-set winner. Maybe it is better to have less money in the hand than more in some dreaded legal bush?

Anyway: as a result of the intervention of conciliation officers, about 60 per cent of cases are withdrawn at that stage. There are no records as to how many simply disappear because the employee is told that he is on to a loser and how many in which the employers make payments.

As to the cases that proceed, the failure rate has always been enormous. In 1978 it reached 72 per cent. Some are lost because they should never have been brought. As employers often point out, what has the employee to lose? The chances of his having to pay costs are minimal and he will even get his expenses paid.

On the other hand, no one knows what proportion of dismissed employees with excellent cases prefer not to bring them. Ordinary people are afraid of courts and tribunals. And well-informed employees know that if they are looking for alternative employment, it is no help to be branded a trouble-maker who takes disputes to courts or tribunals.

Whatever the reason, claimants' chances of winning before a tribunal have always worked out at least two to one against. This is fine if you happen to be the employer; not so good if you are the claimant. Either way, you should not be taken in by complaints that unfair dismissal protection for employees strangles employment prospects. Certainly no employer who recognises how low the odds have always been against him and how easily and how cheaply he can insure against them should allow them to have any substantial effect on his employment strategy. And as surveys show, few do.

If that was the position before the 1980 Act, what will happen as a result of the shift in the burden of proof? Probably, very little. Curiously, the employee's prospects of success have varied little over the years, in spite of changes in the burden of proof. As we shall see from many of the changes made by the 1980 Act, this one is likely to prove more psychological than real.

Still, while we can expect about one third of those unfair dismissal cases which reach trial to be successful, the number of dismissed employees qualified to bring cases at all has already fallen by some 23 per cent, through the increase of the qualifying period of employment from 26 to 52 weeks. If an employee is dismissed after 12 months, then his prospects of winning an unfair dismissal claim will probably be not much less than they were before — which is scarcely in any event an inducement to joy for those who are sacked, whatever their level.

Finally: management should not forget the industrial relations implications of dismissal practice and procedures. The fact that you are now entitled to dismiss an employee during his first 12 months, as unfairly or as unreasonably as you wish, does not mean that you can necessarily do so with impunity. Because you may sack for any reason or for none without giving him any remedy in law other than a claim for his proper notice or pay in lieu, it does not bind his union to accept such an arrangement, without protest or action.

As the law cuts down employees' rights to take their cases to court or tribunal, so it increases their incentive to join unions and to make use of their facilities — which, in its turn, is a curious twist in events. After all, it is Conservative

Governments that create legal frameworks and encourage people to deal with disputes through the law, and unions which press for shop-floor negotiation and settlements. So indirectly, the legislation which is designed to reduce legal pressure on employers by lowering the barriers that protect employees will help the unions in their efforts to recruit.

Chapter 9

The burden of proof — a summary

In criminal cases, the prosecution must normally prove that the accused is guilty 'beyond all reasonable doubt'. Main exceptions:
1. Under the Health and Safety at Work Act, where the prosecution proves the hazard, then the accused must show that he has taken such steps as are 'reasonably practicable' to avoid it.
2. If a foreign body is found in food, then (under the Food and Drugs Act) it is for the accused to show that this was not due to his fault.
3. If you are found in possession of 'recently stolen' property, then the goods are 'hot' and you must prove, if you can, that you did not feel the heat.
4. If you give or attempt to make a gift to someone employed by local or national government, then corruption will be presumed against both giver and receiver.

In a civil action, the burden of proof rests on the plaintiff. He who seeks the help of the court must prove that he is in the right. For instance, the fact that an employee is injured at work will not of itself give him any right to damages against his employers or anyone else. He must prove that his injury was caused by the negligence or breach of statutory duty of the employer, his servant or agent.

Only *the Employers' Liability (Defective Equipment) Act, 1969*, imposes 'strict liability' on employers. If your employee is killed or suffers personal injury through a defect in equipment you supply, then you are deemed to have been negligent. Not only does the burden of proof rest upon you, but — so far as the employee is concerned — it is absolute. You may get a contribution or an indemnity from the manufacturer or supplier, the erector, installer or maintainer of the equipment concerned, if you can show that all or part of the fault lay with him. But the plaintiff employee (or his widow) can look to you for his damages.

If you are injured through a defect in a product, it is not sufficient for you to prove the defect and the injury. You must also prove negligence. Unless and until (as is extremely likely) 'strict liability' (or 'product liability', as it is commonly called in relation to defective products) enters our law, the burden of proof rests on the plaintiff in product liability negligence cases in the same way as it does in all others.

What, then, of the burden in unfair dismissal claims? Since the rules were first introduced by *The Industrial Relations Act, 1971*, the employee has had to prove that he was qualified and that he was 'dismissed' — actually or constructively. If the employer wishes to avoid making a payment, he must then show that he dismissed for an approved, statutory reason. In 1971, the employee then had to prove that this reason was insufficient to warrant depriving him of his livelihood. The 1974 Act reversed the burden, requiring the employer to show not only the reason for the dismissal but that he acted reasonably (and hence 'fairly' — see Chapter 4) in dismissing the employee.

It was then for the employer to show that he had followed a fair procedure; that he had listened to the employee's case; that, where reasonably practicable, he had given at least one warning, preferably in writing; that he had, if possible, given the employee the opportunity of appealing to a higher level of authority — that he had acted in a decent, kindly, responsible way.

Now the pendulum has been swung back — but only half way. The burden of proving qualification and dismissal rests on the employee; the employer must still show the reasons for the dismissal; but then the tribunal must consider all the facts and circumstances and decide whether or not the dismissal was fair.

Chapter 10

Fixed-term contracts

An employee is 'dismissed' if his employer terminates his contract of employment. As we have seen (in Chapter 7), a dismissal may be 'actual' or 'constructive' or due to the expiration of a fixed-term contract when the employee is not re-employed.

Suppose, then, that you are offered a position as (say) personnel director of a company in a different part of Britain. You have to tear up your roots, move your family, buy a new home. You say: 'What security will you give me?' Your prospective employers reply: 'We will give you an initial contract for two years'. You accept; move; and do your job as best you can.

When your two-year term is over, your employers decide not to keep you. Even though your contract has come to an end through the expiry of the time limit and without any action on their part, you are still 'dismissed'. And if the dismissal was 'unfair', then you will be entitled to your remedies.

In practice, it is very unlikely that any employee on a fixed-term contract will get any remedy if he is not re-employed. This certainly applies to short-term contracts for a particular purpose.

Suppose, for instance that you take on a consultant for 12 months — or, for that matter, until he has completed a particular job which in fact takes a year. When his task is completed, his work is no longer needed. So you thank him, pay him and his job is done. He may take you to a tribunal because you have dismissed him; he may allege that the dismissal is unfair; but (as many decisions have shown) he will lose — provided that you can show that he knew both the short-term (or the fixed-term) nature of his job and that there was no alternative work available for him.

To encourage employers to give long-term, fixed-term contracts, the rules (since 1971) have always allowed employees to contract out of their unfair dismissal and of their redundancy rights, if their terms were sufficiently long. Previously, the limit has been two years; the 1980 Act reduces it to twelve months for unfair dismissal — but not for redundancy where the limit stays at two years. In the past, a contracting out clause in a fixed-term contract for two years or more has been effective, while a similar clause in a shorter-term contract has been a dead letter. Today, you may insert a valid, binding, contracting-out clause into a fixed-term contract for as short a time as twelve months.

Legal argument has ranged over what is or is not a 'fixed-term' contract. Suppose, for instance, that you have a two-year contract but either party may put an end to it by giving six months' notice to the other. Is the fixed term six months or twenty-four? In a case involving a BBC Foreign Service announcer, the Court of Appeal held that a contract of that sort was not 'fixed term' — or, at least, that the fixed term was not longer than the period of notice by which either party could put it to death. This decision has been overtaken and today a contract is 'fixed term' even if it can be terminated by notice at an earlier date.

Still, these rules are in the melting pot and if you run into them in your particular case, whether as employer or employee, you should take specific and skilled legal advice before committing yourself.

Finally, remember that an employee can still only 'contract out' of his unfair dismissal and redundancy rights in two circumstances. The first is in fixed-term contracts for twelve months or more. The second is where the parties come to an agreement to settle a claim, and that agreement is recorded by a Conciliation Officer. In any other case, even if an employee does agree not to take action, that agreement will not be binding on him.

Chapter 11

Written reasons

While the qualifying period for unfair dismissal protection has gone up from 26 to 52 weeks, a dismissed employee is still entitled to written reasons for his dismissal after only 26 weeks' service. This will not only help him to launch an unfair dismissal claim in those rare cases where discrimination (sex, race or trade union) may be provable. But he may also be helped to show that he was dismissed 'wrongfully' (that is, without proper notice or pay in lieu). And if adequate reasons are not supplied within fourteen days of the request, he may have an independent claim for two weeks' pay.

An employer who is asked to give 'written reasons' should always do so with care. The dismissed employee is considering litigation and he will probably have been advised by a lawyer to ask for particulars. Even if the application is in the employee's own clumsy words, they may well have been drafted for him by a lawyer.

If the employer has given previous written warning to the employee, he should quote that warning in the notice and complain of non-compliance. But it has been held that mere reference to the warning is not enough. Reasons for the dismissal must still be set out in full.

The aggrieved, dismissed employee who has not received written reasons should certainly ask for them. If he receives none — or if those given are inadequate — he will be entitled to claim two weeks' pay. And it seems that a claim under this heading may be brought, even if the employee does not qualify for unfair dismissal protection.

If, on the other hand, particulars are supplied, the employer will be tied to them. He will find it difficult, if not impossible, to claim at a later stage that the reasons for the dismissal were different from those contained in the notice. Either way, the employee cannot lose by demanding written details. The employer has two weeks within which to provide them.

So dismissed employees should make use of their power to demand particulars. Their employers should provide those particulars, with care and circumspection. They should only draft those particulars themselves if they are quite sure of their ground. Otherwise, they should take legal advice.

Once the employee has received the particulars, he is then able to assess the strength of his position. That position can only be strengthened because the particulars, adequate or otherwise, have been supplied — or even, paradoxically, if the request has gone unanswered.

Chapter 12

Redundancies

In broad terms, an employee is dismissed as redundant when his job goes along with him. He is not to be replaced because there is no longer a need for employees to do that job in that place or at that time. How, then, do the recent changes in the law affect the position of the redundant employee?

First: where an employee is dismissed as redundant, he is entitled to redundancy pay. His qualification remains unchanged: he must have been continuously employed by the same employer (or an associated one) for at least two years after reaching the age of 18. Maximum statutory redundancy pay is frequently adjusted to reflect the decrease in the value of the £ and is currently £3,600 — reached after continuous service for 20 years.

Many redundant employees receive more (and often far more) than the statutory minimum. An employee who is made redundant is entitled to agreed redundancy pay, subject to the statutory minimum. As always, agreement may be reached by individual or by collective bargaining. If the individual is left to his own devices and bargaining strength, he is likely to get the statutory minimum only. His union may well win more.

For instance: many employees who have been on the books for less than the required minimum of two years do in fact receive redundancy pay. Many of their colleagues get more than the statutory minimum — sometimes because the employer wishes to reduce the impact of the unwanted misery; sometimes as an inducement to voluntary redundancies; sometimes so as to avoid battle with the unions which could lead to disruption of production either at the unit which is to close or to remain in operation with a smaller workforce, or in associated units — and sometimes for all or some of these reasons.

Most employers try to achieve voluntary redundancies, for the avoidance of unnecessary hardship and ill-will. In practice, there are often too many volunteers, some of them people whom the employer would prefer to keep. After all, here is the employee's chance (and probably his only chance) to receive a lump sum (probably untaxed).

If the employee genuinely accepts voluntary redundancy, then if his employer is wise he will have the agreement properly recorded by a Conciliation Officer (on form CO3) and it will then (and only then) result in an effective contracting out by the employee of his rights to claim that he was unfairly selected for redundancy.

The fact that an employee is dismissed as redundant does not of itself make the dismissal fair. Redundancy is a statutory reason for dismissal; but the employee may still claim that he was selected unfairly. If he is right, he is entitled to his unfair dismissal remedies, in exactly the same way as if he had been unfairly dismissed on any other ground.

Suppose, then, that you make an employee redundant. He claims that dismissal on that ground was unfair. You show that redundancy was the reason for the dismissal. He maintains that you used redundancy as an excuse for getting rid of him . . . that the real (and unfair) reason for the dismissal was that you did not like him or that you (unfairly) criticised his performance . . . or that you operated on a 'last in, first out' basis for your selection, but took him out of turn. . . .

In the past, you, the employer, would have to prove fairness. Under the 1980 Act rules, that burden is lifted. The tribunal will consider the balance of probabilities, the scales of proof being weighted neither on one side nor on the other.

Second: the 1975 Act rules still require consultation, where an employer proposes to make an employee redundant who is either a member of a recognised trade union or affected by its bargaining. If even one relevant employee is to be made redundant, consultation must take place as soon as possible. If between 10 and 99 employees at one establishment are to be made redundant, within a period of 60 days, then the period of required consultation with the trade union was 60 days. It was reduced (in 1979, by Statutory Instrument) to 30 days. If the number of proposed redundancies at one establishment is to be 100 or more, then the consultation period was and remains at 90 days.

These consultations must be held with any appropriate 'recognised, independent' trade union. They are not required unless the union is recognised (substantially, for the purposes of collective bargaining), nor with a staff association or other organisation which is not 'independent', i.e. free from your control and certified as such by the Certification Officer — see Chapter 22.

In addition and in any event, an employer must notify the Department of Employment of any major intended redundancy, i.e. one of 10 or more at one establishment. The numbers and the periods of notification are the same as those for trade union consultation.

If an employer fails to comply with the redundancy consultation rules, then the union concerned may apply for a 'protection award' for any members affected. An industrial tribunal will make an award unless the employer can show some 'special circumstances' which made it impossible for him to consult within the required period. If, for example, a major customer collapses unexpectedly, so that employees have to be laid off without warning, that might be regarded as a 'special circumstance'.

The object of a protective award is to protect innocent employees, not to punish erring employers. The award is intended as compensation and is likely to equal the amount of pay which the employees concerned would have got during the period when the employers should have consulted, but failed to do so.

If an employer fails to inform the Department of Employment of proposed redundancies in accordance with the rules, then he may be fined up to £400 or (and this is potentially far more important) he may lose up to 10 per cent of the current redundancy rebate.

When an employer pays out statutory redundancy pay (as opposed to any voluntary redundancy money, whether or not this is additional to a statutory payment), he may claim back 41 per cent of such payment from the Redundancy Fund. So he will only have to bear 59 per cent of the statutory redundancy payment from his own pocket.

The figure of 41 per cent was reached because of a Parliamentary anomaly. When the Bill which was intended to reduce redundancy rebates to 40 per cent was introduced by the Labour administration and was on its way through the Commons, the Conservatives set up an ambush and defeated the Bill. It had to be reintroduced but you cannot have the same Bill with the same terms in the same session so the original 40 per cent went up to 41 per cent.

An employer is bound to consult the union, not to comply with its wishes nor (still less) to accept any form of dictation. Common sense and good management require maximum consultation, for the avoidance of unnecessary hardship ... so as to seek ways in which redundancies may be avoided ... or, at worst, to minimise industrial unrest. Redundancy decisions remain firmly in the hands of management. These decisions are generally the industrial and commercial worlds' most miserable, and the wish of employees to leave them in the bosses' hands provides one of the most powerful union arguments against worker participation at boardroom level.

The 1980 Act, then, has no direct impact on redundancy situations — unless you happen to believe that it creates an atmosphere of industrial unrest which leads to disharmony, increases ill-will between unions and management and so makes the soil fertile for those situations which lead to a decrease in productivity and to an increase in redundancy. The industrial relations results of legislation are incalculable and controversial.

The reduction in individual rights caused by the transfer of the burden of proof — plus, of course, the allied reduction in the qualifying period and the removal of rights of employees of some smaller outfits — will not make life better or easier for the individual made redundant. Nor will the reduction in the period of consultation do other than harm to him, although it may (in theory at least) ease the path of some employers who prefer to consult less.

Chapter 13
Maternity rights, old and new

The Employment Protection Act, 1975, gave working mothers-to-be two rights: (1) to maternity pay; (2) to maternity leave. As we shall see in the next chapter, the 1980 Act has made both harder to get.

To qualify for either right, the employee must have been employed for at least two years, as at the beginning of the eleventh week before the date of her expected confinement. To qualify for maternity leave she must also, where reasonably practicable, notify her employer of her intention to return to work, where reasonably practicable not less than three weeks before her departure.

Maternity pay has presented few problems and no direct expense to employers. They pay any qualified mother-to-be up to six weeks at nine-tenths of her normal rate of pay, minus the maximum current maternity allowance (whether or not she is entitled to it). They then reclaim the lot from the Maternity Fund.

What, then, has been the effect of maternity leave? I can find no evidence that the number or percentage of mothers returning to work after childbirth has changed. It appears to remain at about 13 per cent. But some experts believe that the maternity leave rules have provided a disincentive to the employment of women at managerial or executive level. Whether that argument remains sustainable now that the qualifying period for unfair dismissal has been increased from six to twelve months is doubtful, because temporary replacements are now rarely protected against unfair dismissal.

Suppose, then, that a woman in your employment becomes pregnant. If she will have been with you (or with any associated

Individual rights and protection 35

employer) for two years as at the beginning of the eleventh week before the date of her expected confinement, then (if she knows of her rights) she asks: 'Do I give notice of intention to return?' The answer must be: Yes.

If the employee says that she intends to return and then changes her mind, she loses nothing. Even if the employer has kept her job open while she was away, he has no remedy against her.

Conversely: If she gives no notice of her intention to return, she gives up her right to her job, in return for nothing.

Now suppose that a prospective mother does not intend to return because she wants to stay at home and look after her baby. The child is stillborn. So she is desperate to get her job back. Unless she has given notice of an intention to return, she will have lost her rights — to no avail and for no reason.

So any wise and qualified mother-to-be will give notice of intention to return to her job, even if she has no wish to come back. If you are a woman executive or manager, you should certainly state that intention. If you are advising your wife or anyone else's, tell them: give notice. Indeed, as the law and morality are (on this occasion as on so many others) not identical, these rights are not confined to married women. So the same advice should be given to unmarried mothers-to-be, perhaps with even greater force.

If the employee does not give notice of her intention to return, within the specified time, she will not lose her rights if it was 'not reasonably practicable' for her to do so. This is the same rule which protects people who do not claim their unfair dismissal rights within the statutory limit of three months from the date when their employment came to an end.

Courts have held that it is 'reasonably practicable' to claim if you know that you have unfair dismissal rights, even if you do not know or appreciate their extent or the procedures required to claim them. If, for instance, you negotiate with your employers and they do not deny liability but you are still haggling over the amount when the three-month period has passed without you putting in your claim, you will have lost your rights. If you did not know that you had any rights at all, then it will not be 'reasonably practicable' for you to exercise them.

Although there seems to be no reported, binding decision on

the point, a court would probably take the same view on maternity leave. If the employee knows that she is entitled to leave, then she must give her notice of intention to return within the specified period, or lose that right altogether. If she is ignorant not only of the procedure, but also of the existence of the right, then she cannot exercise it.

So what has happened in practice? These rules were introduced in 1975. How have they affected the employment of women?

At shop-floor or typing-pool level, the effect has probably been nil. After all, only about one mother in eight actually wants to return to her job and (to use the phrase so charmingly prevalent in personnel management circles) women 'turn over' so fast that a job can nearly always be found for the returning mother, without too much difficulty.

At higher levels, the problem was (and to a much lesser extent, still is) much greater. Suppose that your assistant goes off to have a baby. You have to replace her. You must train in someone to do the job. But if notice of intention to return has been given, you must inform the replacement or risk an unfair dismissal case if you have to dismiss her when the mother comes back.

Suppose that you move up the next employee in line. If you then try to force her to move back down to make way for the mother and she refuses, she may leave and claim that you have dismissed her constructively.

Nowadays, this problem with the replacements is much less than it was. First, a mother is entitled to return to 'her job', but that does not in normal cases mean that she is entitled to do the same work under precisely the same supervision and circumstances or at the same desk or machine. Provided that the job is substantially the same, that will suffice. Second (and much more important), if you take on a new employee to replace the absent mother, she will not normally have acquired her unfair dismissal protection by the time that the mother must exercise her right to return, which may be assessed as follows:

1   Normally, the mother-to-be must remain at work until the beginning of the eleventh week before the date of her expected confinement. If she is dismissed earlier because of her condition, then she retains her rights. If she leaves

earlier, without being 'dismissed' she loses her rights. Anyway: in normal circumstances she may properly and easily be away for eleven weeks before the baby is born.

2   She then retains her right to return after a period of 29 weeks after the birth of her child; this is subject to a further extension of four weeks, if she cannot take up her job because she is ill or to allow the employer time to make room for her.

It follows that (unless the employee is dismissed because of her condition at an earlier stage she can properly be away for a maximum of 11 plus plus 29 weeks plus 4 weeks making a total of 44 weeks. If a replacement is taken on immediately she leaves, he or she will not have qualified for unfair dismissal protection by the time she gets back.

So the previous worry of some employers in appointing women of childbearing age to executive or managerial posts — anxiety largely caused through problems about replacements — should have been dissipated. And just to make sure that employers are not overburdened by maternity leave problems, the 1980 Act has directly excluded many employees of smaller firms and indirectly ensured that many other women, who are insufficiently advised or equipped to give proper notice in specified forms within stated times, will lose the rights they had.

Chapter 14
Maternity notices*

The law frequently requires people to 'give notice' to others, if they wish to exercise their rights. Once a person is 'put on notice', he can take such steps as are necessary in order to prepare himself for the event which he is then in a position to have noticed. It now imposes a formidable series of notices on mothers who wish to exercise their right to return to work.

In the past, an employee was required to give notice of her intention to return to work at least 21 days before her absence for pregnancy or confinement began but she only had to do so *in writing* if so requested by her employers.

All employers always were wise to make that request, both by including the appropriate term in the written particulars of employment and by having a proper maternity procedure (see later). The 1980 Act requires an employee to give her notice 'where reasonably practicable' at least three weeks before leaving (see previous chapter), and to do so in writing whether requested or not. In addition:

1 Not less than 49 days after the week or date of confinement, the employer may give the mother a written request to confirm her intention to return. She must do so in writing within 14 days of receiving the request, or as soon thereafter as is reasonably practicable; and
2 She must give written notice to her employers at least 21 days before exercising her right to return — instead of the previous 7 days.

*For precedent notices, see Appendix 10.

In addition, an employer with five or fewer employees* is relieved of his obligation to reinstate an employee after maternity leave, where it is not 'reasonably practicable' for him to do so, The mother will also lose her right to return if she 'unreasonably refuses' reasonably suitable alternative employment offered to her by an employer of any size.

In practice, how many women anxious to return will know about and follow the procedures regarding notice? Mainly those who are better educated, more intelligent and/or at higher levels — plus those whose trade unions or staff associations provide procedures and reminders. The rest will lose their rights.

Once again, individual employees are likely to suffer but in the long run unions will gain. It should not take too long for the word to get around that if you want to preserve your rights, you should join a union. Once again, then, the statute which the Government has clearly intended to reduce union power may actually increase it.

NB Even to qualify for maternity pay an employee must give notice to her employer that she will be away "due to pregnancy or confinement" where reasonably practicable at least 21 days before her departure. This notice need only be in writing if the employer so requests.

Wise employers will now request written notice — both in the employees contract of employment or written particulars and as part of normal maternity procedure.

Wise *employees* will give timely written notice both for maternity pay and leave and will keep a copy.

---

* Part-timers are included in the minimum. So if a business employs more than five people, *including part-timers*, the usual maternity leave provisions apply.

Chapter 15

Guarantee pay

The purpose of guarantee pay is to guarantee to most non-salaried employees a little of the security that their salaried colleagues inevitably enjoy. If your outfit goes on to a short working week (or, to use the statutory phrase, if there are 'workless days' caused by a 'diminution' in the need for workers), you will continue to get your money. Those who clock in or who are only paid for those hours they actually work will be out of luck and out of money. No work, no pay.

So the 1975 Act introduced some measure of protection for those employees who suffer from workless days, provided that they have been on the books for at least four weeks. The main exception: where the 'workless day' results from a trade dispute involving employees of their employers (or of any 'associated' employer, which means, in broad terms, an employer in the same group or under the same control).

If, for instance, your company has to operate a short working week because your tool room or your delivery men go on strike, your employees will have to rely on unemployment benefit. If the same employment hiccup was caused through an external stoppage — perhaps caused by the powermen or by someone else's strike, causing non-delivery of your essential materials — then guarantee money will be payable.

These rules have never been particularly popular with anyone. Employers do not like them because they have to make the payments. Employees are not thrilled with joy because guarantee pay is taxable, while unemployment benefit is not. Anyway: the amount of guarantee pay has always been limited.

The maximum has always been fixed at a modest, daily rate (at present £8.00) and for a maximum of five days during any set period. This period was a fixed three months, commencing on the first of May, August, November and February. So an employee might get (for instance) five days' guarantee pay during the last week in April and another five days during the first week in May.

The 1980 Act has introduced a 'rolling' three-month period. An employee cannot get guarantee pay for more than five days in any three-month period. So if he has a five-day batch, he will have to wait three months before he gets the next one. Otherwise, the guarantee pay system remains unaffected by the new rules.

Chapter 16

Discrimination

Every executive and manager must be a successful 'discriminator', or he did not deserve to leave the lower ranks. The law only attempts to prevent discrimination on an anti-social basis.

In practice, discrimination in employment matters is restricted only if it is on any of three improper bases — sex, race and trade union. The first two are not affected by the 1980 Act; the third lies at the root of both the legislation and its underlying, political and philosophical intent.

The Equal Pay Act and the Sex Discrimination Act have between them sought to outlaw sex discrimination in employment. Briefly:

1 Men and women are entitled to equal pay for equal work — you must not discriminate against a woman by paying her less for work which is either the same or assessed on the same basis. This was laid down in *The Equal Pay Act, 1970*, and has been amended and strengthened by *The Sex Discrimination Act, 1975*, so that a 'non-discrimination' clause is now implied into every employee's contract.

2 It is unlawful to discriminate against an employee because he is a man or woman or because he or she is married. This applies to selection, appointment, training, promotion and dismissal alike. Discrimination remains permitted on the ground that a person is *unmarried.*

3 It is unlawful to discriminate against an employee in any of the above respects (appointment, etc.) because of his or her

race, nationality, colour or ethnic or national origin. To some extent, these definitions have yet to be judicially defined. For example, is it unlawful to discriminate against a Jewish employee? Would that be discrimination on grounds of religion only? Religious discrimination is not banned — presumably because of the basic human rights of people in Northern Ireland to discriminate on that basis.

4 It is unlawful to discriminate against an employee because he wishes to join or to take part in the activities of an independent trade union, or not to join or participate in the activities of a non-independent union, staff association or other workers' organisation.

So important are these rights that their infringement not only gives the person discriminated against the right to bring an action to an industrial tribunal, but if he is dismissed on grounds of discrimination, the normal 52-week qualifying period for unfair dismissal protection does not apply. In addition, if he can obtain a certificate from a trade union official that he has been dismissed on grounds of discrimination, the tribunal may (and very occasionally does) order that he be kept in the employer's employment until the unfair dismissal case is heard.

In addition, the statutory provision which enables a tribunal to order that the employee be reinstated in his job was mainly introduced so as to make discrimination more expensive.

How, then, are these rules affected by the new changes in the law?

With the doubling of the qualifying period for unfair dismissal protection, the discrimination exceptions have become potentially more important, but there is no evidence that their use has increased. Indeed, it has proved very difficult to establish discrimination on grounds of sex and almost impossible on grounds of race. This sort of discrimination clearly exists, but is difficult to prove.

There are also several important exceptions to the rules. One of them is hilariously expressed as follows. You may discriminate on grounds of sex where 'sex is an essential qualification for the job' — like your secretary? 'Race' — we are told in a Department of Employment explanation — is an 'essential qualification' for the job of a waiter in a Chinese restaurant because that is part of the decor. The same, please note, does not apply to a chef. English people may be quite as good at cooking Chinese delicacies. . . .

The 1980 Act brings real change in the area of trade union discrimination. In the past, the emphasis has been entirely on giving people the right, if they so wish, to join and to take part in the activities of an independent union — and to penalise employers who interfered with that right. Now comes the counter-effort to prevent discrimination against employees who prefer *not* to join independent trade unions, in closed-shop situations.

'It's Rule 15 of the revised disputes procedure. . . !'

Part Two
TRADE UNION, COLLECTIVE AND CORPORATE RIGHTS

Chapter 17
Introduction

As discussed at the start of this book, the mainstream of industrial relations law conveniently divides into two separate channels. The waters mix and intermingle and the currents almost invariably run in the same direction. But the channels are still sufficiently separate for both the law — and this book — to keep them apart. One deals with the individual rights of the employee. His basic, statutory protection has been consolidated into the 1978 Act. As we have seen, this has now been amended by *The Employment Act, 1980*. The 1978 Act — together with the Court decisions which have interpreted and explained it — forms the bulk and the background of the first part of this book. We now move on to corporate rights.

The other stream of law — which scarcely existed before 1971, but which has now almost reached flood level — attempts to create a framework for the operation of industrial relations, including union organisation; recognition; closed shops; collective bargaining; industrial disputes; and the participation of workers and their organisations in the decision-making process (often referred to as 'worker participation'). With that, we begin — because it lies at the root of the 1980 Act. That Act — combined with other changes in the rules effected by statutory order — makes important but largely peripheral changes in the laws affecting individual rights. But its effect on trade union relations will be mighty, not only because of its words, standing alone, but especially through their impact on the atmosphere of the industrial relations scene.

It is inevitable that governments, lawyers and writers should try to divide up the rules, if only to fit them into Acts of Parliament, or on occasion (as in this case) into chapters and parts of books. But please remember once again that the division is essentially artificial. For instance: closed shops may be a matter of overall trade union relations, but the rights of an individual to contract out could scarcely be more personal, particularly when they are based on 'grounds of conscience or other deeply held personal conviction' (and anyway, what do those words mean?).

Again: the new rules on secondary action have emerged after much Court battle and following the miseries and confusion of the 'long, hard winter' of 1978-79. They are now in legal form. But they could scarcely be more political in their impact. And while they lie at the root of a trade union's right and power to organise industrial action, they obviously affect most profoundly the individual rights not only of the union organiser (and what, now, is his protection against prosecution and civil suit, if he flouts the rules?), but also the individual picket.

It is therefore inevitable that the waters will splash over from one part of this book to the other. Indeed, some of the rules will need explanation in both contexts — that of industrial relations and that of personal rights and remedies.

For instance, the individual who is hurt at work through the negligence or breach of statutory duty of his employer, director or another employee may claim his remedy in a civil court. At the same time, society has set up a new structure of basic law with which the employer and every 'director, manager and secretary' must comply. Failure to do so may lead to prosecution in a criminal court.

Above all, though, Parliament and successive governments have (individually and through the excellent Health and Safety Commission) sought to involve trade unions in the effort to preserve and to protect the life and limb of their members. Safety representatives and safety committees are operating throughout the country. They, too, must be put into the context of employment law. There, too, individual and collective rights and wrongs come and go together.

The Government believes that great restraint and protection should be given to employees who do not belong to trade unions. At one time, there were rumours in the corridors of power that it intended to reintroduce the section originally in *The Health and Safety at Work etc. Act, 1974*, but repealed by

The Employment Protection Act, 1975, giving the Employment Secretary the power to make Regulations requiring employers to consult with elected representatives of the shop floor. Recognising that the implementation of such a suggestion would almost certainly cause the collapse not only of the united efforts of the Health and Safety Commission itself, but also of the current safety representative arrangements, all is at present quiet on that front. The 1980 Act makes no reference to it. But even so, we all know of occasions when disputes over safety have been used or abused by one side or the other or both, for purposes which have little to do with their current origins.

So, as the origin of the 1980 Act was the Government's dissatisfaction with the current state of trade union law and power, that is where we now begin.

Chapter 18

The background

Trade union and labour relations law, like all other branches of our legal rules, has two sources. The first is statute — Acts of Parliament. Parliament is supreme; no Court has the power (such as that wielded by the Supreme Court in the United States) to declare a statute 'unconstitutional'. When Parliament acts, it may overrule any previous law, whether made by Parliament itself or by the Courts.

'Judge-made law' is our second source. Courts are bound to follow precedents established by any equivalent or higher Court, from the High Court upwards. Only the House of Lords may overrule its own precedents.

Under this so-called 'common law' system, Judges who wish to overrule previous decisions must do so by a roundabout route. A Judge will say (as Lord Denning does, most frequently): 'This case is not the same as the other one. I must "distinguish it" on the facts.' He will seek a way to do what he regards as justice, through his interpretation of existing decisions.

Nor has any Judge the power to overrule any statute. He may say: 'This section has the most unfortunate consequences, which surely were not foreseen by the legislature. I hope that it may be repealed or amended. Meanwhile, I have no alternative other than to give judgment in accordance with the law as it stands.' Or the Judge may interpret the law — sometimes in the oddest of ways.

Parliament and the Courts act and interact, rule and overrule, interpret, reinterpret and sometimes misinterpret. Meanwhile, employers and their industrial relations and personnel executives and managers must try to cope as best they can, within the rules and the framework made for them by others. Equally, whenever rules are made, those who dislike them will seek, with the help of their lawyers, to get around them.

In the field of finance, tax evasion is a crime but tax avoidance has been described as a 'lawful art'. It is proper 'so to arrange your affairs as to attract the least possible tax'. It is both a proper and an inevitable commercial tactic, regarded by most businessmen as both lawful and essential.

So why is it either wrong or unexpected for trade unions to look for ways to avoid the effect of laws which *they* regard as harmful to *them* in *their* work? Employers who ignored the Industrial Relations Act rules banning closed shops may have done so because they wished to keep their businesses going or (and this was surprisingly common) because they preferred to work in a closed-shop situation*. But no one accused them of being wicked law breakers.

Whether you like or agree with the process or not, you must expect trade unions to seek ways of avoiding or ignoring or circumventing the rules created by the new Act. It is not enough to see what Parliament has created and how the Courts have interpreted the rules. You must also examine how they will be used, tactically.

Next, then: an outline of and a basic skeletal guide to industrial relations law, as it has evolved since 1971.

* See Chapter 28.

Chapter 19
Industrial relations law — a quick guide

The Industrial Relations Act, 1971 created a legal framework for industrial relations, largely adapted from the American system. It was repealed by *The Trade Union and Labour Relations Act, 1974*, and has largely disappeared, with three major exceptions:

1 It was this (Conservative) statute which first introduced the *unfair dismissal rules*. These were re-enacted in and strengthened by *The Trade Union and Labour Relations Act, 1974*; they were re-enforced by *The Employment Protection Act, 1975*; the rules were then brought together into *The Employment Protection (Consolidation) Act, 1978*; and they were subsequently reweighted in the employer's favour by:
a Regulations that establish the qualifying period for unfair dismissal protection (unless the dismissal was on grounds of sex, race or trade union discrimination) as continuous employment of 52 weeks (as defined), instead of the previous 26 weeks.
b The 1980 Act, which provides that the burden of proving fairness no longer rests on the employer; and which reduces the employee's potential 'basic award' rights.

2 *The Trade Union and Labour Relations Act, 1974*, was the first stage in the implementation of the agreement between the new Labour government and the trade union movement (called by its proponents 'the social contract' or 'social compact' — by its opponents, the 'conspiracy': have it your own way, but recognise its existence and importance). As we have seen, the 1974 Act repealed the Industrial Relations Act and re-enacted the unfair dismissal rules, in strengthened form.

3   *The Employment Protection Act, 1975* increased the powers of 'independent' (and generally of 'recognised') trade unions, as well as the protection of individual employees. The latter changes are now in the Employment Protection (Consolidation) Act. The former include:

A   *Rights that are unaffected by the 1980 Act or recent regulations* including:
a   Disclosure of information to independent, recognised trade unions, during the course of collective bargaining, and their rights to be consulted concerning proposed redundancies.
b   Right of individual employees to itemised pay statements.
c   Right of an individual employee to a written statement of reasons for his dismissal — after six months' service (this period remains unchanged).
d   Right of officials of independent, recognised trade unions to time off work for trade union duties; and of individual employees to time off for public duties.
e   Rights of individual employees against insolvent employers — including claims against the Redundancy Fund, for the bulk of the money owing to them.

B   *Provisions now amended or supplemented* including:
a   The power of the Advisory, Conciliation and Arbitration Service (hereafter called 'ACAS') to make Codes of Practice — now supplemented by a similar power given to the Employment Secretary.
b   Maternity rights — maternity pay and maternity leave (now made harder for employees to obtain) due to new required procedures.

C   *Provisions repealed* including:
a   The entire recognition procedures, formerly regulated by ACAS and the Central Arbitration Committee (hereinafter called 'CAC').
b   Schedule 11 (of the 1975 Act), which gave unions the right to claim improved terms and conditions for members where these were below those 'recognised' or 'received' by 'comparable workers' in the trade or industry and in that district or area.

The third stage in the Labour government's agreement was to have been the introduction of worker participation legislation. The Bullock Commission sat and reported. Partly through divisions within the ranks of the Labour party and the trade union movement, but largely through the absence of any Parliamentary majority, the Bullock Report was not implemented. Other proposals (including the latest: for a supervisory board arrangement) were tabled; but worker participation arrangements have emerged through the side door, rather than by the main (Westminster) entrance. These now include:

1 *Collective bargaining.* What business with trade union representation can take major decisions (or, on occasion, even minor ones) without consultation and (where possible) agreement?
2 *Disclosure of information* for collective bargaining.
3 *Consultation regarding proposed redundancies.*
4 *Safety representatives and committees.*
5 *Union representation* among trustees of pension schemes.
6 *Informal participation* through (non-required) works committees, etc.

The three-year period of wage restraint resulted from (almost unanimous) union agreement and consent. That restraint was (almost totally and miraculously) enforced without legislative backing. But when the agreement collapsed, so did the Labour government.

The Employment Act, 1980 has swung back the pendulum, reducing (in theory at any rate) the power of trade unions.

The Code of Industrial Relations Practice, made under powers contained in the Industrial Relations Act, has been retained. But its rules are being gradually overtaken by later ACAS Codes, which deal with discipline, disclosure of information to trade unions during the course of collective bargaining and time off work (see Appendices 7, 8 and 9).

Atmosphere and attitudes changed profoundly. The 1980 Act is a reflection of its 1971 predecessor. Much of this book is concerned with atmosphere, which (as any theatrical expert will tell you) requires as careful and as subtle handling as the more tangible scenery on any stage, not least that on which the performers of the industrial relations world carry on their activities.

Chapter 20

Laws, regulations and codes

The 'Secretary of State' (which, in this context, means the Employment Secretary) is now empowered to make Codes of Practice. Why? What does this mean and what effect will it have on the industrial relations scene?

Parliament imposes its will in three main ways:

1. Directly, by statute (Parliament 'acts' — it en*acts* Acts of Parliament).
2. By 'enabling' others to make legislation on its behalf — 'delegated legislation' — generally contained in regulations.
3. Through Codes of Practice — also made by others and merely 'laid' before Parliament.

Obviously, if a rule is contained in a statute, it is the law of the land. Not so obviously, delegated legislation has precisely the same effect. The Health and Safety Commission, for instance, may promulgate regulations. Offend against the Protection of Eyes Regulations, for example, and it is no excuse to say: 'Well, these rules were not in the Act. . .'.

Delegated legislation is dangerous because it is expanding, expansive and as difficult to control as it is inevitable, particularly now that Parliament is meant to scrutinise EEC legislation, as well as its own.

Codes do not have the same force as rules contained in statutes or regulations. The offender will not be prosecuted or sued merely for breach of a code. But if he is involved in any civil or criminal proceedings to which that breach is relevant, it may — and probably will — be used in evidence against him.

Authorised codes have proliferated. Filling the gap between enforceable regulations and mere guidance, they began with the Highway Code; continued with the Code of Industrial Relations Practice, made under the Industrial Relations Act; then (as we have seen) came the ACAS Codes. Then we have the Code which, together with the Regulations and Guidance Notes, lays down the rules for safety committees and representatives. Other authorised safety codes are on their way.

All these codes are 'approved', which means that they have legal effect. You or your employers' association or a trade union or the TUC or anyone else may put out a code, for the guidance of members or others or even laying down standards of conduct which are expected from the people concerned. These may be very important within your own set-up but they have no legal weight. Such is the TUC Code on Picketing.

Now the Government has decided that power to make codes specifically concerning industrial relations should not rest entirely with ACAS. That body will only put out a code with the agreement of both the CBI and the TUC nominees, included among its governing authority. In other words: without the consent of the trade unions, there will be no ACAS Code on picketing, nor on any other contentious subject. ACAS works and succeeds through consensus.

So in addition to the new legal rules contained in the 1980 Act, there will soon be codes to supplement them.* The Government will provide guidelines to the conduct it expects. Those who act in breach of a code are liable and likely to have their conduct or misconduct used in evidence against them.

Before an authorised code comes into effect, it must normally be 'laid' before Parliament. It must receive the seal of Parliamentary approval. However, as Parliament has no power to amend the code but can only say 'yea' or 'nay'; as the Government's majority will ensure that such a code is sped on its way; and as no code laid before Parliament has ever been rejected, the gesture of 'laying' before the two Houses is just that — a gesture and no more.

---

* The first two will deal with picketing and closed shops, respectively. They are likely to be approved by Parliament in October 1980 and implemented soon after — probably within a month or two. See Appendices 13 and 14 for Drafts.

Chapter 21
'Independent' trade unions

One proclaimed object of the Industrial Relations Act was to strengthen the hand of 'independent' (or, as they were often then called 'responsible') trade unions, while weakening the power of 'wild-cat strikers'. The then Government received no thanks for its efforts from the trade union movement, especially when the Registrar of Trade Unions replaced the Registrar of Friendly Societies and was given power to peruse and to require change in the rules of those unions which wished to be on the register.

When the 1971 Act was repealed, the Registrar was replaced by the Certification Officer, whose main task was and is to certify that a particular union is 'independent'. This remains his main function, even though the 1980 Act also makes him administrator of the scheme to provide payments out of public funds towards expenditure incurred by independent trade unions in conducting secret ballots.

It is the 'independent' trade union which enjoys most of the legal benefits. So consider:
1   What is a 'trade union'?
2   When is it 'independent', in law?
Section 28 of the 1974 Act defines a trade union as meaning *'an organisation (whether permanent or temporary) which either —*

(a) Consists wholly or mainly of workers of one or more descriptions and is an organisation whose principal purposes include the regulation of relations between workers of that description or those descriptions and employers or employers' associations; or which

   (b) Consists wholly or mainly of —
      (1) Constituent or affiliated organisations which fulfil the

conditions specified in paragraph (a) above (or themselves consist wholly or mainly of constituent or affiliated organisations which fulfil those conditions) or

(2) Representatives of such constituent or affiliated organisations;

and in either case being an organisation whose principal purposes include the regulation of relations between workers and employers or between workers and employers' associations, or include the regulation of relations between its constituent or affiliated organisations.'

In a word: a 'trade union' is a workers' organisation which is designed to regulate relations between workers of the description concerned and their employers. A union unites workers of a particular category, giving them the strength together which individually they eminently and obviously lack.

A trade union may or may not be 'independent'. Many staff associations may properly be defined as 'trade unions', but they are essentially under the thumb (or, more happily, the wing) of their employers — benevolent or otherwise.

Section 30 of the 1974 Act defines an *'independent trade union' as meaning 'a trade union which —*

(a) is not under the control or domination of an employer or of a group of employers or of one or more employers' associations; and

(b) is not liable to interference by an employer or by any such group or association (arising out of the provision of financial or material support or by any other means whatsoever) tending towards such control.'

The Certification Officer decides on independence on the basis of 'domination' or 'control' and not because a union is or is not affiliated to the TUC. However: the application by a non-affiliated union is bound to be opposed by the TUC. If the opposition is unsuccessful (as, for instance, in the well known case of the United Kingdom Association of Professional Engineers — UKAPE), then the opponents have no right of appeal. If, however, an application is turned down by the Certification Officer, appeal lies to the Employment Appeal Tribunal. And it is from the decisions of the Tribunal that the criteria for 'independence' have been established.

Chapter 22

When is a union 'recognised'?

It is enough for a union to be 'independent' for its officials to enjoy a measure of legal protection, when acting 'in contemplation or furtherance of a trade dispute' (as defined and limited). But it is not enough, if the union wishes to enjoy other major rights and privileges — including, for instance, the right to be consulted about proposed redundancies, the right to disclosure of information during the course of collective bargaining, or the right to appoint safety representatives and to require the setting up of safety committees. So what does 'recognition' really mean?

You do not 'recognise' a trade union merely because you accept that it is independent — any more than you 'recognise' its leader by being on 'Hello, Clive' terms with him. Recognition means recognition to any substantial extent for the purposes of collective bargaining.

In the case of *Transport and General Workers' Union* v. *Andrew Dyer*, three driver members of the TGWU were made redundant. The union complained that it ought to have been consulted in accordance with Section 99 of the Employment Protection Act. The employers maintained that they had not recognised the union although they had held discussions with them over the earlier sacking of a union member, which had resulted in the member being reinstated.

The Employment Appeal Tribunal decided that although there was no necessity for a formal act of recognition, if recognition was going to be inferred then the acts should be 'clear and unequivocal'.

In *National Union of Tailors and Garment Workers* v. *Charles Ltd*, the EAT held that not only must the acts be clear and unequivocal, but must also give rise to the clear inference that the employers have recognised the union. The question of what amounts to recognition is one of both fact and law.

The most recent and important decision was given in *National Union of Gold, Silver and Allied Trades* v. *Albury Brothers Ltd.* Again there was no formal recognition agreement, but the company was a member of a trade association which had negotiated terms and conditions of employment with the union. When four employees were made redundant, the union complained that they had not been consulted. The case reached the Court of Appeal, where Lord Denning proclaimed: 'An act of recognition is such an important matter involving such serious consequences for both sides, both for the employers and for the union, that it should not be held to be established unless the evidence is clear upon it, either by agreement or by actual conduct clearly showing recognition'.

In this case, the Court of Appeal decided there was insufficient conduct to constitute recognition. They could not infer recognition without clear and cogent evidence that it was intended by both parties.

Chapter 23

Recognition procedures

Employees generally join unions because they wish to be represented by a workers' organisation for the purposes of collective bargaining. Recognising that individually they are weak, they wish to replace *individual* bargaining about terms and conditions of work with bargaining on a *collective* basis by those who are 'recognised' by the employer as acting for them and on their behalf.

Suppose, then, that a union applies for recognition. What do you do?

Obviously, you first assess whether or not you are prepared to grant that recognition and, if so, with what limitation (if any) upon it. If it is clear that a majority of people in your business or in the particular sector or shop, stratum or area or trade — belong to that union, then you will probably agree. But you may wish to refuse recognition for many reasons, including the following:

1   Because you do not consider that there are enough of your employees in the category or area concerned with their terms and conditions to be decided on a collective basis rather than individually.
2   Because to recognise the union making the claim would offend other unions (recognised or unrecognised), so that your agreement would cause more trouble than it avoided.
3   Because you wish to avoid collective bargaining — either for the present or (as in the Grunwick case) permanently.

If you and your union can agree on recognition, then you should put that agreement into writing in the appropriate form; you should expand it into appropriate procedural agreements — especially for the conduct of collective bargaining and for the regulation of disagreements or disputes.

Recognition will, of course, produce an increase in the power of the union concerned. You will inevitably be involved in a form of worker participation. Hopefully, this will be welcome to you. Anyway, it is inevitable, and you will no doubt have considered the consequences of recognition before you agreed.

Conversely: you must consider what would happen if you refuse recognition. Until the 1980 Act, at least the procedures were clear. Today we are back to the pre-1975 era of industrial negotiation and the flexing of muscles.

Until the new Act, the procedures (in brief) were as follows:

1 The union or the employer consulted ACAS, which would advise, conciliate or (if that failed) set up a secret ballot among the appropriate employees to find out whether or not they wished the union concerned to represent them.

2 If the ballot showed what ACAS (in its discretion and wisdom) regarded as a sufficient majority for recognition, then it would recommend recognition to the employer. Its discretion was very wide, though. When the UKAPE applied for recognition in one company and won a substantial majority among the engineers, ACAS still declined to recommend recognition because the AUEW threatened industrial action. This ACAS decision was upheld by the House of Lords. ACAS is in business to improve industrial relations and not to make them worse and it considered that recognition in this case would do damage.

Unfortunately, while ACAS had a very wide discretion in making its recommendations, it had little power in working with or against employers who failed or refused to co-operate. In the Grunwick case, the House of Lords held that Mr George Ward, proprietor of the business, was acting within his legal rights when he refused ACAS access to the names and addresses of his employees. As the ACAS ballot was necessarily taken only among those employees who were on strike because their employer refused to recognise the union, it was hardly surprising that they voted in favour of recognition. But as the recommendation was made without full consultation with the workforce, it was held to be invalid.

With inadequate power and short of staff, ACAS had no

love for the recognition procedures. Its Chairman, Jim Mortimer, frequently deplored them. Employers disliked the procedures because on occasion they were forced into recognition which they wished to avoid. Trade unions disliked the arrangements which tended to be slow and cumbersome. Now the procedures have disappeared, repealed by the 1980 Act — which replaces them with nothing.

So we are back to shop-floor bargaining. If an employer disliked an ACAS recognition recommendation, he could refuse to implement it. The union would then go to the Central Arbitration Committee. If the CAC upheld the ruling and the employers still failed to comply with it, a term was implied into the contract of employment of each employee which (in effect) was meant to ensure that he would be entitled to terms and conditions which should be not less satisfactory to him than those which he would have received, had the union been recognised.

This procedure has also gone and has not been replaced. We are back to bargaining and to trials of strength. True, the union or the employer may still bring in ACAS which can and will attempt to resolve a dispute. In accordance with its powers, it will advise, as requested. But it can only conciliate with the consent of both sides. It has no power other than that accorded to it by the consent of the parties.

So, in this area at least, we are back to pre-1975 methods, with ACAS replacing the officials of the Department of Employment. You must make your decision and your peace as best you can; accept conciliation where you wish it; and judge each case on its own facts.

If a recognition application is made, here is a checklist of the major considerations which you should take into account:

1   What is the strength of the union? How many members does it have in your business as a whole and/or in that section or department or division or category in respect of which recognition is sought; and what percentage of the workforce in that area is unionised?
2   What other unions are *(a)* represented among your workforce, and *(b)* recognised by you, for the purposes of collective bargaining? What attitude would they take if you *(a)* recognised the applicant or *(b)* refused recognition?

3   What would be the industrial relations effects of recognition? What changes would result and to what extent would these be *(a)* welcome or *(b)* unwelcome to you?
4   What would be the industrial relations results of refusal to recognise? What action would the union be likely *(a)* to wish to take or *(b)* to be able to take, in support of its claim? What strength, support and finance could it command? To what extent would it be assisted at local or national level? Would these effects overflow into other sections or branches or works, within your undertaking?
5   What advice have you sought and received and from whom? Have you sufficiently consulted your own colleagues, within your own organisation?

Remember: a recognition decision is one of vast importance, not only for its immediate impact on your business but for its potential future effects. From recognition flows contact, co-operation and mutual effort — and also procedure agreements, union membership agreements and potential conflict. You cannot expect both to recognise and to work with workers' organisations, while carrying on as if you were running a business dictatorship, however benevolent.

Finally: if you wish to refuse recognition in the long run, how can you do it? There is only one answer — and it is that successfully shown by such organisations as IBM and Marks & Spencer. You must provide terms and conditions of work which are regarded by your workers as being at least as good as those which a union could achieve for them. In that case, they will probably not wish to spend any of their pay on union dues. Otherwise, union membership and recognition will inevitably come in time, whether on the shop floor or within management itself.

Chapter 24

Fair wages and 'recognised' and 'comparable' terms

The Fair Wages Resolution was passed by Parliament in 1946. In general terms it provided that Government contracts should not be given to those who pay their employees less than the 'recognised' rate for the job or whose terms and conditions are below those of 'comparable' workers, in the same trade, industry and area. If public money is to be expended, then its recipients should not be paying their workers less than the rates negotiated by their unions (and hence 'recognised' or generally received by comparable workers).

Schedule 11 of the 1975 Act extended this concept to all employees, whether or not (and to whatever extent, if any) their employers receive payment from public funds.

In addition, the 1975 Act repealed the whole of *The Terms and Conditions of Employment Act, 1959*. This Act provided (among other things) that industrial organisations registered under the 1971 Act could make a report to the Employment Secretary that certain employers were not observing agreements in respect of employment of the nature covered.

Schedule 11 is now repealed. So there is no power left for trade unions to apply for improved terms and conditions where employees are receiving less than recognised rates or the general level in the area. And the situation is even worse than it was before the 1975 Act came into effect, because of the repeal of the 1959 Act.

What, then, will be the practical result of the Schedule's repeal? Curiously (once again) good employers may (in the long run, at least) be as aggravated by its disappearance, as workers and their unions may lose as a result. Employers do not welcome competition from those who pay employees less than the going (or recognised or comparable) rate for the job. And if and when major restraint reappears, the prospects of avoiding industrial dispute through the submission of an acceptable claim will disappear.

A Schedule 11 claim had to be brought by a trade union. In practice, though, in an estimated 50 per cent or so of all claims brought during the years of wage restraint, employers and employees connived. The employers would have been happy (or at least willing) to meet the union's claim for higher pay, but they were prevented from doing so by the rules of the anti-inflationary game. But Schedule 11 awards, like tribunal and court decisions awarding equal pay to women, had priority over pay 'guidelines' or any other then current restraint on pay increases.

With the return of free collective bargaining, the Schedule 11 queue outside the Central Arbitration Committee would inevitably have shrivelled. But if (perish the thought) wage restraint (by any other name — perhaps, such as 'counter-inflation' measures) were to return, then that avenue of escape of (in the main) the poorly paid would have reopened.

Meanwhile, Schedule 11 would still have been useful to those whose terms and conditions were less than those 'recognised' or commonly paid to others in their sphere. Today, the plight of the worst-off is as parlous as their strength is reduced. The fair wages resolution remains, but Schedule 11 has gone.

In one way, then, its disappearance has caused fewer real problems than appears on the surface. Some of its usefulness had in any event disappeared, along with wage restraint. In another way, though, its death will do more harm than people realise. The fact that this remedy was available itself made its impact. We know that 1,600 Schedule 11 cases were decided by the CAC. We can and shall never know how many were threatened but never needed to be brought, nor still less how many employers improved the pay of some or all of their workforce, knowing that if they did not do so, Schedule 11 was there to help.

Chapter 25
Collective bargaining, disclosure of information and worker participation

There is more than one way of running a business. You can do it from the boardroom, from the executive or managerial chair — or from the union HQ. Indeed, you can to some extent run Britain from the IMF or a company from the office of the managing director of its main customers.

Employers frequently proclaim that employees should take an interest in the success of their undertakings. 'Only if workers are involved can we hope to achieve good industrial relations and the best results for the business. . . .' But suggest that involvement is impossible without at least a degree of power over decision-making and enthusiasm wanes rapidly.

Equally, unions sometimes demand 'industrial democracy', which means adequate power in the decision-making process. But point out that some decisions (and especially those involving redundancies) are exceedingly unpleasant and the union may regard itself as happier on its own, traditional side of the bargaining table.

In theory, then, both management and unions are in favour of 'participation' (or 'industrial democracy' or call it what you will). In practice, the concept of involvement is far more complicated and, in some ways, more revolutionary than most people realise. Its advance depends upon trust. The 1980 Act does not deal directly with participation, in any form. In this respect, its atmospheric effect does the damage.

As part of its pledge to introduce worker participation, the Labour Government set up the Bullock Committee. Its eventual report may be summarised in a simple formula: $2x + y$. Boards of companies (said the majority of its members) should include an equal number of representatives of the shareholders (x) and of unions (the other x), plus a number of independent nominees (y).

The Bullock Report died because neither side wanted it. Management feared loss of power, public confidence and investment. Unions feared that if their leaders joined boards, their members would lose confidence. Some regarded board membership as a form of corruption; others denounced this form of participation as designed to preserve a system which ought to be destroyed.

So both parties retreated to their traditional, opposing and essentially conservative positions. A change may be painful; the familiar comforteth.

That does not mean, though, the death of worker participation, either in the narrow or (still less) in the broader sense. The latter already exists, largely unrecognised. The former will almost certainly reappear, in one form or another, if a Labour administration is elected with a sufficient parliamentary majority. Meanwhile, some experts believe that the present Conservative Government will introduce some form of participation — if only through works committees and if only to ward off participation at boardroom level. Meanwhile: no business with active union participation can take many major decisions without at least consultation and, in many cases, without agreement.

Collective bargaining is the main form of participation. It is more highly developed in Britain than in most other countries and many experts (including ACAS Chairman, Jim Mortimer) regard it as the most important and the best way in which workers can and should take part in the decision-making process.

The law interferes as little as possible with either individual or with collective bargaining. The parties hammer out their own agreements as best they can, either on their own or, where necessary, with the help of ACAS or of any other catalyst, public or private.

Once struck, the individual, private or business bargain is normally enforceable by law. Not so the collective deal.

The Industrial Relations Act made formal collective bargains legally binding, except those in which the parties had specifically contracted out of legal enforceability. A 'contracting-out clause' became in practice an inevitable part of every collective agreement. Legal enforceability was a dead letter. It was repealed, along with the Industrial Relations Act. In its place, the parties to a collective bargain may 'contract in' to legal enforceability. No one ever does.

So no court can grant an injunction to restrain unions from breaking an agreement nor, still less, an order for specific performance, requiring compliance. Unlike the case of a commercial contract, it cannot award damages to compensate the innocent party for loss suffered.

Disputes must be sorted out at shop-floor level . . . through negotiating machinery . . . by agreed procedures. . . . The courts cannot intervene.

This arrangement, of course, works both ways. The doors of the court are closed to unions and to employers alike.

Nor does it remove a union's intention to comply with its agreement. It is a great mistake to regard legal sanctions as man's most mighty motivation. How many bargains do businessmen enter into among themselves, saying to themselves (although, of course, not to each other): 'Well, if it goes wrong, they'll never take us to court. . .'? Or: 'Never mind. We've built in some splendid loopholes. . . .'

Unions and employers alike comply with their agreements for quite different reasons. Briefly, they regard a bargain as fair. Anyway, the moral pressures to comply are great and failure to do so may lead to unnecessary unrest.

Still, just as many bargains — private, commercial, national and international — are often 'renegotiated', the same applies to a collective agreement. Parties may agree, disagree . . . negotiate, renegotiate . . . decide and decide again. . . . The great difference between collective and other bargains is that the law lets the parties get on with it. Lawyers ('bloody' or otherwise — see Chapter 37) may help or hinder in the making of the agreement, but enforcement is not a matter for judges.

Chapter 26
Secret ballots and union procedures

Unions are proudly independent bodies which regulate their own activities within the limits of the law. Every company has its own rules, designed and created for its own purposes and contained in its memorandum and articles of association. Many of these rules are required by law; many differ widely, from one company to another.

As with business organisations, so with unions. They are regulated by their rules.

All union rules necessarily provide procedures, among others for qualification for and disqualification from membership; election to membership; election of officers at every level; and for the taking and for the discontinuance of industrial action. Some provide for secret ballots for some or all elections or major decisions; others do not.

Not surprisingly, unions — like companies or countries — deeply dislike and distrust interference in their internal management. It was probably the then Government's insistence that the Registrar of Trade Unions have power to require changes in union rules that provided the main impetus to keeping unions off the register created under the Industrial Relations Act, in spite of resultant tax and other disadvantages. There is no more certain way to upset a union than to attempt to meddle with its rules from the outside.

Why, then, does the 1980 Act give unions the right in many cases to apply for payment of the cost of secret ballots out of public funds, at a time when public expenditure is being severely cut? The Government says: 'Because we wish to encourage secret ballots, both in the election of union officers and especially in the making of decisions to call or to call off industrial action'. The more people who take part in such decisions and the more secretly they do so (it is believed) the more likely it is that 'the moderates' will win and 'the militants' lose.

The major (and largely unrecognised) result of the ACAS Code on time off work is the huge and almost universal proliferation of union election meetings in working hours. Those who attend are normally paid on exactly the same basis as if they were at work. Maximum attendance is welcomed by the unions and by the management alike.

Now arrange the same election by secret ballot. Even if you hand the employees their ballot papers at their workplace, it is unlikely that the number or proportion will be as great. Certainly if you post the ballot papers to people's homes, the 'turn-out' is unlikely to be particularly great.

As for ballots on industrial disputes, many unions' rules already provide for these, No miners' strike, for instance, can begin without a secret ballot.

Once industrial action is begun on a decision taken by secret ballot, then it can normally only come to an end in the same way. So while some strikes may be avoided by balloting, others will be extended and prolonged through the same method.

Again: when the Government had the power to impose compulsory strike ballots during the days of the Industrial Relations Act, it only did so on one occasion — the same railwaymen's strike which it fended off for a short time by using (again, on that unique and solitary occasion) its power to impose a compulsory cooling-off period. Once the ballot is imposed from above, the odds are that the members will rally around their leadership. That is what happened in the railwaymen's strike and the method was never again used.

Under the 1980 Act, compulsion has been rejected. The Government has *not* taken powers to impose ballots, secret or otherwise, on unions who do not want them. Instead, it hopes to encourage secret ballots by at least ensuring that they can be carried out without cost to the union.

Likely practical result? Those unions which already ballot will continue to do so — but as they have been forbidden by the TUC, they are most unlikely to claim the costs from the public via the Certification Officer, as provided for in the new rules.

But will others follow suit and bring in ballots where there were none? We shall see.

Finally: what do we make of the provision that, before issuing a code of practice 'containing practical guidance for promoting the improvement of industrial relations', the Minister must 'consult'?

The Minister will prepare a draft code; submit it to ACAS and consult with them; and 'consider any representations made to him' about it. No doubt if he is a good Minister, he will listen to reason. But as the advice and the representations will be wide and varying, there will certainly be enough backing among them for his own views.

The law requires 'consultation' with trade unions about proposed redundancies. It does not require the employer to accept the advice of any union regarding any or all of the redundancies.

Still: it is better for the Minister to be required to listen, even if he may prove hard of hearing. And certainly it is the democratic right of all concerned not only to have a case but to argue it. Then at least when things go wrong, those consulted can say: 'We told you so...', which will not prevent trouble but which may at least provide some solace and avoid any adequate plea in mitigation to those in authority over those who did not listen.

Note: as a result of a House of Lords amendment to the Act, employers are required to set up proper facilities for secret ballots, at independent trade union request. However, this applies only to trade unions 'recognised' by the employer and to an employer where the number of workers employed by him (or by an associated employer) is 20 or more.

Chapter 27

Time off work — and union elections

The more Parliament creates the possibilities for industrial disruption, the more important it becomes to create, preserve and encourage good relations. Conversely, the greater the opportunities for disharmony, the more time off work union officials are likely to need — for the avoidance and, if necessary, for the resolution of disputes. So while the time off work rules contained in the 1978 Act and in the ACAS Code have not been directly affected by the 1980 Act, their importance has grown and their urgency has become far more apparent.

Any employee who is an official of an independent trade union, recognised for the purposes of collective bargaining, is entitled to time off work during working hours and at his normal rate of pay for two purposes:

1   To carry out official duties 'concerned with industrial relations between the employer and any associated employer and their employees' or

2   To undergo 'training in aspects of industrial relations relevant to the carrying out of those duties'.

Again, the amount of time off that must be allowed will be that which is reasonable in all the circumstances — and in considering reasonableness, regard will be had to the Code of Practice issued by ACAS (Appendix 9).

A trade union official given time off for industrial relations purposes (as opposed, for example, to engaging in general organisation for his union) is entitled to his normal remuneration. That means he should get the normal pay which he is in effect guaranteed under his terms of service. Frequently, though, this pay is itself subject to negotiated agreement between management and union.

As to the rule that the official may take 'reasonable paid time off' during working hours, we come once again to the barrier of 'reasonableness'. How much time will be 'reasonable' will depend upon all the circumstances of the case.

Again: the Act requires employers to permit members of trade unions to take reasonable time off during working hours for the purpose of taking part in an appropriate trade union activity. Such activities do not include those 'which consist of industrial action, whether or not in contemplation or furtherance of a trade dispute'. There is no requirement that an employee be paid while given such time off. But can you in practice dock his pay? And anyway, what 'trade union activity' is covered?

The Code suggests that an official should be permitted reasonable paid time off during working hours for such purposes as 'collective bargaining; informing members about negotiations or consultations; meetings with officials or union officers; interviews with employers on grievance or disciplinary matters; appearances on behalf of members before industrial tribunals; and explanations to new employees about the role of the union in the workplace industrial relations structure'.

The scope of these purposes is potentially massive and those employers who do not already provide paid time off for such purposes are in for a rude shock. They may argue that the official is asking for 'unreasonable' time off. What is or is not 'reasonable' will depend not just on the Code (which carefully does not define that most common word) but on all the circumstances of the particular case.

Again: in order to achieve 'the active participation of members', as opposed to 'officials' — their 'reasonable time off' should include taking part as representatives 'in meetings of official policy-making bodies of the union, such as the executive committee or the annual conference, or representing the union on external bodies such as the committees of industrial training boards'.

Above all: 'Voting at the workplace in union elections' should be permitted in company time. And there may be occasions when it is reasonable for unions to hold meetings during working hours 'because of the urgency of the matter to be discussed or where to do so would not adversely affect production or services'. Employers, concludes the paragraph, 'may also have an interest in ensuring that meetings are representative'.

The word 'may' is a mighty understatement. Employers *do* have such an interest. And many progressive employers have long provided time off for union meetings in working hours.

Naturally, you cannot dock officials' pay for their trade union activities. But is it good industrial relations policy to reduce the pay of the ordinary member who attends a union meeting, to take part in its considerations or (perhaps more important) to vote? Once again, an increasing number of lively managements are allowing trade union members time off on a paid basis, for all such activities. A successful, happy enterprise requires not only a skilled, intelligent management, but a well run, representative trade union body.

The 1978 Act also requires time off work to be given in two other circumstances — to an employee who is carrying out a 'public duty'; and to an employee who is made redundant and requires time off work in order to search for work or new training for that work.

'An employer shall permit an employee of his who is a Justice of the Peace, a member of a local authority, a member of a statutory tribunal, a member of (in England and Wales) a Regional Health Authority or Area Health Authority (or, in Scotland, Health Board)', or a manager of a local education authority educational establishment (or, in Scotland, a school or college council or the governing body of a central institution or a college of education), or a member of a water authority or river purification board — to take time off during that employee's working hours.

The object of the time off? 'The performance of any of the duties of his office or, as the case may be, his duties as such a member.'

The duties referred to are:
1 Attendance at a meeting of the body or any of its committees or sub-committees; or
2 The doing of any other thing approved by the body, or anything of a class so approved, the purpose of the discharge of the functions of the body or any of its committees or sub-committees.'

How much time, then, is an employee to be permitted to take off? On what occasions and subject to what conditions must you allow him to take time off?

The answer depends in each case upon what is 'reasonable in all the circumstances'. Special regard, says the Act, must be had to the following:

a   How much time off is required for the performance of the duties of the office or as a member of the body in question, and how much time off is required for the performance of the particular duty?

b   How much time off has the employee already been permitted either for carrying out trade union duties or activities?

c   The circumstances of the employer's business and the effect of the employee's absence on the running of that business.

For the larger firm with many employees, the absence of one man or woman for an occasional public duty will go almost unnoticed. Remove the same employee for the same time from a small outfit and it may come to a temporary halt. Again, the employee must not be unreasonable in his demands for time off, while the employer must be reasonable in acceding to his sensible requests. Note, too, that it is up to you whether you pay employees who take time off for their public duties.

Of course, the list of public duties is limited — but the Employment Secretary may add to it. Although jury duty is not included, it need not be — you cannot refuse to permit your employees to sit on juries. They may, though, ask for their jury duty to be postponed if it would create difficulties for the business for them to be away, and courts do try to oblige.

Finally: 'An employee who is given notice of dismissal by reason of redundancy shall ... be entitled before the expiration of his notice to be allowed by his employer reasonable time off during working hours in order to look for new employment or to make arrangements for training for future employment'. This right is given to employees of two years' standing who would qualify for redundancy pay.

Once more, the employee is only entitled to time off as and when it is 'reasonable' for him to take it to seek work and training, but not to train.

What are an employee's rights if he does not get the time off to which he considers that he is reasonably entitled — for trade union or public duties or to replace the job which is about to disappear? As usual he may complain to an industrial tribunal. Where reasonably practicable, the employee (again, as usual) has three months from the date when the complaint arose within which to bring it to the notice of the tribunal.

In the case of time off for public or trade union duties, the tribunal may award a successful claimant such compensation as it considers 'just and equitable in all the circumstances, having regard to the employer's default in failing to permit time off to be taken by the employee and to any loss sustained by the employee which is attributable to the matters complained of'. In addition, if the employer has failed to pay the employee the whole or part of any amount required to be paid as remuneration, if he properly took time off for trade union duties, then the tribunal may order the employer to pay the employee the amount which is due to him.

Where a redundant employee is not given time off to hunt or make arrangements for training for other work, he may be awarded up to two-fifths of a normal week's pay.

Finally, Section 13 of the 1980 Act contains a happy and uncontentious addition to time off work rights. A pregnant employee who — on the advice of a doctor or a registered midwife or health visitor — makes an appointment to receive ante-natal care is entitled 'not to be unreasonably refused time off during her working hours to enable her to keep the appointment'. Other than for the first appointment, she must on request produce a certificate of pregnancy from the doctor or other expert, plus an appointment card. While away, she will be entitled to her normal pay. An employee who maintains that she has been wrongfully deprived of her rights under this Section may claim compensation from an industrial tribunal.

Chapter 28

Union membership agreements and closed shops

Not surprisingly, unions seek to obtain the agreement of employers to a closed shop or Union Membership Agreement (UMA). More surprisingly: while employers (and their managers) frequently have philosophical objections to UMA arrangements, the majority prefer to work with them.

In practice, it is generally easier to deal with unions in a closed-shop situation. An integrated workforce, represented by stewards or other officials who speak on behalf of them all, is normally a better bargaining partner than people representing only part of the workforce. Fragmentation and divisions among trade unions are much harder for employers to cope with. Nor is any dispute more difficult for an employer to solve than one between unions. Demarcation is one problem: membership disputes is another. Neither is likely in a closed shop.

Why, then, all the argument and dispute over closed shops and the rights of individuals to contract out of union membership? Because of a classic clash between freedoms.

On the one hand, unions object to 'free riders'. Their members say: 'Why should we pay our union dues for a bargaining set-up which benefits those who will not belong? Why should they benefit if they will not join?'

Often, the members and officers of the union have made considerable sacrifices in order to achieve representation, recognition, rights and benefits, for those members. Why (they ask) should we not have the freedom to say: 'We do not want to work with anyone who will not join our union'?

So what of the freedom of an individual not to join? Why should he lose his job? 'He is free', says the union, 'to find other work elsewhere'.

Set against the freedom of the union and of its members not to work with non-joiners, you have the freedom of people not to join — the right to say: 'I object to belonging to a union. I will not join — nor am I prepared to contribute to a set-up which I consider to be wrong.'

These two views are, of course, entirely irreconcilable. They also have profound political implications. The Labour Party receives its mass support and finance from the trade unions. They favour closed shops. Labour Governments therefore legislate in favour of the freedom of people to organise in trade unions and to refuse to work with those who will not join.

Conservative Governments receive their major financial support from industry — from the owners of capital, from those who basically oppose the power of trade unions. Conservative Governments legislate against closed shops.

With certain, complicated and almost impossible exceptions, the Industrial Relations Act banned closed shops. Result: in practice, nil. Trade unions ignored the ban and expected employers to do the same — which they did. It was business as usual. The closed shop remained open.

The 1971 Act provided that when closed shops were lawful, people could still contract out on grounds of religion or conscience, paying the amount of the union dues either to the union itself or to a nominated charity. But the scheme was ignored and did not work.

In 1974, the Labour Government repealed the Industrial Relations Act and closed shops became lawful. This time, individual employees could contract out on grounds of religion only. As we shall see, this exception has now been highly expanded.

Whatever the law, *you* must consider your tactics. If a union presses you to enter into a closed-shop arrangement, what should you do? I suggest the following steps:

1 Assess whether or not you would prefer to have a closed-shop agreement. Have you any philosophical or political objections to one? Do you recognise that in your case, a UMA would bring you managerial benefits, including perhaps a reduction in friction or (more positively) an improvement in industrial relations?

2   Consider: what is the strength of the union within your workforce? Even if you are agreeable to a UMA, would it command the support of a substantial majority of the workers concerned? This is important not only because the answer will affect the union's strength if you refuse, but also the consequences if you agree.

3   Consult your colleagues. It is almost always a mistake to make this sort of agreement (or, in fact, any other of major consequence) without consultation. As is so often the case, communications with unions are both important and generally satisfactory; communications between different levels of management or management in different places are often a disgrace.

4   If you decide to agree to a UMA, try to make sure that it will apply to future employees and not to existing ones. Almost every dispute in practice arises where a UMA is applied to those who are already employed and who then refuse to join. Have you consulted the appropriate precedents? Have you prepared the necessary documentation? Has your agreement covered all essential points?

5   If you are likely to be under persistent pressure to accept a closed-shop agreement, will you be able successfully to resist it? If not, then you must be prepared to give way while the union is still willing to accept an agreement which applies (as above) to future and not to existing employees.

Chapter 29

Closed shops — the new rules

A 'shop' is closed when the employers and union or unions concerned agree that only members of the appropriate union or unions will be employed within that unit. As a 'closed shop' invariably results from an agreement relating to the union membership, the Act correctly refers to 'Union Membership Agreements' (UMAs).

A UMA, like most other business arrangements, usually arises after negotiation, bargaining, pressure and counter-pressure, threat and counter-threat. But no closed shop can operate without an agreement.

The government believes that UMAs provide too much strength to unions and too powerful an infringement of the rights of individual employees to work without joining. Rejecting union arguments that their members should have freedom *not* to work with those who wish to benefit from their efforts without contributing to their cause, as well as the pleas of many practical personnel and industrial relations managers who prefer to work in an integrated, unionised situation, the Act makes UMAs more difficult to create and easier to avoid.

Suppose, then, that a particular union is dominant among your workforce, a majority of whom are members. The steward or convenor may come to you and say: 'We ask you to agree that in future you will not take on new employees who are not already members of our union'. If you make such an agreement, you will have a 'pre-entry' closed shop among your employees. If the deal is that every employee must 'be or become' a member, then it is a 'post-entry' closed shop. Either way it is based on an 'agreement'.

The Government has remembered lessons from the

Industrial Relations Act, which banned all UMAs other than so-called 'agency shop agreements', which were extremely limited and, in practice, confined in the main to seamen and actors. But UMAs continued to operate and even to grow. Few managements are prepared to risk closing down their closed shops and their businesses at the same time. And anyway, as already indicated, a high percentage of involved managers were happy to work in closed-shop situations.

So the Act does not ban closed shops. But it does extensively widen opportunities to opt out and strictly limits their growth.

The Trade Union and Labour Relations Act, 1974 (as amended by the 1976 Act) gave any affected employee the right to contract out of a UMA only 'on grounds of religious belief'. Now it will be unfair to dismiss a non-joiner if he 'genuinely objects on grounds of conscience or other deeply held personal conviction to being a member of any trade union whatsoever or of a particular trade union'. This extended right not to join or to belong applies to existing as well as to future closed shops. Its extent is so wide that — subject to the restraints of pressure from fellow workers — membership of a union in a closed-shop situation may almost be voluntary.

The Act does not define 'conscience', nor (still less) what is or is not a 'deeply held personal conviction'. But any genuine belief that membership of the union concerned or any union would be wrong, should suffice. For instance:

Mr A has a profound dislike of socialism and has always voted against the Labour Party. He would regard his belief as a genuine one of 'conscience', but in any event, it is certainly long and 'deeply' held, personal and would amount to a 'conviction'. So he might well be entitled not to join a union affiliated to the Labour Party — which means nearly all of them. The fact that individual union members are entitled to 'contract out' of their Labour Party contributions (and a majority of members of some unions make use of that right) would not alter his right to keep out of the union altogether.

Mr B is a Catholic who has long, hard and conscientiously campaigned against abortion. He is unwilling to join a union which proclaims the right of women to have abortion 'on demand'. He would prefer to join a religiously based union, along the lines of those operating in many continental countries. The Act implicitly gives him freedom not to join any of our British unions.

Mr C is a member of (say) the United Kingdom Association of Professional Engineers (UKAPE). He has a 'deeply held personal conviction' that membership of the AUEW would be wrong for him, because of its TUC affiliation . . . because he regards himself as a 'professional engineer', better represented by UKAPE . . . or simply because he has a profound belief in his right to be different.

So the exit door from compulsory union membership is wide open. Almost any affected employee can walk through it, no matter how long the union membership agreement may have been in operation.

Naturally, if employees do accept Parliament's invitation to leave unions, the industrial relations effects may be profound. You would have to consider, for instance, what you would do to protect these lawful 'free riders' — and to keep your business going if unions concerned exercise their right to withdraw the labour of their men, so as to force you to dismiss people whom the law now says are entitled to stay on.

Chapter 30

Future closed shops

Closed shops which came into existence before the 1980 Act remain lawful, although their members may opt out on grounds of conscience or 'deeply held personal conviction'. What of new UMAs. These remain lawful — but only those which are 'approved' will be legally binding on the employees concerned. Unless the UMA is 'approved', a non-joiner cannot be 'fairly' dismissed for his 'free riding'. So when is a UMA 'approved'? And how will these arrangements work?

To be 'approved', there must be:

1 A secret ballot of all those 'entitled to vote', conducted so as to secure 'so far as reasonably practicable' that all such people have the right to vote — secretly.
2 Approval by 'not less than 80 per cent of those entitled to vote in the ballot', of the agreement's application to them.

In other words: 80 per cent of those entitled to vote in the secret ballot must cast their vote in favour of the closed shop. I repeat: 80 per cent of those *'entitled* to vote' — not 80 per cent of those who *do* vote.

It is sometimes possible to achieve a very high turnout in a workshop ballot. This may be done by handing ballot papers personally to each employee who turns up at work and by sending (or better, by delivering) ballot papers to those who are away sick. And postal votes are sometimes arranged for people in hospital or on holiday.

However: even if everyone has a ballot paper, he is not bound to use it. Some folk have a religious, a conscientious objection or even a 'deeply held personal conviction' which restrains them from voting at all. Even in Australia, where voters are required to turn out at the polling station, not everyone votes when he gets there.

So we start from the proposition that it is not easy to obtain an 80 per cent turnout of those entitled to vote. To obtain a majority of 80/20 in favour (or, for that matter, against) a closed shop — or anything else in a free society — is highly unlikely.

It therefore follows that 'approved' UMAs will be a rarity. Existing closed-shop agreements remain in force, subject to the opting-out rules which themselves will be subject to workshop pressures. And new UMAs are likely to arise by tacit, unwritten, informal arrangements, rather than through ballots which everyone is likely to recognise are unlikely to produce an 80 per cent majority of those 'entitled to vote'.

The extent to which these new rules will restrict future closed-shop arrangements is both arguable and much argued. The new Code (see Draft in Appendix 14) and its implementation will have some effect. But union strength and persistence and managerial preference and necessity are likely to remain decisive, tomorrow as they are today.

Chapter 31

Dismissing the 'free rider'

Obviously, it is 'unfair' to dismiss an employee because he exercises his legal right not to belong to a trade union in a closed-shop/UMA situation. His 'genuine objection' may be to joining the particular union, for which he has a peculiar dislike; or he may wish to keep out of unions altogether. Either way, he exercises that right and if you dismiss him, then his dismissal will be unfair.

Indeed, the qualifying period for unfair dismissal protection (now 52 weeks — as defined, which may mean a little less) does not apply where the dismissal is for 'an inadmissible reason'. Sacking for refusal to join a trade union where the employee opts out on the basis of a genuine, conscientious objection or a deeply held personal conviction would be an 'inadmissible reason', so even a new employee could claim his unfair dismissal remedy.

The major and most likely claim by the sacked employee would be for compensation, now reaching a maximum of £6,250. The employee must 'mitigate' his loss, keeping it to the minimum by obtaining other work, if he can. And his own conduct is taken into account — but the exercise of his legal right not to join could scarcely be regarded as 'contributory conduct'.

If the employee is long term, then he will also be able to claim a 'basic award'. The Act would remove his right to the former maximum of two weeks' pay at up to £120 per week, if no loss was suffered. But it retains the right to lost statutory redundancy entitlement. Many employees who opt out of new closed-shop arrangements are in fact old-timers. After 20 years' service at the appropriate age and pay, the basic award may reach £3,600.

Trade union, collective and corporate rights 89

Finally: the dismissed employee may claim to be re-engaged or reinstated. Obviously, that claim would be fiercely contested by his employers, who would say (with apparent justification) that taking him back onto the payroll would spell disaster in industrial relations. Anyway, only in the famous case of the sleeping night-shift worker at Vauxhall has a tribunal made an 'additional award' for unreasonable refusal to obey an order for reinstatement or re-engagement. Still, it could happen. And if the reason for the dismissal was (as in this case would be likely) discrimination, the additional award could be £6,240.

Suppose, then, that one of your employees lawfully opts out of a closed-shop/UMA arrangement. The union concerned threatens industrial action which could paralyse your production. What do you do? First: you add up the possible cash cost of a dismissal. This (as we have seen) could amount to the grand total of £16,090. Then you look at Section 10 of the Act.

'*If in proceedings before an industrial tribunal on a complaint against an employer . . . the employer claims —*
  (a) that he was induced to dismiss the complainant by pressure which a trade union or other person exercised on him by calling, organising, procuring or financing a strike or other industrial action, or by threatening to do so, and
  (b) that the pressure was exercised because the complainant was not a member of any trade union or of a particular trade union
the employer may before the hearing of the complaint require the person who he claims exercised the pressure to be joined . . . as a party to the proceedings.'*

You sack a non-joiner under union pressure? Then you can bring the union or official into the action as a 'third party' and seek a contribution in respect of any sum which you may have to pay to the claimant. That contribution 'shall be such as the tribunal considers to be just and equitable in the circumstances, and may constitute a complete indemnity'.

So you may claim a complete indemnity from the union or its officer against any compensation which you may have to pay — and 'compensation' includes *(a)* a compensatory award; *(b)* a basic award; and *(c)* an additional award.

It is, of course, both possible and often intelligent to have rights which you do not necessarily use. The fact that you may

* See also Chapter 36

have access to union funds to compensate you will not necessarily induce you to seek your contribution or indemnity from that union. You will have to balance the likely amount of the award to the employee against the likely or potential cost of any possible or probable industrial action which the union would take if you tried to attack its funds. Most industrial relations observers believe that only eccentric and very determined employers (such, perhaps, as a latter-day Ward of Grunwick) would be likely to make use of this procedure.

Most will shrug; pay off the non-joiner; and continue to produce. But of course, the greater the movement against joining, the more major the potential cost of sacking those who exercise their new rights not to join.

* * *

Can an employer discipline an employee who refuses to join a union?

Until now, the law has ensured that an employee should not have action taken against him by his employer 'to compel him to belong to a union which is not independent'. The words 'which is not independent' are now repealed.

If an employee wishes to opt out of a closed shop, then you may discipline him unless he had one of the following reasons:
1   He acted because of 'conscience or other deeply held personal conviction'. In practice, there are few situations which may not be covered by these words; or
2   He was already employed by you when the closed shop came into existence; or
3   The (post-1980 Act) closed shop was not 'approved' by 80 per cent in a secret ballot.

In the case of a post-Act UMA, you may not discipline an employee who is a member of a closed shop, for taking part in its activities, if the UMA is 'approved'.

In the same way as you can claim a complete indemnity from the union for any compensation you may have to pay a claimant in respect of an unfair dismissal claim, so you can in any action by an employee for disciplinary action that you have taken against him, short of dismissing him.

Chapter 32

Picketing — in law and in practice

Picketing is a form of pressure designed to increase the effect of your own industrial action by inducing others to extend or at least not to destroy it. Theoretically, it is lawful — in spite of new limitations. In practice (and here is where we begin) it takes place by consent of the local police.

Even under the old rules, under which peaceful picketing was permitted anywhere other than outside a person's residence, the police could still stop it. This was largely thanks to a ruling laid down in a parking prosecution, brought long ago against a barrister who is now a distinguished judge.

The lawyer parked his car on a road where there were no yellow lines or other restrictions. He was charged with 'obstruction'. He challenged the police to show that he had prevented any other vehicle from passing freely to or fro. 'That', said the Court, 'is not the point. Your car was stationary on a patch of road? Then no other vehicle could pass over that patch, which was therefore obstructed. You caused the obstruction and are therefore guilty of the offence charged.'

So if a picket remains stationary on a road, he is obstructing a highway. If he stands on a pavement, he is obstructing that pavement. The fact that he gets in no one's way is irrelevant.

Along comes a policeman. 'Move along, there', he says. Unless the picket complies, he is (by definition) obstructing that police officer in the execution of his-duty.

So the police require no law to ban picketing of any sort. In the dark days of the 1978-1979 winter, a very senior police officer told me: 'We do not need new laws. We police by consent.'

Anyway: new laws there are — directed against 'secondary'

picketing. Picketing is said to be 'primary' if it is outside the place of work of the people in dispute. It is 'secondary' if it is outside someone else's.

Some of your employees are on strike and they are trying to persuade other workers or other people's delivery vehicles to keep away so as not to prejudice their efforts through carrying on deliveries as if no dispute were taking place? Then clearly that picketing was, is and will remain both direct and in obvious 'contemplation and furtherance' of the dispute.

Now let the same pickets move to your suppliers' premises. They are still 'picketing' and they may even be approaching some of the same people. But that picketing is 'secondary' and, under the new rules, it is unlawful.

Similar terms are applied to other sorts of boycott. For instance: some Arab countries still refuse to trade with Israel. This is a 'primary' boycott. They may also threaten not to do business with your company, if you yourself trade with or invest in that country or its enterprises. That is the 'secondary' boycott.

In some cases (one example being a company that manufacture containers), they say: 'If you supply to those who supply to the State of Israel, we will boycott your goods'. That is a 'tertiary' boycott.

Should secondary or tertiary boycotting or blacking or picketing be allowed? Once again, we run into the clash of freedoms. On the one hand, in the industrial scene, workers say: 'Why should we not be free to attempt to persuade others not to destroy that industrial action which we are free to take to preserve, protect or extend our interests?' On the other, a stranger to the dispute replies: 'Why should you be free to ruin my business, because you are in dispute with yours?' Or even: 'Why should our employees risk unemployment because they are hazarding our freedom to earn our living and to keep our business going?'

In the clash over closed shops, the differences between the political parties were, are and will doubtless remain clearly defined. In the scene of the industrial secondary picket, the sides are more erratically arrayed.

The Labour Government and the TUC both recognised the general, public outrage during the 1978/79 winter against the effects of secondary picketing during the lorry drivers' strike.

That administration was under pressure from some people to bring in anti-picketing legislation. It refused, for the following reasons:

1. Because it would not have worked. When picketing was unlawful during the days of the Industrial Relations Act, the powers vested in the police were only used on a handful of occasions, resulting in most cases in riot and rampage. At the suggestion of the Minister then responsible for public order, the police let their new powers lie dormant.
2. Because (as we have seen) the police already have sufficient anti-picketing power, if they see fit to use it — which, normally, they do not. Had the Government wished to stimulate police intervention, it could no doubt had done so. Sensibly, it did not.
3. Because to do so would have divided its own ranks. The outcry against a new law with potential criminal consequences, banning the use of a traditional (if disliked) method of strengthening the arm of strikers, could have caused dismay on the Left, of the sort induced by that ill-fated document produced in the late 1960s, *In Place of Strife*.

This reasoning has failed to convince the new administration. Whether they are right or wrong, those who deal with industrial relations must now cope with a new scene, which they have set.

Chapter 33

Picketing and secondary action — the new rules*

The new picketing rules are designed to restrict pickets in the main to their own places of work. Primary picketing remains lawful; secondary and other picketing is banned. Primary pickets and their union officials remain protected because their action is 'in contemplation or furtherance' of the trade dispute concerned. Those who picket elsewhere (or 'black' other peoples' premises or goods) are unprotected — the dispute is now 'too remote' from the action to be covered. This, in effect, puts the law back where it was when established by a series of decisions of the Court of Appeal, presided over by Lord Denning — and before those decisions were overruled by the House of Lords.

The law (in this case, *The Trade Union and Labour Relations Act, 1974*) protects unions and their employees, when acting in accordance with the 'golden formula' — 'in contemplation or furtherance of a trade dispute'. The Court of Appeal held that if you picket outside other people's premises (that is, engage in 'secondary' rather than in 'primary' action), your activities are not necessarily 'in contemplation or furtherance' of the trade dispute in question — physically and in law they may be too removed therefrom. The House of Lords (in a series of decisions culminating in *Express Newspapers* v. *McShane*) ruled (in effect) that a decision as to whether or not a particular action is 'in contemplation or furtherance' of a particular trade dispute is one essentially for the trade union people concerned. Their officers or members are picketing or blacking one place in order to sharpen the impact of industrial action elsewhere? Then secondary action is an extension of the primary action and both are 'in contemplation or furtherance' of the trade dispute concerned.

*See Appendices 13 and 14 — the draft Codes contain useful explanations of the official view of the meaning of the relevant Sections. In addition, watch out for amplification such as the 6 picket suggested limit.

The Court of Appeal held (in broad terms) that a careful distinction must be made between industrial and political action (respectively). Where (for instance) the trade union demands cannot possibly be met, the action is political and hence not in contemplation or furtherance of a 'trade dispute'.

The House of Lords decided that this distinction could not properly be drawn. Just as people frequently start the bargaining at a level far away from that which they expect eventually to attain, so in the end bargaining decisions must be left to them. Assuming that there is a genuine 'trade dispute' — that is, a dispute of difference between employers and employees or between employees and between different employers), then the employees and their unions are entitled to the protection of the law and it is not for courts to draw the boundary lines between political and industrial relations decisions.

Parliament is entitled at any time to overrule decisions of Courts — and it has now done so regarding picketing and blacking. The method? To remove the protection of pickets and their union organisers against legal action. Instead of merely being liable to prosecution (generally by the police) for obstruction (of the pavement, highway or of police officers in the execution of their duties) or for intimidation, blackmail or assault, they now become far more liable to civil action, brought by employers harmed.

First: the new rights, subject of course to the old restrictions regarding obstruction and the like:

'It shall be lawful for a person in contemplation or furtherance of a trade dispute to attend —
  (a) at or near his own place of work, or
  (b) if he is an official of a trade union, at or near the place of work of a member of that union whom he is accompanying and whom he represents,
for the purpose only of obtaining or communicating information, or peacefully persuading any person to work or abstain from working.'

In the past, peaceful picketing was permitted anywhere other than outside a person's own residence. Today, it must be 'at or near' the 'place of work' concerned. There is an exception (as we have seen) for union officials accompanying members.

There is another one for mobile, peripatetic workers — erectors, installers, maintenance men, sales representatives ... for one of them, his 'place of work' will be 'any premises of his employer from which he works or from which his work is administered'. Note: he is protected when he pickets outside his own HQ, but not if he joins with workmates at the place where he is actually working.

* * *

Apart from curbing secondary picketing, the Act also restricts the immunities given to trade union officials and their members when using other forms of 'secondary action' to promote the success of their primary industrial action. In particular, employers who suffer from secondary industrial action may sue the individual concerned in the civil courts, claiming an injunction to restrain the continuation or repetition of the wrong or damages, where the action has resulted in interference in or the breach of commercial contracts.

Unfortunately, Section 17 is incredibly abstruse and difficult to interpret. Consider for instance the Employment Secretary's explanation to the Commons of the alleged meaning of the Section, in so far as it applies to associated companies:

'Where a firm is in dispute with its employees and the firm seeks to transfer work to an associated company belonging to the same group, it would be unfair if the employees of the associated company were not able to take action to prevent that additional work being done to break the strike in that manner. ... Action taken against a customer who is receiving goods is a secondary action and that action should have immunity, provided that it is directed principally towards the original dispute and not for other motives ... that should be so not only in respect of a customer but in respect of a supplier....

'I have always conceded that the clause is difficult and complex because we seek to steer a course between *The Trade Union and Labour Relations Act, 1974,* and the 1976 Act, which gives immunity to trade unions for practically any purposes that they like to perform in any direction and however distant it is from the original dispute, so long as the trade union official feels that it has some relevance to the original dispute ... we have sought to narrow that provision. . . .

'We also recognise that to take immunity right back so that it allows only for breaches of contract in primary disputes goes to the other extreme. . . .'

Remember, though, that a person who engages in secondary action will still be protected if, but only if, it comes within the legally complicated provisions of Section 17.

'Secondary action' as defined by the Act occurs where someone induces another to break a contract of employment or interferes or induces another to interfere with its performance *or* threatens to do so, 'if the employer under the contract of employment is not a party to the trade dispute'. So these rules do not apply as between the parties to the dispute.

Next, 'the purpose or principal purpose of the secondary action' must be 'directly to prevent or disrupt the supply during the dispute of goods or services between an employer who is a party to the dispute and the employer under the contract of employment to which the secondary action relates'. Normally, this means 'blacking'.

In addition, the secondary action must be 'likely to achieve' its purpose.

The Section then goes on to pile complexity upon complication. If and when employers see fit to attempt to sue trade unions or their employees whose immunities are now restricted, courts will have to attempt to unravel the legislators' meaning. Who, for instance, is 'an employer who is party to the dispute'? As the words 'trade dispute' are widely defined in Section 29 of the 1976 Act, the Section may be less powerful than it appears.

Anyway, my advice remains unchanged — let someone else be the test case.

Also, if you do run into actual or potential trouble over secondary action, as the Section is so difficult to construe and as any current Codes of Practice will have to be taken into account, you will certainly need skilled legal help in its interpretation and experienced advice in the practical effect which the issue of a writ will be likely to have on your industrial relations and whether or not it would be likely to promote or to delay a satisfactory solution to your industrial troubles.

Chapter 34

Trade union immunities — and further legislation?

The status of a trade union is an odd one. It is capable of making a contract. All property belonging to it is vested in trustees, who hold it in trust for the union. It is capable of being sued and can sue in its own name. And it may be prosecuted in its own name. Judgments, awards and orders may be enforced against any property held in trust for the union.

Again, the general law concerning contempt of court applies to trade unions. As Sir John Donaldson said in the case of *Heaton* v. *Transport and General Workers' Union*: 'Once it is alleged that a court order has been disobeyed, the matter ceases to be a dispute between the parties and becomes one that involves the court itself'.

If a union or its official is held to have committed a wrongful act which was not 'in contemplation or furtherance of a trade dispute' under the new rules, what then? How can Court orders be enforced against them?

Unions, their officers and members are citizens like all others and in the absence of some special protection, the ordinary enforcement rules apply. In practice, unions and those people connected with them normally comply with Court orders. It is the exception that causes the problems.

In one famous Industrial Relations Act battle, AUEW engineers refused to pay a massive fine imposed upon them by the National Industrial Relations Court. If it was to be enforced (they said) they would bring all engineering work to a halt.

There is no law to prevent one person from paying the fine of another. Unknown benefactors — rumoured to be not unconnected with Fleet Street — paid the fine for them.

If necessary, unions have funds which may be subjected to attack. But their vulnerability is not clear. In a television interview, the Prime Minister said that if the proposals on secondary industrial action do not work, 'let us go for trade union funds'. If further employment legislation follows the 1980 Act, it will probably be directed at union funds.

Meanwhile, failure to comply with a Court order is, of course, a 'contempt' of Court. Learning inevitable lessons from the sad case of the Pentonville five, jailed for refusing to obey an order of the National Industrial Relations Court and later released on the application of the Official Solicitor, it is unlikely that protestors will be jailed. But if an individual refuses to obey an order of the Court and has no money to meet a fine, then his contempt must be 'purged' — and normally, that means imprisonment.

Once the full weight of the law is imposed on an individual, his martyrdom attracts immediate support, often from those who in other circumstances would deplore his methods and philosophy. It is to avoid this outcome that Courts and Governments will do their best to impose their wishes by any available method other than jail.

* * *

The decision of the House of Lords in the sad case of *British Steel Corporation* v. *Granada* has now brought most journalists into potential conflict with the law. Courts now have limited power to order a journalist to disclose the source of information published. There was justification for requiring the *Daily Mail* reporter, Brendon Mulholland, to disclose his source in the Vassel case because security and the public interest were involved. Now this power may be used to protect private interests, including those in the public sector.

As no journalist could or would disclose a source, each is now liable to be in contempt of court and, like Mr Mulholland, to be imprisoned as a result.

So martyrdom has ceased merely to be an attraction for extremists. It has become a peril for employers and for employees alike, in each and all of the media.

Chapter 35
'Unreasonable exclusion or expulsion'

One of a trade union's most cherished powers is the right to regulate its own membership. Who may and who may not be members; how applications are made and who considers them and in what manner; when and why a member may be expelled — provisions for all these are inevitably contained in the rules of all unions.

Why, then, should any Government try to interfere in a union's freedom to choose its own members? Because (this Government replies) in a closed-shop situation, if a union will not admit a person to membership or if it expelled a member, he will lose his job. Yet again, we are balancing two freedoms — that of the union to decide on its membership and that of the individual to hold his job where a Union Membership Agreement applies.

So the regulation of unions' rights to choose members is limited to 'employment . . . in respect of which it is the practice, in accordance with a Union Membership Agreement, for the employee to belong to a specified trade union or one of a number of specified trade unions'. In such a case, a person who 'is, or is seeking to be' employed in that undertaking 'shall have the right —

(a) not to have an application for membership of a specified trade union unreasonably refused; and

(b) not to be unreasonably expelled from a specified trade union.'

Once again, the law applies the standard of 'reasonableness'. A restraint clause in a contract of service will only be enforceable if it is 'reasonable'. Dismissal will be fair if it is 'reasonable' in all the circumstances to deprive the employee of his livelihood. You may use 'reasonable force' to eject a trespasser. An occupier must take 'reasonable care' for the safety of his visitors.

An exclusion clause in a business contract for the sale of goods will be voidable if it is 'unfair or unreasonable' and in a contract for the provision of services, it will be void unless it 'satisfies the test of reasonableness' if the contract is either with a consumer or made on the supplier's 'own, standard, written terms'.

Under the Health and Safety at Work Act, an employer must take such steps as are 'reasonably practicable' to protect his own employees and others 'affected by his undertaking' and the individual employee must take such steps as are 'reasonably practicable' for his own protection and for that of his colleagues. And so on. . . .

Reasonableness is a concept which tends to be strictly personal. That which I believe to be right is 'reasonable'. If you disagree with me, then are you not unreasonable?

The law has created a so-called 'reasonable man', whose judgment is applied in these situations. He used to be called 'the man on the Clapham omnibus', in the days when omnibuses flowed through Clapham. American lawyers sometimes call him 'the man who comes home at the end of the day, rolls up his shirt sleeves and mows the lawn. . .'.

If a dispute arises on what is or is not 'reasonable' and the parties cannot resolve that dispute and it gets to a court or tribunal, then the person or people enthroned in the seat of justice will apply the test of 'reasonableness' — according to their likes and in the light of their experience. The outcome is unpredictable and will differ according to the individual or individuals hearing the case.

This applies, of course, to all decisions of all courts at all times. The judge, magistrate, tribunal member or other person in judicial authority attempts to be objective. But (as we shall analyse in Chapter 37), that objectivity is itself subject to that individual's own views, background and experience.

So who is to decide on whether or not a trade union has acted 'reasonably' in refusing membership or in expelling an existing member? First: the union itself. It must comply with its rules and if the member considers that the rules are being improperly applied, he will have appropriate remedies and appeals either within the union itself or via the TUC. And he may also take the union to court, claiming that it is in breach of its rules or that it has acted 'contrary to natural justice'.

Take, for instance, the celebrated action brought by a professional musician called Bonsor, against the Musicians' Union. A lifetime member of the union, he was expelled for alleged failure to pay his subscriptions. He maintained that the Branch Secretary had removed his name from the register without complying with union rules, in particular without consulting the Branch Committee.

The House of Lords agreed with him; granted him an injunction, restraining the union from excluding him; and also awarded him damages as compensation for his financial loss. The union and he had a contractual relationship; the union had broken that contract; and he was therefore entitled to compensation.

In the case of *Ridge* v. *Baldwin*, Lord Hodson stated that there are three features of natural justice:
1   The right to be heard by an unbiased tribunal.
2   The right to have notice of charges of misconduct.
3   The right to be heard in answer to those charges.

In *Radford* v. *Natsopa*, the Court held that any union rule which provides for an automatic forfeiture of membership without the necessity for a charge and hearing would be void as *ultra vires*, i.e. beyond the powers of the union.

When a charge is made against a member, he must be heard *before* any decision is taken. In *Leary* v. *National Union of Vehicle Builders*, Mr Leary was dismissed from his union under a rule that members who were six months in arrear with their contributions would be excluded at the discretion of the branch committee. Mr Leary was not told of the meeting of the committee which excluded him. He appealed and was given a full hearing by the appeals council but his exclusion was upheld. He appealed to the High Court, claiming that his exclusion was contrary to the rules of natural justice. The Court held that in order to fulfill the requirements of natural justice, it is not enough to have a complete hearing at the appeal stage. There must be a hearing before the original tribunal. The appeal was allowed and the exclusion overruled.

In the recent case of *Stevenson* v. *United Road Transport Union*, Lord Justice Buckley formulated the test: 'Where one party has a discretionary power to terminate the tenure or enjoyment by another of an employment . . . is that power conditional on the party invested with the power first being satisfied on a particular point which involves investigating some matter on which the other party in fairness ought to be heard or to be allowed to give his explanation or put his case? If the answer is yes, then, unless, before the power purports to have been exercised, the condition has been satisfied after the other party has been given a fair opportunity of being heard or of giving his explanation or putting his case, the power will not have been well exercised.'

The new rules supplement and do not replace the old ones. An employee who considers that he has been mistreated by his union still may and should follow the trail laid down by its own rules. These are remedies provided by his contract. He can and should also look to the trade union movement as such to provide him with his remedy, through its own procedure. He may also pursue the new remedy, provided by the 1980 Act.

A union's rules may give it the right to exclude or to expel a person from membership, in its sole and absolute discretion, as reasonably or as unreasonably as it pleases. So the employee's new right to bring a complaint to an industrial tribunal not only gives him an entirely new avenue of appeal on grounds already existing but it also extends those grounds themselves.

'A union shall not be regarded', says the Act, 'as having acted reasonably only because it has acted in accordance with the requirements of its rules' — nor 'unreasonably', only because it has acted in contravention of them. 'Reasonableness' stands apart and becomes even more difficult than usual to define.

As in the case of unfair dismissal applications, so here — the complaint must be brought within three months from the date of the act (of refusal or expulsion) complained of, unless it was not 'reasonably practicable' for the complaint to be presented before the end of that period.

As usual, a dissatisfied party may appeal to the Employment Appeal Tribunal (EAT). But whereas in all other cases appeal lies only on a point of law, here the employee may appeal 'on any question of law or fact arising from any decision of, or arising in any proceedings before, an Industrial Tribunal under this section'.

Suppose that a tribunal makes a declaration that a complaint is 'well founded'. After a four-week interval, the complainant may apply for compensation. If by that time the complainant has been admitted or readmitted to the membership of the union, his claim goes to the tribunal, which will award such compensation as it considers 'appropriate for the purpose of compensating the applicant for the loss sustained'.

If, though, the claimant has not been admitted or re-admitted to membership of the union, his application goes to the Employment Appeal Tribunal. The EAT will then award such amount as it considers 'just and equitable in all circumstances'.

As in the case of compensation for unfair dismissal, the applicant must 'mitigate his loss'. He must take reasonably active steps to replace the employment that he has lost.

The maximum compensation payable will be 30 weeks' pay at the current maximum rate for the assessment of calculating a basic award in an unfair dismissal case; plus the current maximum compensatory award (at present, £6,250). Appeal against an award of compensation again lies to the EAT, but on a question of law only.

Chapter 36
Indemnities from unions*

The 1980 Act has provided the newest and most remarkable way for an employer to earn the undying enmity of his trade unions. In broad terms, if union pressure induces him to dismiss an employee, and if that employee brings an unfair dismissal complaint to an industrial tribunal, he may require that the person who he claims exercised the pressure be joined, or in Scotland 'sisted', as a party to the proceedings. The tribunal may then order that party (inevitably, the union) to pay a contribution towards any compensation payable by the employer or even to provide that employer with a complete indemnity.

It is not unusual in law to require one person to indemnify another, if he was really at fault. Suppose, for instance, that you are poisoned by defective food, from a supermarket. You will get your rights against the retailer who will claim an indemnity against the manufacturer or perhaps from his supplier.

An employee is injured through defective equipment which you have supplied to him? Then [thanks to *The Employers' Liability (Defective Equipment) Act, 1969*] you will have to pay damages, irrespective of fault. But if that equipment was defective when you bought it, you will be able to claim your indemnity against your supplier.

In law, employers are liable to compensate those who suffer from the results of negligent acts or omissions of their employees, perpetrated in the course of their employment. If your employee harms someone else in the course of his work and you are sued, it is no answer for you to say: 'Don't blame me — it was my employee'. You get the benefit of all that he does right and you are also 'vicariously liable' for his negligence, within the scope of his employment.

Nor, in practice, can you obtain an indemnity from him, if his negligence causes you to suffer loss. As Lord Denning once said: 'If that were the law, then every employee would expect to be paid an addition to his wage or salary, so that he could take out his own insurance'. So employees do not generally

* See also Chapter 31.

indemify employers.

There are still a few contracts of employment under which the employee agrees to accept personal responsibility where (for instance) stock in his charge goes astray. These contracts are as unpleasant as they are rare. But in general, those who make their living through the efforts of others must get their indemnity (if any) from their insurers.

Equally, employers have had to bear their own responsibility for their own actions, when deciding whether or not to dismiss. They may or they may not take advice from or consult ACAS, unions, lawyers or anyone else. They take their decision and accept its consequences.

Naturally, such decisions are nearly always taken under 'pressure', of one sort or another. Maybe the foreman 'presses' to get rid of an irritating, unpleasant or unmanageable member of his team. Maybe he even threatens to resign, if the employee is kept on. If the employer gives way to that pressure, no one has ever suggested that the foreman should contribute towards or indemnify him against loss suffered, if unfair dismissal proceedings result.

Equally, unions may 'press' for the dismissal of an unwanted colleague or workmate. If sweet words are insufficient, then they may threaten or even take industrial action. Until now, they have been no more liable than the individual foreman — or manager, executive or director — in similar circumstances.

Indeed, if the action of the union officials concerned was 'in contemplation or furtherance of a trade dispute', his protection was greater than that of the manager.

The 1980 Act now removes that protection. If, then, industrial action or its threat forces you to dismiss and if that dismissal leads to an award by an Industrial Tribunal in favour of the sacked employee, you may join the union or its official as a party to the action. If the tribunal decides that the dismissal was not only unfair but also resulted from the union's threatened or actual industrial action, the union will have to repay you any money that you have to pay the employee.

Naturally, before you use your legal rights, you will consider the industrial relations consequences. Even if you have a legal entitlement, will it be wise to seek it? Or is the Government by giving you this new power really inviting you (legally) to court disaster? Is the remedy worth having? Is anyone who invites you to exercise it not like the man who asked the cat to leap off a cliff into a stormy sea, to catch a fish to rescue it from drowning?

Anyway: the law now provides you with your right and your remedy. My advice: think many times before you exercise it. Success in this sort of proceedings may be vastly more expensive than failure. Even the act of joining the union to the proceedings may (rightly or wrongly) be regarded by the union as sufficiently provocative to spark off trouble, infinitely more expensive than the sum (if any) which you may have to pay to the dismissed employee.

Finally: your problem is made no easier because you will have to decide whether or not to join the union to the proceedings before you even know whether the employee will succeed — and, if so, then how much compensation he will be awarded. Even if the dismissal was unfair, he may have obtained other work very swiftly. He will have mitigated (that is, kept to a minimum) *his* loss. By joining the union, you may have magnified *yours* beyond the measure of good industrial relations — and for little or no purpose.

Wise employers will allow this new parliamentary fruit to wither on the vine.

* * *

The Act in its final form gives similar rights to a claim, contribution or indemnity in dismissal cases arising out of 'trade union labour only' contracts with contractors or subcontractors. In brief, where an employer enters into a 'trade union labour only' contract and as a result cannot employ a particular non-member; if the employer requests the contractor to waive the union membership requirement but he refuses; if there is no other work for the employer to give to the non-member; and if as a result he has to dismiss the non-member, who claims that the dismissal was unfair — then the employer may join the contractor to the proceedings, seeking contribution or indemnity from him. In his turn, the contractor may join the union whose pressure he alleges prevented him from waiving the union membership clause.

In practice, the employer is far more likely to seek his indemnity against the contractor than the contractor against the union. But practical employers, anxious to avoid industrial trouble are unlikely to make due use of these new powers.

Chapter 37

Trade unions, courts and lawyers

Any executive or manager who wishes to understand the trade unions' approach to the law, old and especially new, must also recognise their deep dislike, distaste and distrust for the law in all its manifestations — which includes courts, tribunals, judges and (alas) lawyers. We are an unloved lot.

If an employee is dismissed, he still has two remedies in two different venues. He may bring a complaint to an Industrial Tribunal which may award him compensation or other remedies if he was qualified to claim and if the dismissal was 'unfair'. He may also claim damages for wrongful dismissal. This is an ordinary claim for breach of contract and it goes to a civil court — generally, to the County Court if it is for £2,000 or less; to the High Court if it is for a higher sum.

In practice, once an employee has become qualified for unfair dismissal protection (briefly and normally, by 52 weeks' service on a full-time basis — working at least 16 hours a week or 8 hours after 5 years' continuous service), then he can claim cheaply and swiftly. His total cash winnings may (in theory at least) exceed £16,000. To bring a claim in a civil court is slower, more expensive and unless he has either legal aid or the financial backing of his union, usually an impossibility.

As the two actions would involve the same witnesses giving the same evidence, why not combine them? *The Employment Protection Act, 1975*, gave the Government power to transfer to tribunals all claims arising out of contracts of employment, including not only disputes for wrongful dismissal but also over holiday pay and other terms of work.

Early in 1979, the Labour law officers (the Lord Chancellor, the Attorney General and the Solicitor General) decided that the time had come to remove the nonsense of two claims for the same unlawful dismissal. They consulted the views of the TUC which replied: 'Nothing doing'.

With back-bench persistence, I had been nagging successive governments to consolidate the two rights and bring them together before the tribunal. I was now referred to the TUC, at whose HQ I met a top official, expert in trade union and employment law. 'Sorry', he said. 'You fellows have got enough work without our agreeing to your getting any more!'

There was no personal animosity, of course. Many of his best friends are lawyers. But his view and that of most of his allies is clear. The more disputes that are settled on the shop floor, the better; and the more that come before any court or tribunal, the worse for the worker.

I pointed out that his own members were not getting their wrongful dismissal rights because of the cost of proceedings. He said: 'That, I am afraid, is part of the cost that we pay for keeping disputes away from courts'.

'But we are only trying to remove these disputes from courts and judges', I said, 'and to bring them before tribunals — one of whose members is almost always a TUC nominee and whose decisions are almost always unanimous'.

'Sorry', he said. 'We are trying to keep cases away from legal forums. We will not agree to any increase in litigation.'

The reasons for this attitude are several and complex. Their root lies in their lack of confidence in the decisions of courts and tribunals, even though the legally qualified chairman of a tribunal is outnumbered by laymen, two to one. Add the CBI representative and his vote to that of the lawyer chairman and we are back at two to one. . . .

The situation then gets worse when you ask: 'Who are the judges?' Lawyers, of course. And how are they qualified to understand the viewpoint of trade unionists and those whom they represent? Most are products of public or grammar schools and of ancient universities, with a background which is neither lower income nor working class. Through their sheltered (and often boarding) schools, they have emerged perhaps via the Army, through the gates of ivory towers of higher learning and into the work of a barrister, without even a pause at the factory, the office or the construction site.

As one trade union leader told me: 'Of course judges and the rest do their very best to do justice, as they see it. But few of them have any feeling for or conception of our approach to the problems of working life.'

Then (say the unions) look at the words and the decisions of judges since the days of the Taff Vale case. How often do they reflect our view? When do we get justice from the courts? At which stage, he drew my attention to some recent edict of Lord Denning.

It was against this background that Geoffrey Howe led the 1971 effort to introduce into Britain a legal framework for industrial relations, imported from the USA. Its failure was doomed. And so it is that while unions objected fiercely to the rights of employees being whittled away through the increase in the qualifying period for unfair dismissal protection and through the reduction in the basic award (see Chapter 14), they are themselves the nation's top opponents of any further intrusion of courts, tribunals or lawyers into what they regard as the proper area for shop-floor negotiation and for those procedures and precedents established by them and their managers, on behalf of their members and their employers.

We must be careful, though, not to confuse dislike of the law and lawyers with lawlessness or failure to recognise the necessity for the preservation of the rule of law. By their nature, most trade unions and most of their leaders are well set in their ways and far from revolutionary in their style. They control their own organisations by consent and they are exceedingly sensitive to any loss of influence. They dislike the tearaway much more than their employers — he has, after all, torn away from their leadership.

Equally, they are democrats by training, nature, instinct and necessity. The vast majority wish to live and to work within the law and have no desire to bring down this or any other government (however disliked) through industrial means. 'We have enough trouble keeping our own house in reasonable shape', a union chief told me, 'without trying to overrule what your House has seen fit to mishandle!'

The 1980 Act has not made the task of their leaders any easier nor the lot of their rank and file any pleasanter. The basic industrial relations question must now be: How will they react in practice to the new restrictions on their powers and (in most senses, at least) on the rights of their members?

Chapter 38

All the best — from ACAS

The Advisory, Conciliation and Arbitration Service (commonly known as ACAS) provides a magnificent, free service. Under the leadership of Jim Mortimer, it is doggedly independent. Put onto a statutory basis by the 1975 Act, it is neither the right arm of management nor the puppet of unions. With nominees of the TUC and the CBI dominating its governing body, it makes decisions by consensus and helps others to decide wherever possible by agreement.

The 1980 Act has removed the powers of ACAS to make recommendations of recognition (Chapter 22). Otherwise its position remains unaffected by law but, more crucial by far, as the tide of industrial relations problems surges forward, so ACAS is successor in title to King Canute — but with a success rate which he would have envied.

So consider: how can you make the best use of ACAS, in the light of any current darkness? Indeed, the greater the problem, the more important it is to know the powers, the duties and the possibilities of this service.

'The Service shall as it thinks fit', says *The Employment Protection Act, 1975*, 'on request or otherwise, provide, without charge, to employers, employers' associations, workers and trade unions such advice as it thinks appropriate on any matter concerned with industrial relations or employment policies'.

You have a problem over unfair dismissal? You would like to revise your grievance procedures? You do not know how to establish a friendly relationship with a particular union or its area officers? You have any other industrial relations or employment policy worries? Then write to or telephone your

112 Guide to The Employment Act, 1980

local office of ACAS or of the Department of Employment. Ask for a conciliation officer to call round and see you.*

The Service is not bound to comply with your request — it will do so 'if it thinks fit' (but this escape clause is seldom used). It may, of course, come in on its own initiative — but this is unlikely. Anyway, any help that it does provide will be 'without charge' and the scope of its potential advice is almost unlimited. The Act specifically includes the following matters upon which advice may be provided:

1 'The organisation of workers or employers for the purpose of collective bargaining.' Have you received an application for a closed shop? Is your bargaining machinery in working order? Could you not do better — with top advice?

2 'The recognition of trade unions by employers.' The Service has now lost its powers to deal with recognition disputes (see Chapter 23). But it may still advise.

3 'Machinery for the negotiation of terms and conditions of employment, and for joint consultation.' Have you new machinery to be set up — or does your old machinery require oiling?

4 'Procedures for avoiding and settling disputes and workers' grievances.' Both individual and collective disputes and grievances are included. 'Questions relating to communication between employers and workers.' Have you any — and if so what — committees or councils, and how effective are they? Are your lines of communication really open?

5 'Facilities for officials of trade unions.' With employers now required to provide reasonable time off on a paid basis for trade union officials to carry out duties in respect of industrial relations, this provision is particularly important.

6 'Procedures relating to the termination of employment.' Not, note, merely relating to dismissals. 'Termination' should,

*The address of ACAS HQ is Cleland House, Page Street, London SW1P 4ND (Tel: 01-211 3000). Details of its nearest local office from HQ or the Department of Employment (Tel: 01-213 3000).

where possible, be by agreement... without rancour or dispute
.... The time to seek the help of the Service is before trouble breaks out.

7 'Disciplinary matters.' Can you, perhaps, benefit from the experience of others in your industry (or in any other industry, for that matter), in dealing with breaches (express or implied) of your rules?

8 'Manpower planning, labour turnover and absenteeism.' The Service looks to good relations, the planning of a labour force, the reduction in labour turnover (particularly where due to dissatisfaction, or other avoidable factors) — and the reduction of absenteeism (likewise, where avoidable).

9 'Recruitment, retention, promotion and vocational training of workers.' From the industrial womb to tomb, the ubiquitous Service is available — free of charge.

10 'Payment systems, including job evaluation and equal pay.' The Equal Pay Act and Sex and Race Discrimination Acts are in full force. Do you need advice on their interpretation or implementation?

In addition to individual help, the Service 'may publish general advice on any matter concerned with industrial relations or employment policies' — including any of the matters referred to above. It may also, if it thinks fit, enquire into 'any question relating to industrial relations generally or to industrial relations in any particular industry or in any particular undertaking or part of an undertaking'. All or part may be enquired into.

Naturally, the Service will produce results from its enquiry. These findings — together with any advice given by the Service in connection with them — may be published by the Service. But publication will only be made *(a)* 'if it appears to the Service that publication is desirable for the improvement of industrial relations, either generally or in relation to the specific question enquired into' and *(b)* 'after sending a draft of the findings to, and taken into account the views of, all the parties appearing to the Service to be concerned'.

Normally, the advice of the Service is given in total confidence. If, however, the Service sets up an enquiry, it may publish the results of that enquiry, so that others in similar circumstances to the undertaking concerned may benefit. In practice, though, if either of the parties to the enquiry object to the findings and advice being published, that objection will be sustained.

So you need not normally be concerned about the confidentiality of your discussions with the Service. The conciliators may not be able to avoid seeing evil or hearing evil — but speaking evil is no part of their job. Indeed, it is their tact and impartiality which makes their service so useful.

ACAS officers vary in their skill, experience and ability. Jim Mortimer advises that if you are dissatisfied with the service you receive, you should contact your ACAS area headquarters. Tell them your problem; explain what has gone wrong; and ask them to send in someone else.

To get the best from ACAS, do not simply telephone for help. Outline your problem and ask for the assistance of an officer who is expert in that particular territory.

Better still: why not make friends with your ACAS people before you need their help at all? Drop in and see them — or invite them to visit you. Once you have established contact, you can let them know your problems and you can also appreciate some of theirs.

Chapter 39
Conciliation and arbitration

Conciliation means the bringing together of parties with opposing views and helping them to reach agreement. Obviously, this cannot be done without the consent of those parties.

Arbitration means the placing of a dispute before an independent arbitrator, and agreeing in advance to accept his ruling. Once again, there can be no arbitration without consent.

Whilst ACAS is primarily an 'advisory' service, it may also help through conciliation and arbitration — help that has never been more needed than it is, since the 1980 Act. It provides the main channel of communication between employers and employees, when normal routes are blocked.

'Where a trade dispute exists or is apprehended, the Service may — at the request of one or more parties to the dispute or otherwise — offer the parties to the dispute its assistance with a view to bringing about a settlement.'

Note: either party may request the help of the Service, which may also intervene on its own initiative.

'The assistance offered by the Service may be by way of conciliation or by other means, and may include the appointment of a person other than an officer or servant of the Service to offer assistance to the parties to the dispute with a view to bringing about a settlement.'

Conciliation — as opposed to arbitration — means the bringing together of the parties . . . the intervention of a catalyst, enabling the different elements to mix . . . neither legally nor morally is either party bound to accept the view of the conciliator. Indeed, he may prefer to express none.

In exercising its conciliatory functions, the Service 'shall have regard to the desirability of encouraging the parties to a dispute to use any appropriate agreed procedures for negotiation or the settlement of disputes.' If there are agreed procedures, these should, where possible, be used. If either party is loath to do so, the conciliator may help the parties to create new arrangements, to bring peace by agreement and to avoid industrial disruption.

'The Service shall designate officers to perform the functions of conciliation officers under any enactment (including any provision of this Act. . . .) in respect of matters which are, or could be, subject to proceedings before an Industrial Tribunal.'

Conciliation officers bring about the settlement or withdrawal of well over 40 per cent of all claims for compensation for unfair dismissal. Individual conciliation — as opposed to helping employers and employees in organised bodies — to settle differences remains the most frequent job of the conciliator.

If conciliation fails, how then can a dispute be settled? Where an individual considers that he has been unfairly dismissed, he may bring his claim before an industrial tribunal. The tribunal (independent chairman and two lay members) will settle the matter — subject to a right to appeal to the Employment Appeal Tribunal, on any point of law.

Collective disputes are different, though. As the Industrial Relations Act fiasco showed that (for whatever reason), a compulsory legal framework for the solution of industrial disagreements in Britain brings disaster. Courts can only operate where the parties are at least prepared to accept that the power of the law must be exercised in the interests of the community as a whole.

Arbitration provides an alternative forum to courts and tribunals. The parties agree to their dispute being settled by a third party, an 'arbitrator'. He only acquires his power through the 'submission' of the parties. Under the Arbitration Acts, where parties have submitted their dispute to an arbitrator, in writing, then his decision may be enforced through the courts. Indeed, rights of appeal against arbitrators' rulings are fewer and less likely to succeed than those against the decisions of judges. You can only successfully appeal against an arbitrator's award if you can show an error of law in the award or (in rare cases) if you can prove improper conduct on the part of the arbitrator.

The 1975 Act says that:

'Where a trade dispute exists or is apprehended the Service may, at the request of one of more parties to the dispute and with the consent of all the parties to the dispute, refer all or any of the matters to which the dispute relates for settlement to the arbitration of

    (a) one or more persons appointed by the Service for that purpose (not being an officer or servant of the Service); or
    (b) the Central Arbitration Committee. . . .'

Either party to an industrial dispute may request arbitration, but the arbitrator only acquires his powers through the consent of all concerned — all of whom agree to accept his decision.

Not long ago, a railwaymen's dispute was submitted to arbitration, but the union declared that it did not agree in advance to accept the arbitrator's decision. The result may have been called an arbitration, but it was not. It was an enquiry, with one party but not the other agreeing to act in accordance with the umpire's edict.

In exercising its functions in connection with arbitration, the Service is then required 'to consider the likelihood of the dispute being settled by conciliation'. Almost always, Parliament hopes that the parties will agree among themselves.

'Where there exist appropriate agreed procedures for negotiation or the settlement of disputes (the Service) shall not refer the matter for settlement to arbitration . . . unless those procedures have been used and have failed to result in a settlement or unless, in the opinion of the Service, there is a special reason which justifies arbitration . . . as an alternative to those procedures.'

If the parties decide to refer the matter to arbitration by someone outside the Service, that is their affair. But if they want the Service to appoint someone — not being 'an officer or servant of the Service' — or to refer the matter to the CAC, the agreed procedures must first have been tried and found wanting, unless there is some special procedure.

In England or Wales, the man who (by agreement) decides on the dispute is called 'an arbitrator', in Scotland, an 'arbiter'. Either way, he is an industrial Solomon whose verdict the parties must agree in advance to accept.

Chapter 40

EEC industrial relations law

EEC industrial relations laws vary greatly and are seldom harmonised. For example, the difference between the highly sophisticated worker participation rules in Germany and our own pragmatic and haphazard efforts is remarkable. The 1980 Act neither refers to nor is affected by EEC efforts. But so as to complete our picture and because EEC rulings may affect our industrial relations and employment law, here is a brief summary of the overall set up.

The EEC makes rules in one of five ways:
1   *Regulations* — binding on all, as if they formed part of the law of the member nation.
2   *Directives* — which are binding, but each member state may decide on 'the choice of form and methods' by which the result required is achieved.
3   *Decisions* — of the Council of Ministers or Commission — addressed to individuals or to one or more member states — not normally enforceable without national legislation.
4   *Opinions* and *recommendations* — of persuasive effect only.
5   *Conventions* — entered into between member states.

Rulings to date

In the employment field, the following are the main current rules:

1   *EEC Regulation 1463/70* — requiring a tachograph ('spy in the cab') to be operative in any new lorry over $3\frac{1}{2}$ tonnes

brought into service from 1 January 1976, or which carries dangerous goods — and to be operative on all such lorries, whatever their age, from 1 January 1978.

2 *Directives* — on *(a)* equal pay — mostly covered by our Equal Pay Act and Sex Discrimination Act; *(b)* equal treatment for married women — also, no problem for the UK; *(c)* mass dismissals — covered by notification requirements in the 1975 Act, i.e. to consult with independent, recognised trade unions regarding any intended redundancy, and in addition with the Department of Employment for any major redundancy, involving more than 10 people at one establishment; *(d)* recommendations for a 40-hour week — already in operation in most sectors of British industry, other than agriculture; *(e)* recommendation for four weeks' annual holiday — here, the UK is far behind but not for long, if the unions have their way.

3 *Directive* — giving employees rights where a business is transferred or merged — usually called 'acquired' rights. The 1978 Act goes some way in that direction — but further legislation in this area is likely in due course.

In addition: UK employers are beginning to make calls on 'the Social Fund' — available for training or re-training for 'new, stable employment' with 'public authority support'. With special help provided for textile, clothing and agricultural industries; for immigrant, disabled and young workers; and for 'less developed' or, in the UK 'assisted' areas, such money is available. If you may be entitled to dip into this helpful kitty, telephone the EEC's London office — 01-727 8090.

Finally: the Treaty of Rome requirements concerning the free movement of workers within the Common Market area are already in force. The UK treats nationals of other EEC countries in the same way as its own and there are no restrictions on such persons entering Britain and remaining here for the purpose of employment.

Chapter 41

A martyr's charter?

The most important photograph in the recent history of industrial relations shows a docker called Bernie Steer, standing outside the walls of Pentonville Prison, arms outstretched, and proclaiming: 'It's a bloody liberty!' He was not complaining of being locked-up. On the contrary: he was furious at his release. When the British worker is angry at being set free from prison, you know that there is something very wrong with the law and with its enforcement.

Mr Steer was one of a group of dockers involved in a demarcation dispute which was not even between different unions. The battle raged between two branches of the giant Transport and General Workers Union, to decide whether other dockers or the drivers should unload the new containers at the docks. The unfortunate employers were caught in the nut-cracker. Unwisely, they used their undoubted right under the Industrial Relations Act to take the strikers to the National Industrial Relations Court (now happily deceased).

The Court ruled that Mr Steer and his fellow docker pickets were acting unlawfully. They granted the employers an injunction restraining the pickets. Bernie Steer and his colleagues ignored the injuction and carried on picketing.

The employers returned to the Court, asking that the injunction be enforced. The Court clearly could not permit its orders to be flouted. Were the dockers in contempt? Then the normal rules would apply. Until that contempt was 'purged' and the Court's order obeyed, the strikers would have to be imprisoned.

In its essence, the Industrial Relations Act was a civil statute. It created civil rights and remedies and set up a civil court. The framework was civil and not criminal. Nevertheless, breach of a court order made under that Act led to criminal consequences. Mr Steer and his colleagues were locked up. And at that stage, they received the broad trade union backing they sought and which until then they had signally lacked.

Other dockers who did not share the extreme left-wing views of Mr Steer and his friends were unwilling to allow them to be sent to prison for an industrial action. They threatened an all-out dock strike, which could easily have turned into a general strike.

Immediately, the Government saw the danger. It brought forth that distinguished gentleman known as the Official Solicitor, propelled him into the limelight, whence he applied for the release of the dockers. To everyone's relief except their own, the application was granted.

Mr Steer's lesson was well learned — not least by one Robert Relf, who put up a sign outside his house, in breach of the Race Relations Act; was brought by the (then) Race Relations Board* before a court, which granted an injunction against him; he flouted the injunction and was duly consigned to prison, where he went on hunger strike. The Board then applied for his release and he emerged, to a hero's welcome from leaders of the very far right.

So the question for all of us must now be: Will the new Act provide yet another invitation to martyrdom? If so, then what happens to the rule of law?

In its main outlines, the 1980 Act will probably have less effect than most people expect. In practice, the restrictions on the closed shop and on secondary picketing will be largely ignored; payment out of public funds for secret ballots may be gratefully received by some of those who would have secret ballots anyway, but few unions are likely to change their rules as a result; and the main unfair dismissal and maternity structures will remain basically unaffected, even though fewer people will be able to benefit from them, and that benefit will be less.

What really matters about the new rules is how they will be implemented and the extent to which they will bring back the sort of ill-will and mistrust which poisoned the air of the world of employment relations from 1970 to 1974. The days of the Industrial Relations Act are likely to return.

* Now the Commission for Racial Equality.

Happily, good industrial relations in most enterprises will depend not so much on the law as on individual good relations between management and workforce, between personnel and industrial relations executives and managers and trade union representatives. Those who must contend with the new legislation at shop-floor level must know its terms and work within or without them as best they can. With specific guidance, adequate knowledge of the law, good luck — and, I hope, with the continued help of this book — peace remains possible.

'Not here Mr Jenkins – if the man from ACAS comes in, we may get caught in the act!'

Part Three
APPENDICES

Appendix 1

The Employment Act, 1980 — a summary

Arrangement of Sections

Like all statutes, the 1980 Employment Act starts with an 'Arrangement of Sections' — like the headings of Parts and Chapters in a book, they provide an overall guide. No statute contains an index.

Trade union ballots and codes of practice

Section 1 - Payments in respect of secret ballots The Employment Secretary is given power to make regulations to permit the Certification Officer to make payments towards expenditure incurred by independent trade unions in respect of ballots for all or any of the following five purposes:
1   Decisions on calling or ending a strike or other industrial action.
2   Elections to management committees, etc.
3   Elections of union officials.
4   Amendment of union rules.
5   Decisions on amalgamation or transfer.
Such payments will be made by the Certification Officer on application by the trade union concerned.

Section 2 - Secret ballots on employer's premises Where an *independent* trade union, *recognised* to any extent for the purposes of collective bargaining, intends to hold a secret ballot, then it may request the employer to permit his premises to be used to give his workers a convenient opportunity of voting. The employer must then, so far as is reasonably practicable, comply with that request.
  Firms with less than 20 employees are excluded from this obligation.

Complaint by a trade union that an employer has not complied with its request when it is reasonably practicable to do so, must be made to the Industrial Tribunal, within three months, unless not reasonably practicable to do so.

Section 3 – Codes of Practice to be issued by the Employment Secretary Section 3 gives the Employment Secretary power to make Codes of Practice, i.e. unlike ACAS codes, etc., without obtaining concurrence of trade unions, etc. He must, however, consult ACAS — and lay a code before Parliament. For Draft Codes, see Appendices 13 and 14.

Section 4 – Unreasonable exclusion or expulsion from trade union Section 4 applies where there is a union membership agreement (or closed-shop agreement). Actual or prospective employees (as the case may be) are entitled to complain to an industrial tribunal that a trade union has unreasonably refused his application for membership or has unreasonably expelled him. As always, 'reasonableness' depends on all the circumstances of the case — but compliance by the union with its own rules is not the sole criterion.

Appeal against the tribunal's decision will lie on a question of fact or law to the Employment Appeal Tribunal.

Section 5 – Compensation for unreasonable exclusion or expulsion Where an industrial tribunal (or, on appeal, the Employment Appeal Tribunal) finds that an employee has been unreasonably excluded or expelled, compensation may be awarded according to specified rules — subject (as in the case of unfair dismissal) to:
1   The applicant's duty to mitigate his loss, i.e. by finding other work if he can.
2   Reduction to allow for the applicant's contributory behaviour (if any).

Section 6 – Unfair dismissal An employer/respondent no longer has to satisfy an industrial tribunal that a dismissal was fair. Nor is the burden of proving fairness transferred to the employee. Instead, the tribunal must consider the question of fairness 'in accordance with equity and the substantial merits of the case'.

Section 7 – Dismissal relating to trade union membership In a UMA closed-shop situation, it is unfair to dismiss an employee if he objects to joining the union 'on grounds of conscience or other deeply held personal conviction'. This rule applies to existing as well as to future closed shops — so (union pressures apart) employees who object to closed shops may effectively opt out, even of existing arrangements.

As to the future, Section 7 provides that it will only be fair to dismiss an employee for refusing to join an *approved* UMA. A UMA will only be considered as approved if:
1 A secret ballot is held of all relevant employees.
2 At least 80 per cent of those eligible to vote, do vote in favour of the closed shop. Even if you come to an agreement with the union or unions concerned, that agreement is not binding on its members in the absence of 80 per cent vote in favour.

Section 8 – Small undertakings The employees of many small 'undertakings' are excluded from unfair dismissal protection. To qualify for exclusion:
1 The employee must have been employed for not more than two years.
2 The 'undertaking', i.e. the entirety of the business, irrespective of the number of units or companies in it, must not have employed more than 20 people at any time.

An employee is entitled to contract out of his unfair dismissal protection if he has a fixed-term contract for one year or more (reduced from two years or more).

Section 9 – Basic award Entitlement to a 'basic award' when dismissed unfairly is reduced in various respects — the most important being: the repeal of the previously existing right to receive up to two weeks' pay at a maximum (latterly, of £120 per week), if dismissed unfairly, even where no loss was suffered. The award may also be reduced:
1 If the complainant has unreasonably refused an offer of alternative employment which would have had the effect of reinstating him 'in his employment in all respects as if he had not been dismissed'; or
2 If it would be 'just and equitable' to reduce the amount of the basic award due to the complainant's conduct 'whether before or after the dismissal'.

Section 10 – Contribution or indemnity from trade union An employer who is ordered to pay compensation to a dismissed employee may in certain circumstances apply to the tribunal to 'join' his trade union to the proceedings and to claim a contribution towards (or even a complete indemnity) in respect of any award made against him. The following circumstances must apply for this right to exist:
1   The employer must prove that he dismissed the employee as a result of union pressure, exercised 'by calling, organising, procuring or financing a strike or other industrial action, or by threatening to do so'.
2   Pressure was exercised because of the employee's refusal to join or to remain a member of a trade union.

The amount of any contribution ordered to be paid under this section will be such as the tribunal considers to be 'just and equitable in the circumstances, and may constitute a complete indemnity'.

The employer may also join a contractor as a party to the proceedings if:
1   The employers and the contractor were parties to a contract which required that the work be only done by employees who are members of a trade union or of a particular trade union.
2   The employer requested the contractor to consent to the employment of the claimant, but he refused.
3   That because of the refusal, the employee could not be employed on that work.
4   That no other work was available upon which the employee could be employed.
5   Therefore the employee was dismissed.

If the contractor can prove that he was induced to withhold consent by pressure exercised on him by a union or other person by threatening industrial action, then the contractor may join that person (or union) to the proceedings.

Section 11 – Maternity Two important points to note are:
1   To qualify for maternity *pay* the mother must inform her employer (in writing if he so requests) at least 21 days before her absence begins (or if that is not reasonably practicable, as soon as is reasonably practicable) that she will be (or is) absent wholly or partly because of

pregnancy or confinement. (Note: the wise employer will now request that such notice be given in writing.)
2   In the case of maternity *leave*, the mother-to-be must inform her employer *in writing* at least 21 days before her absence begins (or as soon as is reasonably practicable) that she will be or is absent due to pregnancy or confinement and that she intends to return to work with her employer.

In either case, the employee must inform the employer of the expected week of confinement or of its date. (Note: the employee must inform her employer *in writing*, whether or not the employer so requests.)

An employer is now also entitled to request the mother *in writing* to give him written confirmation that she intends to return to work. If he does so not less than 49 days after the beginning of the expected week of confinement then — unless the mother gives that confirmation within 14 days of receiving the request (or as soon as is reasonably practicable thereafter) — she will lose her right to return.

(A new system should now be introduced, with due diary entries as appropriate.)

Finally: an employee who intends to exercise her right to return to work must notify her employer of her intention so to do *in writing* at least three weeks before she does so, otherwise the employer cannot be required to take her back.

(Note: have you prepared and introduced a new system and taken steps to ensure that employees know their rights and their new obligations?)

Section 12 – Right to return   Mothers employed by small firms lose their right to return if:
1   The number employed in the business does not exceed five; and
2   It is not reasonably practicable for the employer (or his successor) to take her back.

Again: if it is not reasonably practicable (for a reason other than redundancy) to permit the mother to return to her job and she is offered reasonably suitable alternative employment which she either accepts or unreasonably refuses, she will lose her right to return to her former job.

In either of the above circumstances, the alternative

employment must involve work 'of a kind both suitably related to the employee and appropriate to her in the circumstances, and . . . the provisions of the contract as to the capacity and place in which she is to be employed and as to other terms and conditions of her employment' must not be 'substantially less favourable to her' than those which she would have enjoyed in her previous job.

Section 13 – Time off for ante-natal care   A pregnant employee who wants to attend ante-natal instruction on the advice of a doctor, a midwife or a health visitor shall not be unreasonably refused paid time off during her working hours to keep the appointment.

With the exception of the first appointment, an employer can require the employee to produce a certificate from the doctor, midwife or health visitor stating that she is pregnant and proof that the appointment has been made.

Complaint may be made to the tribunal that the employer has unreasonably refused time off or that he has failed to pay her for such time off. This must be made within three months of the date of the appointment or within such time as is reasonable. If the complaint is found to be justified, then the tribunal can order that the employer pay to the employee the amount that she would have received had she had the day off, or if she did take the time off, then her normal pay for that time.

Section 14 – Guarantee pay   No employee can be entitled to guarantee pay for more than five days during any three-month period. Previously, these three-month periods were fixed (commencing on 1 February, May, August and November). Now they 'roll' — so when an employee has had his five days, he must wait another three months before he can qualify again.

Section 15 – Action short of dismissal relating to trade union activities   This Section alters the rights of an employee not to be disciplined by his employer for the purpose of:
1   Preventing or deterring him from being or seeking to become a member of an independent trade union or penalising him for doing so; or
2   Preventing or deterring him from taking part in the activities of an independent trade union at any appropriate time, or penalising him for doing so; or

3   Compelling him to be or become a member of a trade union.

The last right has been widened to include all unions whether or not they are independent.

Section 15(2)(a) states that the rights of an employee who is a member of a union specified in a Union Membership Agreement, not to be disciplined for taking part in union activities on the employer's premises shall not be extended to new closed-shop agreements which have come into being without the secret ballot support.

The Section also extends an employee's rights not to have disciplinary action taken against him to compel union membership when there is a UMA (1) to conscientious objectors, (2) to existing employees when a closed shop is introduced and (3) to those employees covered by a new closed shop agreement which has not been approved by secret ballot.

A right of joinder similar to that found in Section 10 is also provided.

Section 16 – Picketing   Picketing will only be lawful when it is done in contemplation or furtherance of a trade dispute when carried out by:
1   A person picketing outside or near his own place of work (or if dismissed — former place of work) or
2   A trade union official accompanying and representing a member of that union

for the purpose only of 'peacefully obtaining or communicating information, or peacefully persuading any person to work or abstain from working'.

Section 17 – Secondary action   This Section states that secondary action which interferes with, threatens to break or breaks a contract (other than a contract of employment) will not be actionable in tort if the action satisfies the following requirements:
1   That the purpose or principal purpose of the action was to prevent or disrupt the supply of goods and services during the trade dispute between an employer who is a party to the dispute and a supplier or customer with whom he has a contract.
2   That the action was taken by the employees of the supplier.

134 Guide to The Employment Act, 1980

3   The action is likely to achieve the prevention or disruption of supply.

This immunity is also extended to situations where the secondary action involves employees of an associated employer to the employer, but once again the purpose or the principal purpose must have been to disrupt the supply of goods and services.

Section 18 – Acts to compel trade union membership   Immunity which is given to trade union officials and members from legal action shall not apply where 'a person induces an employee of one employer to break his contract of employment in order to compel workers of another employer to join a particular trade union, unless they are working at the same place'.

Section 19 – Repeals: charter on press freedom; recognition procedures; Schedule 11 (terms and conditions of employment)
Section 19 removes three existing rules, at a stroke:
1   The charter on freedom of the press contained in *The Trade Union and Labour Relations Act, 1974*, is repealed;
2   The pre-existing recognition procedures (operated through and by ACAS) are repealed.
3   Schedule 11 of *The Employment Protection Act, 1975* (broadly: giving trade unions the right to claim improved terms and conditions where employees are receiving less than those 'recognised' or those received by 'comparable workers' in the industry and area) is repealed.

Note:
a   None of the existing arrangements are replaced by others. So all now return to shop-floor bargaining; but
b   The Fair Wages Resolution (broadly: no government contracts to go to employers granting less than 'recognised' or 'comparable' terms and conditions) remains in force.

These provisions apply in England, Scotland and Wales but not in Northern Ireland.

The Schedules to the Act only set out or (where appropriate) affect amendements to or repeals of existing legislation, made necessary by the new Act.

Appendix 2

The Employment Act, 1980

ARRANGEMENT OF SECTIONS

Trade union ballots and Codes of Practice

Section
1. Payments in respect of secret ballots.
2. Secret ballots on employer's premises.
3. Issue by Secretary of State of Codes of Practice.

Exclusion from trade union membership
4. Unreasonable exclusion or expulsion from trade union.
5. Compensation.

Unfair dismissal
6. Determination of fairness of dismissal.
7. Dismissal relating to trade union membership.
8. Exclusions of rights.
9. Basic award.
10. Contribution in respect of compensation.

Maternity
11. Notices to employer.
12. Right to return.
13. Time off for ante-natal care.

Other rights of employees
14. Guarantee payments.
15. Action short of dismissal relating to trade union membership and activities.

Restrictions on legal liability
16. Picketing.
17. Secondary action.
18. Acts to compel trade union membership.

Miscellaneous and general

Section
19. Enactments ceasing to have effect.
20. Interpretation, minor and consequential amendments and repeals.
21. Short title, commencement and extent.

SCHEDULES:
Schedule 1—Minor and consequential amendments.
Schedule 2—Repeals.

Employment Act 1980

1980 CHAPTER 42

An Act to provide for payments out of public funds towards trade unions' expenditure in respect of ballots, for the use of employers' premises in connection with ballots, and for the issue by the Secretary of State of Codes of Practice for the improvement of industrial relations; to make provision in respect of exclusion or expulsion from trade unions and otherwise to amend the law relating to workers, employers, trade unions and employers' associations; to repeal section 1A of the Trade Union and Labour Relations Act 1974; and for connected purposes. [1st August 1980]

BE IT ENACTED by the Queen's most Excellent Majesty, by and with the advice and consent of the Lords Spiritual and Temporal, and Commons, in this present Parliament assembled, and by the authority of the same, as follows:—

Trade union ballots and Codes of Practice

1.—(1) The Secretary of State may by regulations make a scheme (below called " the scheme ") providing for payments by the Certification Officer towards expenditure incurred by independent trade unions in respect of such ballots to which this section applies as may be prescribed by the scheme.

(2) This section applies to a ballot if the purpose of the question to be voted upon (or if there is more than one such question, the purpose of any of them) falls within the purposes mentioned in subsection (3) below.

Payments in respect of secret ballots.

(3) The purposes referred to in subsection (2) above are—
   (a) obtaining a decision or ascertaining the views of members of a trade union as to the calling or ending of a strike or other industrial action ;
   (b) carrying out an election provided for by the rules of a trade union ;
   (c) electing a worker who is a member of a trade union to be a representative of other members also employed by his employer ;
   (d) amending the rules of a trade union ;
   (e) obtaining a decision in accordance with the Trade Union (Amalgamations, etc.) Act 1964 on a resolution to approve an instrument of amalgamation or transfer ;
and such other purposes as the Secretary of State may by order specify.

1964 c. 24.

(4) The scheme may include provision for payments to be made towards expenditure incurred by an independent trade union in respect of arrangements to hold a ballot which is not proceeded with but which, if it had been held, would have been a ballot to which this section applies.

(5) The circumstances in which and the conditions subject to which payments may be made under the scheme, and the amounts of the payments, shall be such as may be prescribed by or determined in accordance with the scheme; and the scheme shall include provision for restricting the cases in which payments are made to cases in which the ballot is so conducted as to secure, so far as reasonably practicable, that those voting may do so in secret.

(6) The Secretary of State shall out of money provided by Parliament pay to the Certification Officer such sums as he may require for making payments under the scheme.

(7) Any power to make regulations or orders under this section shall be exercisable by statutory instrument ; and—
   (a) a statutory instrument containing regulations under this section shall be subject to annulment in pursuance of a resolution of either House of Parliament ;
   (b) no order shall be made under this section unless a draft of it has been laid before and approved by resolution of each House of Parliament.

(8) Expressions used in this section and in the 1974 Act have the same meanings in this section as in that Act.

Secret ballots on employer's premises.

2.—(1) Subject to subsection (3) below, where an independent trade union proposes that a relevant ballot be held and requests an employer to permit premises of his to be used for the purpose of giving workers employed by him who are members of the union a convenient opportunity of voting, the employer shall, so far as reasonably practicable, comply with the request.

(2) A ballot is a relevant ballot for the purposes of this section if—
  (a) as respects the purpose of the question (or one of the questions) to be voted upon, the ballot satisfies the requirements of a scheme under section 1 of this Act, and
  (b) the proposals for the conduct of the ballot are such as to secure, so far as reasonably practicable, that those voting may do so in secret.

(3) Subsection (1) above shall not apply where, at the time the request is made,—
  (a) the union is not recognised by the employer to any extent for the purpose of collective bargaining, or
  (b) the number of workers employed by the employer, added to the number employed by any associated employer, does not exceed twenty.

(4) A trade union may present a complaint to an industrial tribunal that it has made a request in accordance with subsection (1) above and that it was reasonably practicable for the employer to comply with it, but that he has failed to do so.

(5) An industrial tribunal shall not entertain a complaint under this section unless it is presented to the tribunal before the end of the period of three months beginning with the date of the failure, or within such further period as the tribunal considers reasonable in a case where it is satisfied that it was not reasonably practicable for the complaint to be presented before the end of the period of three months.

(6) Where a tribunal finds that a complaint under this section is well-founded, the tribunal shall make a declaration to that effect, and may make an award of compensation to be paid by the employer to the union which shall be of such amount as the tribunal considers just and equitable in all the circumstances having regard to the employer's default in failing to comply with the request and to any expenses incurred by the union in consequence of the failure.

(7) An appeal shall lie to the Employment Appeal Tribunal on a question of law arising from any decision of, or arising in proceedings before, an industrial tribunal under this section.

(8) The remedy of a trade union for a failure to comply with a request made in accordance with subsection (1) above shall be by way of a complaint under this section and not otherwise.

(9) Expressions used in this section and in the 1974 Act have the same meanings in this section as in that Act.

Issue by Secretary of State of Codes of Practice.

3.—(1) The Secretary of State may issue Codes of Practice containing such practical guidance as he thinks fit for the purpose of promoting the improvement of industrial relations.

(2) The Secretary of State shall after consultation with the Advisory, Conciliation and Arbitration Service (whether carried out before or after the passing of this Act) prepare and publish a draft of any Code of Practice that he proposes to issue under this section.

(3) The Secretary of State shall consider any representations made to him about a draft prepared under subsection (2) above and may modify the draft accordingly.

(4) If the Secretary of State determines to proceed with the draft he shall lay it before both Houses of Parliament and, if it is approved by resolution of each House, shall issue the Code in the form of the draft.

(5) A Code of Practice issued under this section shall come into operation on such day as the Secretary of State may by order appoint ; and an order under this subsection—
- (*a*) may contain such transitional provisions or savings as appear to the Secretary of State to be necessary or expedient ;
- (*b*) shall be made by statutory instrument, which shall be subject to annulment in pursuance of a resolution of either House of Parliament.

(6) The Secretary of State may from time to time revise the whole or any part of a Code of Practice issued under this section and issue that revised Code, and subsections (2) to (5) above shall apply to such a revised Code as they apply to the first issue of a Code.

(7) If the Secretary of State is of the opinion that the provisions of a Code of Practice to be issued under this section will supersede the whole or part of a Code previously issued by him under this section or by the Advisory, Conciliation and Arbitration Service under section 6 of the 1975 Act or having effect by virtue of paragraph 4 of Schedule 17 to that Act, he shall in the new Code state that on the day on which the new Code comes into operation in pursuance of an order under subsection (5) above the old Code or a specified part of it shall cease to have effect (subject to any transitional provisions or savings made by the order).

(8) A failure on the part of any person to observe any provision of a Code of Practice issued under this section shall not

of itself render him liable to any proceedings; but in any proceedings before a court or industrial tribunal or the Central Arbitration Committee—
  (a) any such Code shall be admissible in evidence, and
  (b) any provision of the Code which appears to the court, tribunal or Committee to be relevant to any question arising in the proceedings shall be taken into account in determining that question.

Exclusion from trade union membership

4.—(1) This section applies to employment by an employer with respect to which it is the practice, in accordance with a union membership agreement, for the employee to belong to a specified trade union or one of a number of specified trade unions. *Unreasonable exclusion or expulsion from trade union.*

(2) Every person who is, or is seeking to be, in employment to which this section applies shall have the right—
  (a) not to have an application for membership of a specified trade union unreasonably refused;
  (b) not to be unreasonably expelled from a specified trade union.

(3) The rights conferred by subsection (2) above are in addition to and not in substitution for any right which exists apart from that subsection; and, without prejudice to any remedy for infringement of any such other right, the remedies for infringement of a right conferred by that subsection shall be those provided by the following provisions of this section and section 5 below.

(4) A complaint may be presented to an industrial tribunal against a trade union by a person that an application by him for membership of the union has been unreasonably refused, or that he has been unreasonably expelled from the union, in contravention of subsection (2) above.

(5) On a complaint under this section, the question whether a trade union has acted reasonably or unreasonably shall be determined in accordance with equity and the substantial merits of the case, and in particular a union shall not be regarded as having acted reasonably only because it has acted in accordance with the requirements of its rules or unreasonably only because it has acted in contravention of them.

(6) A tribunal shall not entertain a complaint under this section unless it is presented to the tribunal before the end of the period of six months beginning with the date of the refusal or expulsion, as the case may be, or within such further period as the tribunal considers reasonable in a case where it

is satisfied that it was not reasonably practicable for the complaint to be presented before the end of the period of six months.

(7) Where a tribunal finds that a complaint under this section is well-founded, the tribunal shall make a declaration to that effect.

(8) An appeal shall lie to the Employment Appeal Tribunal on any question of law or fact arising from any decision of, or arising in any proceedings before, an industrial tribunal under this section.

(9) For the purposes of this section and section 5 below—
(a) if an application for membership of a trade union has been neither granted nor rejected before the end of the period within which it might reasonably have been expected to be granted if it was to be granted, the application shall be treated as having been refused on the last day of that period, and
(b) if under the rules of a trade union any person ceases to be a member of the union on the happening of an event specified in the rules, he shall be treated as having been expelled from the union.

(10) Any expression used in any provision of this section or section 5 below and in the 1974 Act has the same meaning in that provision as it has in that Act, except that any reference in such a provision to a trade union includes a reference to a branch or section of a trade union.

(11) Any provision in an agreement shall be void in so far as it purports to exclude or limit the operation of, or to preclude any person from presenting a complaint or making an application under, this section or section 5 below; but this subsection shall not apply to an agreement to refrain from instituting or continuing proceedings where a conciliation officer has taken action in accordance with section 133(2) or (3) of the 1978 Act.

Compensation. **5.**—(1) A person who has made a complaint against a trade union under section 4 above which has been declared to be well-founded may make an application in accordance with subsection (2) below for an award of compensation to be paid to him by the union.

(2) If at the time when the application under this section is made the applicant has been admitted or re-admitted to membership of the union against which he made the complaint, the application shall be to an industrial tribunal; and if at that time he has not been so admitted or re-admitted, the application shall be to the Employment Appeal Tribunal.

(3) An industrial tribunal or the Employment Appeal Tribunal shall not entertain an application for compensation under this section if it is made before the end of the period of four weeks beginning with the date of the declaration under section 4 above or after the end of the period of six months beginning with that date.

(4) Subject to the following provisions of this section, the amount of compensation awarded on an application under this section—
- (a) in the case of an application to an industrial tribunal, shall be such as the tribunal considers appropriate for the purpose of compensating the applicant for the loss sustained by him in consequence of the refusal or expulsion which was the subject of his complaint, and
- (b) in the case of an application to the Employment Appeal Tribunal, shall be such as the Appeal Tribunal considers just and equitable in all the circumstances.

(5) In determining the amount of compensation to be awarded under this section, the industrial tribunal or the Employment Appeal Tribunal shall apply the same rule concerning the duty of a person to mitigate his loss as applies to damages recoverable under the common law of England and Wales or of Scotland, as the case may be.

(6) Where the industrial tribunal or the Employment Appeal Tribunal finds that the refusal or expulsion which was the subject of the applicant's complaint was to any extent caused or contributed to by any action of the applicant, it shall reduce the amount of the compensation by such proportion as it considers just and equitable having regard to that finding.

(7) The amount of compensation awarded on an application to an industrial tribunal under this section shall not exceed the aggregate of—
- (a) an amount equal to thirty times the limit for the time being imposed by paragraph 8(1)(b) of Schedule 14 to the 1978 Act (maximum amount of a week's pay for purpose of calculating basic award in unfair dismissal cases), and
- (b) an amount equal to the limit for the time being imposed by section 75 of that Act (maximum compensatory award in such cases).

(8) The amount of compensation awarded on an application to the Employment Appeal Tribunal under this section shall not exceed the aggregate of—
- (a) the amount referred to in paragraph (a) of subsection (7) above, and
- (b) the amount referred to in paragraph (b) of that subsection, and

(c) an amount equal to fifty-two times the limit for the time being imposed by paragraph 8(1)(a) of Schedule 14 to the 1978 Act (maximum amount of a week's pay for purpose of calculating additional award of compensation in unfair dismissal cases).

(9) An appeal shall lie to the Employment Appeal Tribunal on a question of law arising from any decision of, or arising in proceedings before, an industrial tribunal under this section.

Unfair dismissal

Determination of fairness of dismissal.

6. In section 57(3) of the 1978 Act (determination of question of fairness to depend on whether employer can satisfy tribunal that he acted reasonably) for the words from " the employer can " to the end there shall be substituted the words " in the circumstances (including the size and administrative resources of the employer's undertaking) the employer acted reasonably or unreasonably in treating it as a sufficient reason for dismissing the employee ; and that question shall be determined in accordance with equity and the substantial merits of the case ".

Dismissal relating to trade union membership.

7.—(1) In subsection (3) of section 58 of the 1978 Act (dismissal of employee for non-membership of a union to be fair where there is a union membership agreement unless he objects to membership on grounds of religious belief) for the words from " unless " to the end there shall be substituted the words " but subject to subsections (3A) to (3C) ".

(2) After subsection (3) of that section there shall be inserted—

" (3A) The dismissal of an employee in the circumstances set out in subsection (3) shall be regarded as unfair if he genuinely objects on grounds of conscience or other deeply-held personal conviction to being a member of any trade union whatsoever or of a particular trade union.

(3B) The dismissal of an employee by an employer in the circumstances set out in subsection (3) shall be regarded as unfair if the employee—

(a) has been among those employees of the employer who belong to the class to which the union membership agreement relates since before the agreement had the effect of requiring them to be or become members of a trade union, and

(b) has not at any time while the agreement had that effect been a member of a trade union in accordance with the agreement.

(3C) Where a union membership agreement takes effect after the commencement of section 7 of the Employment Act 1980 in relation to the employees of any class of an employer, and an employee of that class is dismissed by the

employer in the circumstances set out in subsection (3), the dismissal shall be regarded as unfair if—
> (a) the agreement has not been approved in relation to those employees in accordance with section 58A, or
>
> (b) it has been so approved through a ballot in which the dismissed employee was entitled to vote, but he has not at any time since the day on which the ballot was held been a member of a trade union in accordance with the agreement.

(3D) Where the employer of any employees changes in such circumstances that the employees' period of continuous employment is not broken, this section and section 58A shall have effect as if any reference to the employees of any class of the later employer included a reference to the employees of that class of the former employer.

(3E) In determining for the purposes of subsection (3B) and of section 58A(2) whether a person belongs to a class of employees, any restriction of the class by reference to membership (or objection to membership) of a trade union shall be disregarded."

(3) After that section there shall be inserted—

"Ballots as to union membership agreements.

58A.—(1) A union membership agreement shall be taken for the purposes of section 58(3C) to have been approved in relation to the employees of any class of an employer if a ballot has been held on the question whether the agreement should apply in relation to them and not less than 80 per cent. of those entitled to vote in the ballot voted in favour of the agreement's application.

(2) The persons entitled to vote in a ballot under this section in relation to the application of a union membership agreement to the employees of any class of an employer shall be all those employees who belong to that class, and are in the employment of the employer, on the day on which the ballot is held.

(3) A ballot under this section shall be so conducted as to secure that, so far as reasonably practicable, all those entitled to vote have an opportunity of voting, and of doing so in secret."

8.—(1) After section 64 of the 1978 Act there shall be inserted—

Exclusions of rights.

"Extended qualifying period where no more than twenty employees.

64A.—(1) Subject to subsection (2), section 54 does not apply to the dismissal of an employee from any employment if—
> (a) the period (ending with the effective date of termination) during which the employee was

continuously employed did not exceed two years ; and

(b) at no time during that period did the number of employees employed by the employer for the time being of the dismissed employee, added to the number employed by any associated employer, exceed twenty.

(2) Subsection (1) shall not apply to the dismissal of an employee by reason of any such requirement or recommendation as is referred to in section 19(1), or if it is shown that the reason (or, if more than one, the principal reason) for the dismissal was an inadmissible reason."

(2) In section 142(1) of the 1978 Act (which provides that section 54 does not apply in relation to a contract for a fixed term of two years or more) for the words " two years " there shall be substituted the words " one year ".

Basic award.   **9.**—(1) Section 73 of the 1978 Act (calculation of basic award for unfair dismissal) shall be amended as follows.

(2) In subsection (1) (provisions to which calculation of basic award is subject)—

(a) after paragraph (b) there shall be inserted—

" (ba) subsection (7A) (which provides for the amount of the award to be reduced where the employee has unreasonably refused an offer of reinstatement) ;

(bb) subsection (7B) (which provides for the amount of the award to be reduced because of the employee's conduct) ; " ; and

(b) paragraph (c) shall cease to have effect.

(3) In subsection (3) (calculation by reference to number of years of employment) for paragraphs (b) and (c) there shall be substituted—

" (b) one week's pay for each year of employment not falling within paragraph (a) which consists wholly of weeks in which the employee was not below the age of twenty-two ; and

(c) half a week's pay for each such year of employment not falling within either of paragraphs (a) and (b).".

(4) After subsection (7) there shall be inserted—

" (7A) Where the tribunal finds that the complainant has unreasonably refused an offer by the employer which if accepted would have the effect of reinstating the complainant in his employment in all respects as if he had not been dismissed, the tribunal shall reduce or further reduce the amount of the basic award to such extent as it considers just and equitable having regard to that finding.

(7B) Where the tribunal considers that any conduct of the complainant before the dismissal (or, where the dismissal was with notice, before the notice was given), other than conduct taken into account by virtue of subsection (7), was such that it would be just and equitable to reduce or further reduce the amount of the basic award to any extent, the tribunal shall reduce or further reduce that amount accordingly.".

(5) Subsection (8) (minimum basic award of two weeks' pay) shall cease to have effect.

10. After section 76 of the 1978 Act there shall be inserted—

"Contribution in respect of compensation.

76A.—(1) If in proceedings before an industrial tribunal on a complaint against an employer under section 67 the employer claims—

(a) that he was induced to dismiss the complainant by pressure which a trade union or other person exercised on him by calling, organising, procuring or financing a strike or other industrial action, or by threatening to do so, and

(b) that the pressure was exercised because the complainant was not a member of any trade union or of a particular trade union,

the employer may before the hearing of the complaint require the person who he claims exercised the pressure to be joined, or in Scotland sisted, as a party to the proceedings.

(2) Where any person has been joined, or in Scotland sisted, as a party to proceedings before an industrial tribunal by virtue of subsection (1), and the tribunal—

(a) makes an award of compensation under section 68(2) or 71(2)(a) or (b), but

(b) finds that the claim of the employer (as specified in subsection (1)) is well-founded,

the tribunal may make an order requiring that person to pay to the employer a contribution in respect of that compensation.

(3) The amount of any contribution ordered to be paid under this section in respect of any compensation shall be such as the tribunal considers to be just

and equitable in the circumstances, and may constitute a complete indemnity.

Indemnity in respect of union membership clauses.

76B.—(1) If in proceedings before an industrial tribunal on a complaint against an employer under section 67 the employer claims that—

(a) he and another person (in this section and in section 76C called " the contractor ") were parties to a contract requiring that work done by employees of his for the purposes of the contract should be done only by employees who were members of trade unions or of a particular trade union,

(b) the complainant could not, consistently with that requirement, be employed on that work,

(c) the employer had requested the contractor to consent to the employment of the complainant on that work notwithstanding that requirement,

(d) the contractor had withheld his consent,

(e) apart from the work to which that requirement (or any similar requirement under other contracts to which the employer was a party) related, the employer had no work available which was suitable for the complainant to do, and

(f) the employer would not have dismissed the complainant but for that requirement,

then, subject to subsection (2), the employer may before the hearing of the complaint require the contractor to be joined, or in Scotland sisted, as a party to the proceedings.

(2) An employer may not by virtue of this section require more than one person to be joined, or in Scotland sisted, in proceedings in respect of any complaint.

(3) Where a person has been joined, or in Scotland sisted, as a party to proceedings before an industrial tribunal by virtue of subsection (1), and the tribunal—

(a) makes an award of compensation under section 68(2) or 71(2)(a) or (b), but

(b) finds that the claim of the employer (as specified in subsection (1)) is well-founded, the tribunal shall order that person to pay to the employer an amount equal to the amount of that compensation.

Contribution in respect of indemnity under s. 76B.

76C.—(1) If in the proceedings referred to in section 76B the contractor claims that he was induced to withhold the consent referred to in subsection (1) of that section by pressure which a trade union or other person exercised on him by calling, organising, procuring or financing a strike or other industrial action, or by threatening to do so, the contractor may before the hearing of the complaint require the person who he claims exercised the pressure to be joined, or in Scotland sisted, as a party to the proceedings.

(2) Where any person has been joined, or in Scotland sisted, as a party to proceedings before an industrial tribunal by virtue of subsection (1), and the tribunal—

  (a) makes an order under section 76B, but

  (b) finds that the claim of the contractor (as specified in subsection (1)) is well-founded,

the tribunal may make an order requiring that person to pay to the contractor a contribution in respect of the contractor's liability to the employer by virtue of the order under section 76B.

(3) The amount of any contribution ordered to be paid under this section in respect of any such liability shall be such as the tribunal considers to be just and equitable in the circumstances, and may constitute a complete indemnity."

Maternity

Notices to employer.

11.—(1) In subsection (3) of section 33 of the 1978 Act (which specifies conditions to which the rights to maternity pay and to return to work are subject) for paragraph (c) (information to employer) there shall be substituted—

  " (c) in the case of the right to maternity pay, she informs her employer, in writing if he so requests, at least twenty-one days before her absence begins or, if that is not reasonably practicable, as soon as reasonably practicable, that she will be (or is) absent from work wholly or partly because of pregnancy or confinement ; and

  (d) in the case of the right to return, she informs her employer in writing at least twenty-one days before her absence begins or, if that is not reasonably practicable, as soon as reasonably practicable,—

(i) that she will be (or is) absent from work wholly or partly because of pregnancy or confinement,

(ii) that she intends to return to work with her employer, and

(iii) of the expected week of confinement or, if the confinement has occurred, the date of confinement."

(2) After that subsection there shall be inserted—

" (3A) Where not earlier than forty-nine days after the beginning of the expected week of confinement (or the date of confinement) notified under subsection (3)(d) an employee is requested in accordance with subsection (3B) by her employer or a successor of his to give him written confirmation that she intends to return to work, she shall not be entitled to the right to return unless she gives that confirmation within fourteen days of receiving the request or, if that is not reasonably practicable, as soon as reasonably practicable.

(3B) A request under subsection (3A) shall be made in writing and shall be accompanied by a written statement of the effect of that subsection.".

(3) In section 47 of the 1978 Act, in subsection (1) (employee to exercise her right to return to work by notifying the employer at least seven days in advance)—

(a) for the word " notifying " there shall be substituted the words " giving written notice to ", and

(b) for the word " seven " there shall be substituted the word " twenty-one ";

and in subsections (6) and (7) for the word " fourteen " there shall be substituted the word " twenty-eight ".

<small>Right to return.</small>

12. After section 56 of the 1978 Act there shall be inserted—

<small>"Exclusion of s.56 in certain cases.</small> **56A.**—(1) Section 56 shall not apply in relation to an employee if—

(a) immediately before her absence began the number of employees employed by her employer, added to the number employed by any associated employer of his, did not exceed five, and

(b) it is not reasonably practicable for the employer (who may be the same employer or a successor of his) to permit her to return to work in accordance with section

45(1), or for him or an associated employer to offer her employment under a contract of employment satisfying the conditions specified in subsection (3).

(2) Section 56 shall not apply in relation to an employee if—

(a) it is not reasonably practicable for a reason other than redundancy for the employer (who may be the same employer or a successor of his) to permit her to return to work in accordance with section 45(1), and

(b) he or an associated employer offers her employment under a contract of employment satisfying the conditions specified in subsection (3), and

(c) she accepts or unreasonably refuses that offer.

(3) The conditions referred to in subsections (1) and (2) are—

(a) that the work to be done under the contract is of a kind which is both suitable in relation to the employee and appropriate for her to do in the circumstances; and

(b) that the provisions of the contract as to the capacity and place in which she is to be employed and as to the other terms and conditions of her employment are not substantially less favourable to her than if she had returned to work in accordance with section 45(1).

(4) Where on a complaint of unfair dismissal any question arises as to whether the operation of section 56 is excluded by subsection (1) or (2), it shall be for the employer to show that the provisions of that subsection were satisfied in relation to the complainant."

13. After section 31 of the 1978 Act there shall be inserted— *Time off for ante-natal care.*

" Time off for ante-natal care. **31A.**—(1) An employee who is pregnant and who has, on the advice of a registered medical practitioner, registered midwife or registered health visitor, made an appointment to attend at any place for the purpose of receiving ante-natal care shall, subject to the following provisions of this section, have the right not to be unreasonably refused time off during her working hours to enable her to keep the appointment.

(2) Subject to subsection (3), an employer shall not be required by virtue of this section to permit an employee to take time off to keep an appointment unless, if he requests her to do so, she produces for his inspection—
>   (a) a certificate from a registered medical practitioner, registered midwife or registered health visitor stating that the employee is pregnant, and
>   (b) an appointment card or some other document showing that the appointment has been made.

(3) Subsection (2) shall not apply where the employee's appointment is the first appointment during her pregnancy for which she seeks permission to take time off in accordance with subsection (1).

(4) An employee who is permitted to take time off during her working hours in accordance with subsection (1) shall be entitled to be paid remuneration by her employer for the period of absence at the appropriate hourly rate.

(5) The appropriate hourly rate in relation to an employee shall be the amount of one week's pay divided by—
>   (a) the number of normal working hours in a week for that employee when employed under the contract of employment in force on the day when the time off is taken; or
>   (b) where the number of such normal working hours differs from week to week or over a longer period, the average number of such hours calculated by dividing by twelve the total number of the employee's normal working hours during the period of twelve weeks ending with the last complete week before the day on which the time off is taken; or
>   (c) in a case falling within paragraph (b) but where the employee has not been employed for a sufficient period to enable the calculation to be made under that paragraph, a number which fairly represents the number of normal working hours in a week having

regard to such of the following considerations as are appropriate in the circumstances, that is to say,—

(i) the average number of normal working hours in a week which the employee could expect in accordance with the terms of her contract;

(ii) the average number of such hours of other employees engaged in relevant comparable employment with the same employer.

(6) An employee may present a complaint to an industrial tribunal that her employer has unreasonably refused her time off as required by this section or that he has failed to pay her the whole or part of any amount to which she is entitled under subsection (4).

(7) An industrial tribunal shall not entertain a complaint under subsection (6) unless it is presented within the period of three months beginning with the day of the appointment concerned, or within such further period as the tribunal considers reasonable in a case where it is satisfied that it was not reasonably practicable for the complaint to be presented within the period of three months.

(8) Where on a complaint under subsection (6) the tribunal finds the complaint well-founded it shall make a declaration to that effect; and—

(a) if the complaint is that the employer has unreasonably refused the employee time off, the tribunal shall order the employer to pay to the employee an amount equal to the remuneration to which she would have been entitled under subsection (4) if the time off had not been refused; and

(b) if the complaint is that the employer has failed to pay the employee the whole or part of any amount to which she is entitled under subsection (4), the tribunal shall order the employer to pay to the employee the amount which it finds due to her.

(9) Subject to subsection (10), a right to any amount under subsection (4) shall not affect any right of an employee in relation to remuneration under her contract of employment (in this section referred to as "contractual remuneration").

(10) Any contractual remuneration paid to an employee in respect of a period of time off under this section shall go towards discharging any liability of the employer to pay remuneration under subsection (4) in respect of that period, and conversely any payment of remuneration under subsection (4) in respect of a period shall go towards discharging any liability of the employer to pay contractual remuneration in respect of that period.

1979 c. 36.

(11) Until the coming into operation of section 10 of the Nurses, Midwives and Health Visitors Act 1979, this section shall have effect as if for any reference to a registered midwife or registered health visitor there were substituted a reference to a certified midwife."

Other rights of employees

Guarantee payments.

14.—(1) In section 15(2) of the 1978 Act (which restricts entitlement to five days in any one of the periods of three months beginning on 1st February, 1st May, 1st August and 1st November) for the words from " any " to the end there shall be substituted the words " any period of three months ".

(2) This section shall not have effect in relation to workless days (within the meaning of section 12 of that Act) falling before the commencement of this section except so far as they are relevant in determining entitlement to guarantee payments in respect of days falling after that time.

Action short of dismissal relating to trade union membership and activities.

15.—(1) In subsection (1)(c) of section 23 of the 1978 Act (right of employee not to have action taken by his employer to compel him to belong to a union which is not independent) the words " which is not independent " shall cease to have effect.

(2) After subsection (2) of that section there shall be inserted—

" (2A) Where it is the practice, in accordance with a union membership agreement, for the employees of any class of an employer to belong to a specified independent trade union, or to one of a number of specified independent trade unions, then—

(a) subject to subsection (2B), the right conferred on employees of that class by virtue of subsection (1)(b) in relation to a union's activities shall extend to activities on the employer's premises only if the union is a specified union ; and

(b) employees of that class shall not have the right conferred by virtue of subsection (1)(c) except in respect of action which, if it amounted to dismissal from employment to which section 54 applies, would be regarded as unfair by reason of section 58(3A), (3B) or (3C).

(2B) A union membership agreement which takes effect after the commencement of section 7 of the Employment Act 1980 in relation to the employees of any class of an employer shall be disregarded for the purposes of the application of subsection (2A)(a) to employees of that class of the employer unless the agreement has, for the purposes of section 58(3C), been approved in relation to them in accordance with section 58A."

(3) Subsections (3), (4), (5)(a) and (6) of section 23 and subsection (1)(b) of section 25 of the 1978 Act shall cease to have effect.

(4) After section 26 of the 1978 Act there shall be inserted—

"Contribution in respect of compensation on certain complaints under s. 24.

26A.—(1) Where—

(a) a complaint is presented to an industrial tribunal under section 24 on the ground that action has been taken against the complainant by his employer for the purpose of compelling him to be or become a member of a trade union, and

(b) the employer claims in proceedings before the tribunal that he was induced to take the action by pressure which a trade union or other person exercised on him by calling, organising, procuring or financing a strike or other industrial action, or by threatening to do so,

the employer may before the hearing of the complaint require the person who he claims exercised the pressure to be joined, or in Scotland sisted, as a party to the proceedings.

(2) Where any person has been joined, or in Scotland sisted, as a party to proceedings before an industrial tribunal by virtue of subsection (1), and the tribunal—

(a) makes an award of compensation in favour of the complainant, but

(b) finds that the claim of the employer (as specified in subsection (1)) is well-founded,

the tribunal may make an order requiring that person to pay to the employer a contribution in respect of that compensation.

(3) The amount of any contribution ordered to be paid under this section in respect of any compensation shall be such as the tribunal considers to be just

Restrictions on legal liability

Picketing.

16.—(1) For section 15 of the 1974 Act there shall be substituted—

"Peaceful picketing.

15.—(1) It shall be lawful for a person in contemplation or furtherance of a trade dispute to attend—

    (*a*) at or near his own place of work, or

    (*b*) if he is an official of a trade union, at or near the place of work of a member of that union whom he is accompanying and whom he represents, .

for the purpose only of peacefully obtaining or communicating information, or peacefully persuading any person to work or abstain from working.

(2) If a person works or normally works—

    (*a*) otherwise than at any one place, or

    (*b*) at a place the location of which is such that attendance there for a purpose mentioned in subsection (1) above is impracticable,

his place of work for the purposes of that subsection shall be any premises of his employer from which he works or from which his work is administered.

(3) In the case of a worker who is not in employment and whose last employment was terminated in connection with a trade dispute, subsection (1) above shall in relation to that dispute have effect as if any reference to his place of work were a reference to his former place of work.

(4) A person who is an official of a trade union by virtue only of having been elected or appointed to be a representative of some of the members of the union shall be regarded for the purposes of subsection (1) above as representing only those members; but otherwise an official of a trade union shall be regarded for those purposes as representing all its members."

(2) Nothing in section 13 of the 1974 Act shall prevent an act done in the course of picketing from being actionable in tort unless it is done in the course of attendance declared lawful by section 15 of that Act.

(3) In subsection (2) above "tort" has as respects Scotland the same meaning as in the 1974 Act.

17.—(1) Nothing in section 13 of the 1974 Act shall prevent **Secondary** an act from being actionable in tort on a ground specified in **action.** subsection (1)(*a*) or (*b*) of that section in any case where—
- (*a*) the contract concerned is not a contract of employment, and
- (*b*) one of the facts relied upon for the purpose of establishing liability is that there has been secondary action which is not action satisfying the requirements of subsection (3), (4) or (5) below.

(2) For the purposes of this section there is secondary action in relation to a trade dispute when, and only when, a person—
- (*a*) induces another to break a contract of employment or interferes or induces another to interfere with its performance, or
- (*b*) threatens that a contract of employment under which he or another is employed will be broken or its performance interfered with, or that he will induce another to break a contract of employment or to interfere with its performance,

if the employer under the contract of employment is not a party to the trade dispute.

(3) Secondary action satisfies the requirements of this subsection if—
- (*a*) the purpose or principal purpose of the secondary action was directly to prevent or disrupt the supply during the dispute of goods or services between an employer who is a party to the dispute and the employer under the contract of employment to which the secondary action relates ; and
- (*b*) the secondary action (together with any corresponding action relating to other contracts of employment with the same employer) was likely to achieve that purpose.

(4) Secondary action satisfies the requirements of this subsection if—
- (*a*) the purpose or principal purpose of the secondary action was directly to prevent or disrupt the supply during the dispute of goods or services between any person and an associated employer of an employer who is a party to the dispute ; and
- (*b*) the goods or services are in substitution for goods or services which but for the dispute would have fallen to be supplied to or by the employer who is a party to the dispute ; and

(c) the employer under the contract of employment to which the secondary action relates is either the said associated employer or the other party to the supply referred to in paragraph (a) above; and

(d) the secondary action (together with any corresponding action relating to other contracts of employment with the same employer) was likely to achieve the purpose referred to in paragraph (a) above.

(5) Secondary action satisfies the requirements of this subsection if it is done in the course of attendance declared lawful by section 15 of the 1974 Act—

(a) by a worker employed (or, in the case of a worker not in employment, last employed) by a party to the dispute, or

(b) by a trade union official whose attendance is lawful by virtue of subsection (1)(b) of that section.

(6) In subsections (3)(a) and (4)(a) above—

(a) references to the supply of goods or services between two persons are references to the supply of goods or services by one to the other in pursuance of a contract between them subsisting at the time of the secondary action, and

(b) references to directly preventing or disrupting the supply are references to preventing or disrupting it otherwise than by means of preventing or disrupting the supply of goods or services by or to any other person.

(7) Expressions used in this section and in the 1974 Act have the same meanings in this section as in that Act; and for the purposes of this section an employer who is a member of an employers' association which is a party to a trade dispute shall by virtue of his membership be regarded as a party to the dispute if he is represented in the dispute by the association, but not otherwise.

(8) Subsection (3) of section 13 of the 1974 Act shall cease to have effect.

Acts to compel trade union membership.

18.—(1) Nothing in section 13 of the 1974 Act shall prevent an act to which this section applies from being actionable in tort on a ground specified in subsection (1)(a) or (b) of section 13 in any case where—

(a) the contract concerned is a contract of employment, or

(b) the contract concerned is not a contract of employment but one of the facts relied upon for the purpose of establishing liability is that any person has—

(i) induced another to break a contract of employment or interfered or induced another to interfere with its performance, or

(ii) threatened that a contract of employment under which he or another is employed will be broken or its performance interfered with, or that he will induce another to break a contract of employment or to interfere with its performance.

(2) This section applies to an act done for the purpose of compelling workers to become members of a particular trade union or of one of two or more particular trade unions, if none of those workers works for the same employer or at the same place as the employee working under the contract of employment referred to in subsection (1) above.

(3) Expressions used in this section and in the 1974 Act have the same meanings in this section as in that Act.

Miscellaneous and general

19. The following enactments shall cease to have effect, that is to say— *Enactments ceasing to have effect.*
(a) section 1A of the 1974 Act (charter on freedom of the press);
(b) sections 11 to 16 of the 1975 Act (procedure for dealing with issues relating to recognition of trade unions); and
(c) section 98 of and Schedule 11 to the 1975 Act (extension of terms and conditions of employment) and the Road Haulage Wages Act 1938 (fixing of statutory remuneration). *1938 c. 44.*

20.—(1) In this Act— *Interpretation, minor and consequential amendments and repeals.*
"the 1974 Act" means the Trade Union and Labour Relations Act 1974;
"the 1975 Act" means the Employment Protection Act 1975;
"the 1978 Act" means the Employment Protection (Consolidation) Act 1978.
1974 c. 52.
1975 c. 71.
1978 c. 44.

(2) Schedule 1 to this Act (which makes minor and consequential amendments) shall have effect.

(3) The enactments mentioned in Schedule 2 to this Act are hereby repealed to the extent specified in the third column of that Schedule.

21.—(1) This Act may be cited as the Employment Act 1980. *Short title commencement and extent.*
(2) Sections 2, 4 to 19 and 20(2) and (3) of this Act, and Schedules 1 and 2, shall not come into operation until such day as the Secretary of State may appoint by order made by statutory instrument, and different days may be so appointed for different purposes.

(3) An order under this section may contain such transitional and supplementary provisions as appear to the Secretary of State to be necessary or expedient.

(4) Paragraph 7 of Schedule 1 to this Act shall extend to Northern Ireland, but otherwise this Act shall not extend there.

SCHEDULES

SCHEDULE 1

Minor and Consequential Amendments

The Post Office Act 1969

1. In section 81(1) of the Post Office Act 1969 (exclusion of road haulage workers employed by Post Office from the workers in relation to whom wages councils may operate) the words from the beginning to " the Road Haulage Wages Act 1938 ; and " shall cease to have effect.

The Trade Union and Labour Relations Act 1974

2. In Schedule 1 to the 1974 Act, paragraph 32(2)(*a*) shall cease to have effect.

3. In Schedule 2 to the 1974 Act, in paragraph 32(1) (periodical re-examination of members' superannuation schemes) at the beginning there shall be inserted the words " Subject to paragraph 33A below " and after paragraph 33 there shall be inserted—

" 33A. The Certification Officer, on the application of a trade union or employers' association, may exempt any members' superannuation scheme which it maintains from the requirements of paragraph 32 above if he is satisfied that, by reason of the small number of members to which the scheme is applicable or for any other special reasons, it is unnecessary for the scheme to be examined in accordance with those requirements.

33B. The Certification Officer may at any time revoke any exemption granted under paragraph 33A above if it appears to him that the circumstances by reason of which the exemption was granted have ceased to exist ; and for the purposes of paragraph 32 above the relevant date next following the revocation shall be such date as the Certification Officer may direct."

The Employment Protection Act 1975

4. In section 6 of the 1975 Act, after subsection (10) there shall be inserted—

" (10A) If the Service is of the opinion that the provisions of a Code of Practice to be issued under this section will supersede the whole or part of a Code previously issued by it under this section or by the Secretary of State under section 3 of the Employment Act 1980, it shall in the new Code state that on the day on which the new Code comes into effect in pursuance of an order under subsection (5) or (8) above the old Code or a specified part of it shall cease to have effect (subject to any transitional provisions or savings made by the order)."

5. In section 121(1) of the 1975 Act, for the words " 98 to " there shall be substituted the words " 99 to ".

6. In section 126(1) of the 1975 Act, in the definition of " recognition ", for the words from " has " to " above " there shall be substituted the words " in relation to a trade union, means the recognition of the union by an employer, or two or more associated employers, to any extent, for the purpose of collective bargaining ".

7. In section 127(1) of the 1975 Act, after paragraph (f) there shall be inserted—

" (ff) the Employment Act 1980 ; and ".

The Employment Protection (Consolidation) Act 1978

8. In section 15(5) of the 1978 Act, for the words " relevant periods " there shall be substituted the words " length of the period ".

9. In section 32(1) of the 1978 Act, for " 31 " there shall be substituted " 31A ".

10. In section 55(5) of the 1978 Act, after " 64(1)(a) " there shall be inserted " 64A ".

11. In section 56 of the 1978 Act, after the word " then " there shall be inserted the words " subject to section 56A ".

12. In section 58(5) of the 1978 Act, for the words " subsection (1) or (3) " there shall be substituted the words " subsection (1), (3A), (3B) or (3C) ".

13. In section 66 of the 1978 Act (revocation of exclusion orders under section 65)—

(a) subsection (1) shall cease to have effect ; and

(b) in subsection (2) for the words from " on " to " satisfied " there shall be substituted the words " at any time when an order under section 65 is in force in respect of a dismissal procedures agreement the Secretary of State is satisfied, whether on an application by any of the parties to the agreement or otherwise,".

14. In section 71(3)(a) of the 1978 Act, for the words " section 58(1) or (3) " there shall be substituted the words " section 58(1), (3A), (3B) or (3C) ".

15. In section 121(2)(c) of the 1978 Act, for the words " or 31(3) " there shall be substituted the words " 31(3) or 31A(4) ".

16. In section 128(4) of the 1978 Act, after the word " references " there shall be inserted the word " applications ".

17. In section 133(1) of the 1978 Act, in paragraph (a) after " 31 " there shall be inserted " 31A ", and after paragraph (c) there shall be inserted—

" or

(d) arising out of a contravention, or alleged contravention, of section 4 of the Employment Act 1980 ".

18. In section 134 of the 1978 Act, for subsection (3) there shall be substituted—

" (3) Where—

(a) a person claims that action has been taken in respect of which a complaint could be presented by him under section 67, and

(b) before any complaint relating to that action has been so presented, a request is made to a conciliation officer (whether by that person or by the employer) to make his services available to them,

the conciliation officer shall act in accordance with subsections (1) and (2) above as if a complaint had been presented."

19. In section 136(5) of the 1978 Act, after the words "subsection (1)" there shall be inserted the words "or under section 2, 4 or 5 of the Employment Act 1980".

20. In section 140 of the 1978 Act (restrictions on contracting out of 1978 Act) subsection (2)(b) shall cease to have effect.

21. In section 149 of the 1978 Act—
   (a) in subsection (1)(c), after "64(1)" there shall be inserted "64A(1)";
   (b) in subsection (2), after "58" there shall be inserted "58A".

22. In section 154 of the 1978 Act (orders, rules and regulations)—
   (a) in subsection (1) the words "or an order under section 65 or 66" shall cease to have effect ; and
   (b) in subsection (4) for the words from "section 96" to the end there shall be substituted the words "section 65, 66 or 96".

23. In the subsection set out in paragraph 2(1) of Schedule 2 to the 1978 Act, for the words from "the employer can" to the end there shall be substituted the words "in the circumstances (including the size and administrative resources of the employer's undertaking) the employer would have been acting reasonably or unreasonably in treating it as a sufficient reason for dismissing the employee if she had not been absent from work ; and that question shall be determined in accordance with equity and the substantial merits of the case".

24. In paragraphs 2(4) and 6(3) of Schedule 2 to the 1978 Act, for "58(3)" there shall be substituted "58(3) to (3E), 58A".

25. In paragraph 5 of Schedule 3 to the 1978 Act, for the words "or 31" there shall be substituted the words "31 or 31A".

26. In paragraph 1(2)(a) of Schedule 9 to the 1978 Act, after the word "question" there shall be inserted the word "application".

27. In paragraph 7 of Schedule 9 to the 1978 Act, for sub-paragraph (2) there shall be substituted—

"(2) Any order for the payment of any sum made by an industrial tribunal in Scotland (or any copy of such an order certified by the Secretary of the Tribunals) may be enforced in like manner as an extract registered decree arbitral bearing a

The Employment Act, 1980 163

warrant for execution issued by the Sheriff Court of any Sheriffdom in Scotland."

28. In paragraph 18 of Schedule 11 to the 1978 Act, after sub-paragraph (*a*) there shall be inserted—

"(*aa*) with respect to the manner in which an application to the Appeal Tribunal under section 5 of the Employment Act 1980 may be made ; "

and after sub-paragraph (*c*) there shall be inserted—

"(*d*) for the registration and proof of any award made on an application to the Appeal Tribunal under section 5 of the Employment Act 1980.".

29. After paragraph 21 of Schedule 11 to the 1978 Act there shall be inserted—

"21A.—(1) Any sum payable in England and Wales in pursuance of an award of the Appeal Tribunal under section 5 of the Employment Act 1980 which has been registered in accordance with the rules shall, if a county court so orders, be recoverable by execution issued from the county court or otherwise as if it were payable under an order of that court.

(2) Any order by the Appeal Tribunal for the payment in Scotland of any sum in pursuance of such an award (or any copy of such an order certified by the Secretary of the Tribunals) may be enforced in like manner as an extract registered decree arbitral bearing a warrant for execution issued by the Sheriff Court of any Sheriffdom in Scotland."

30. In paragraph 23(1) of Schedule 11 to the 1978 Act, for the words from "section 14" to "those provisions" there shall be substituted the words "sections 31 and 32 of the Powers of Criminal Courts Act 1973 (powers of Crown Court in relation to fines and forfeited recognisances) shall have effect as if".

31. In paragraph 10 of Schedule 13 to the 1978 Act, for the words "section 47" there shall be substituted the words "section 45(1) or in pursuance of an offer made in the circumstances described in section 56A(2)".

32. In paragraph 11 of Schedule 13 to the 1978 Act, after "64(1)(*a*)" there shall be inserted "64A(1)".

33. In paragraph 7(1) of Schedule 14 to the 1978 Act, after paragraph (*c*) there shall be inserted—

"(*cc*) where the calculation is for the purposes of section 31A, the day of the appointment concerned ; ".

SCHEDULE 2
Repeals

Chapter	Short title	Extent of repeal
1 & 2 Geo. 6. c. 44.	The Road Haulage Wages Act 1938.	The whole Act.
12, 13 & 14 Geo. 6. c. 7.	The Wages Councils Act 1948.	In section 1(1)(c), the words from "Parts II and III" to the end, and Schedule 1.
1968 c. 73.	The Transport Act 1968.	Section 69(4)(d). So much of Schedules 10 and 11 as amends the Road Haulage Wages Act 1938.
1969 c. 35.	The Transport (London) Act 1969.	In Schedule 3, paragraph 1(2)(a).
1969 c. 48.	The Post Office Act 1969.	In section 81, in subsection (1), the words from the beginning to "the Road Haulage Wages Act 1938; and", and subsection (2).
1972 c. 68.	The European Communities Act 1972.	In paragraph 9(4) of Schedule 4, the words from the beginning to "1938" and the words from "after" to "Part VI; and".
1974 c. 52.	The Trade Union and Labour Relations Act 1974.	Section 1A. Section 13(3). In Schedule 1, in paragraph 32(1) the words from "Except" to "below", and paragraph 32(2). In Schedule 3, paragraph 4.
1975 c. 18.	The Social Security (Consequential Provisions) Act 1975.	In Schedule 2, paragraph 4.
1975 c. 60.	The Social Security Pensions Act 1975.	Section 31(9).
1975 c. 71.	The Employment Protection Act 1975.	Sections 11 to 16. In section 17(2), paragraph (b) and the word "or" immediately preceding it. In section 21(5), paragraph (b) and the word "or" immediately preceding it. Section 98. Section 106(1). In section 118(2)(d), the words "16(7)(b) or (c) or", the words from "or paragraph" to "this Act", the words "16 or" and the words from "or, as" to the end. In section 121(1), the reference to section 16. In section 127(1)(g), the words "in paragraphs (a) to (f)". Schedule 11. In Part IV of Schedule 16, paragraphs 4 and 17. In Schedule 17, paragraph 13.

Chapter	Short title	Extent of repeal
1976 c. 3.	The Road Traffic (Drivers' Ages and Hours of Work) Act 1976.	In section 2(3), the words from " the following " to " 1938 " and the word " and ".
1976 c. 7.	The Trade Union and Labour Relations (Amendment) Act 1976.	Section 2.
1976 c. 79.	The Dock Work Regulation Act 1976.	In section 15(1), in the definition of " recognised ", the words from " and a union " to the end.
1977 c. 3.	The Aircraft and Shipbuilding Industries Act 1977.	In section 56(1), in the definition of " relevant trade union ", the words from " or as " to the end.
1978 c. 36.	The House of Commons (Administration) Act 1978.	In Schedule 1, in paragraph 5(6), the words " Part IV of ".
1978 c. 44.	The Employment Protection (Consolidation) Act 1978.	In section 23, in subsection (1)(c), the words " which is not independent ", and subsections (3) to (6). In section 25(1), paragraph (b) and the word " and " immediately preceding it. In section 32(1)(a), the words " not only " and the words from " but " to " 1975 ". In section 33(3), the word " and " at the end of paragraph (b). Section 58(4). Section 66(1). Section 73(1)(c) and (8). Section 97. In section 135(1), the words from " for the purpose " to the end. Section 140(2)(b). In section 154(1), the words " or an order under section 65 or 66 ". In Schedule 6, in paragraph 12(2)(b), sub-paragraph (ii) and the word " or " immediately preceding it.
1979 c. 12.	The Wages Councils Act 1979.	In Schedule 6, paragraph 1.

Appendix 3

Extracts from *The Trade Union and Labour Relations Act, 1974* (as amended)

Status and regulation of trade unions and employers' associations

2.—(1) A trade union which is not a special register body shall not be, or be treated as if it were, a body corporate, but—
  (a) it shall be capable of making contracts;
  (b) all property belonging to the trade union shall be vested in trustees in trust for the union;
  (c) subject to section 14 below, it shall be capable of suing and being sued in its own name, whether in proceedings relating to property or founded on contract or tort or any other cause of action whatsoever;
  (d) proceedings for any offence alleged to have been committed by it or on its behalf may be brought against it in its own name; and
  (e) any judgment, order or award made in proceedings of any description brought against the trade union on or after the commencement of this section shall be enforceable, by way of execution, diligence, punishment for contempt or otherwise, against any property held in trust for the trade union to the like extent and in the like manner as if the union were a body corporate.

(2) A trade union which is not a special register body shall not be registered as a company under the Companies Act 1948 and accordingly any registration of any such union under that Act (whenever effected) shall be void.

(3) No trade union shall be registered under the Friendly Societies Act 1896 or the Industrial and Provident Societies

Act 1965 and accordingly any registration of a trade union under either of those Acts (whenever effected) shall be void.

(4) A trade union (other than a special register body) which, immediately before the commencement of this section, was a body corporate shall, on that commencement, cease to be a body corporate and the provisions of section 19 below (as well as this section and section 4 below) shall apply to the trade union on and after that commencement.

(5) The purposes of any trade union which is not a special register body and, in so far as they relate to the regulation of relations between employers or employers' associations and workers, the purposes of any trade union which is such a body, shall not, by reason only that they are in restraint of trade, be unlawful so as—

    (a) to make any member of the trade union liable to criminal proceedings for conspiracy or otherwise ; or

    (b) to make any agreement or trust void or voidable ;

nor shall any rule of a trade union which is not a special register body or, in so far as it so relates, any rule of any other trade union be unlawful or unenforceable by reason only that it is in restraint of trade.

5.—(1) Subject to the provisions of this section, every worker shall have the right not to be—
    (a) excluded from membership,
    (b) expelled from membership,
of a trade union or a branch or section of a trade union by way of arbitrary or unreasonable discrimination.

(2) The exclusion or expulsion of a worker from membership of a union, branch or section shall not be deemed to be arbitrary or unreasonable if the worker is of a description different from that or those of the majority of the members of that union, branch or section (as the case may be) or does not possess the appropriate qualifications for such membership.

(3) A worker aggrieved by his exclusion or expulsion from any trade union, branch or section may apply to an industrial tribunal in accordance with industrial tribunal regulations for a declaration that he is entitled to be a member of that union, branch or section.

(4) Where any such declaration has been made and has not been implemented by the union, branch or section concerned within any period specified in the declaration or if no such period is specified within a reasonable period, the worker may apply to the High Court or, in Scotland, the Court of Session for an injunction, interdict or such other relief (including compensation) as the Court may think just and expedient in all the circumstances of the case.

(5) Nothing in this section or section 2(5) above shall prejudice or in any way reduce the common law rights of a person who has applied to join, but not been given membership of, or who claims to be and to remain a member of, or who has been expelled from, a trade union.

Restrictions on legal liability and legal proceedings

13.—(1) An act done by a person in contemplation or furtherance of a trade dispute shall not be actionable in tort on the ground only—

    (*a*) that it induces another person to break a contract or *induces any other person to interfere with its performance.*
    (*b*) that it consists in his threatening that a contract (whether one to which he is a party or not) will be broken *or its performance interfered with* that he will induce another person to break a contract of employment to which that other person is a party.*

(2) For the avoidance of doubt it is hereby declared that an act done by a person in contemplation or furtherance of a trade dispute is not actionable in tort on the ground only that it is an interference with the trade, business or employment of another person, or with the right of another person to dispose of his capital or his labour as he wills.

(3) For the avoidance of doubt it is hereby declared that—

    (*a*) an act which by reason of subsection (1) or (2) above is itself not actionable;

---

*words in italics were added by *The Trade Union and Labour Relations (Amendment) Act, 1976,* which extended the protection to *all* contracts – not just contracts of employment.

(b) a breach of contract in contemplation or furtherance of a trade dispute;

shall not be regarded as the doing of an unlawful act or as the use of unlawful means for the purpose of establishing liability in tort.

(4) An agreement or combination by two or more persons to do or procure the doing of any act in contemplation or furtherance of a trade dispute shall not be actionable in tort if the act is one which, if done without any such agreement or combination, would not be actionable in tort.

14.—(1) Subject to subsection (2) below, no action in tort shall lie in respect of any act—

- (a) alleged to have been done by or on behalf of a trade union which is not a special register body or by or on behalf of an unincorporated employers' association; or
- (b) alleged to have been done, in connection with the regulation of relations between employers or employers' associations and workers or trade unions, by or on behalf of a trade union which is a special register body or by or on behalf of an employers' association which is a body corporate; or
- (c) alleged to be threatened or to be intended to be done as mentioned in paragraph (a) or (b) above;

against the union or association in its own name, or against the trustees of the union or association, or against any members or officials of the union or association on behalf of themselves and all other members of the union or association.

(2) Subsection (1) above shall not affect the liability of a trade union or employers' association to be sued in respect of the following, if not arising from an act done in contemplation or furtherance of a trade dispute, that is to say—

- (a) any negligence, nuisance or breach of duty (whether imposed on them by any rule of law or by or under any enactment) resulting in personal injury to any person; or
- (b) without prejudice to paragraph (a) above, breach of any duty so imposed in connection with the ownership,

occupation, possession, control or use of property (whether real or personal or, in Scotland, heritable or moveable).

(3) In this section "personal injury" includes any disease and any impairment of a person's physical or mental condition.

15. It shall be lawful for one or more persons in contemplation or furtherance of a trade dispute to attend at or near—

(a) a place where another person works or carries on business; or

(b) any other place where another person happens to be, not being a place where he resides,

for the purpose only of peacefully obtaining or communicating information, or peacefully persuading any person to work or abstain from working.

16. No court shall, whether by way of—

(a) an order for specific performance or specific implement of a contract of employment, or

(b) an injunction or interdict restraining a breach or threatened breach of such a contract,

compel an employee to do any work or attend at any place for the doing of any work.

17. Where an application for an injunction or interdict is made to a court in the absence of the party against whom the injunction or interdict is sought or any representative of his, and that party claims, or in the opinion of the court would be likely to claim, that he acted in contemplation or furtherance of a trade dispute, the court shall not grant the injunction or interdict unless satisfied that all steps which in the circumstances were reasonable have been taken with a view to securing that notice of the application and an opportunity of being heard with respect to the application have been given to that party.

28.—(1) In this Act, except so far as the context otherwise requires, "trade union" means an organisation (whether permanent or temporary) which either—

(a) consists wholly or mainly of workers of one or more

descriptions and is an organisation whose principal purposes include the regulation of relations between workers of that description or those descriptions and employers or employers' associations; or

(b) consists wholly or mainly of—

(i) constituent or affiliated organisations which fulfil the conditions specified in paragraph (a) above (or themselves consist wholly or mainly of constituent or affiliated organisations which fulfil those conditions), or

(ii) representatives of such constituent or affiliated organisations;

and in either case is an organisation whose principal purposes include the regulation of relations between workers and employers or between workers and employers' associations, or include the regulation of relations between its constituent or affiliated organisations.

(2) In this Act, except so far as the context otherwise requires, " employers' association " means an organisation (whether permanent or temporary) which either—

(a) consists wholly or mainly of employers or individual proprietors of one or more descriptions and is an organisation whose principal purposes include the regulation of relations between employers of that description or those descriptions and workers or trade unions; or

(b) consists wholly or mainly of—

(i) constituent or affiliated organisations which fulfil the conditions specified in paragraph (a) above (or themselves consist wholly or mainly of constituent or affiliated organisations which fulfil those conditions), or

(ii) representatives of such constituent or affiliated organisations;

and in either case is an organisation whose principal purposes include the regulation of relations between employers and workers or between employers and trade unions, or include the regulation of relations between its constituent or affiliated organisations.

29.—(1) In this Act " trade dispute " means a dispute between employers and workers, or between workers and workers, which is connected with one or more of the following, that is to say—

(a) terms and conditions of employment, or the physical conditions in which any workers are required to work ;

(b) engagement or non-engagement, or termination or suspension of employment or the duties of employment, of one or more workers ;

(c) allocation of work or the duties of employment as between workers or groups of workers ;

(d) matters of discipline ;

(e) the membership or non-membership of a trade union on the part of a worker ;

(f) facilities for officials of trade unions ; and

(g) machinery for negotiation or consultation, and other procedures, relating to any of the foregoing matters, including the recognition by employers or employers' associations of the right of a trade union to represent workers in any such negotiation or consultation or in the carrying out of such procedures.

(2) A dispute between a Minister of the Crown and any workers shall, notwithstanding that he is not the employer of those workers, be treated for the purposes of this Act as a dispute between employer and those workers if the dispute relates—

(a) to matters which have been referred for consideration by a joint body on which, by virtue of any provision made by or under any enactment, that Minister is represented ; or

(b) to matters which cannot be settled without that Minister exercising a power conferred on him by or under an enactment.

(3) There is a trade dispute for the purposes of this Act even though it relates to matters occurring outside Great Britain.*

---

*As amended by *The Trade Union and Labour Relations (Amendment) Act, 1976*.

(4) A dispute to which a trade union or employers' association is a party shall be treated for the purposes of this Act as a dispute to which workers or, as the case may be, employers are parties.

(5) An act, threat or demand done or made by one person or organisation against another which, if resisted, would have led to a trade dispute with that other, shall, notwithstanding that because that other submits to the act or threat or accedes to the demand no dispute arises, be treated for the purposes of this Act as being done or made in contemplation of a trade dispute with that other.

(6) In this section—

"employment" includes any relationship whereby one person personally does work or performs services for another;

"worker", in relation to a dispute to which an employer is a party, includes any worker even if not employed by that employer.

(7) In the Conspiracy and Protection of Property Act 1875 "trade dispute" has the same meaning as in this Act.

30.—(1) In this Act, except so far as the context otherwise requires,—

"act" and "action" each includes omission and references to doing an act or taking action shall be construed accordingly;

"collective agreement" means any agreement or arrangement made by or on behalf of one or more trade unions and one or more employers or employers' associations and relating to one or more of the matters mentioned in section 29(1) above;

"contract of employment" means a contract of service or of apprenticeship, whether it is express or implied and (if it is express) whether it is oral or in writing;

"dismissal procedures agreement" means an agreement in writing with respect to procedures relating to dismissal made by or on behalf of one or more independent trade unions and one or more employers or employers' associations;

"employee" means an individual who has entered into or works under (or, where the employment has ceased, worked under) a contract of employment, otherwise than in police service;

"employers' association" includes a combination of employers and employers' associations;

"independent trade union" means a trade union which—

(a) is not under the domination or control of an employer or a group of employers or of one or more employers' associations; and

(b) is not liable to interference by an employer or any such group or association (arising out of the provision of financial or material support or by any other means whatsoever) tending towards such control;

"individual proprietor" means an individual who is the owner of an undertaking;

"1971 Act" means the Industrial Relations Act 1971;

"official", in relation to a trade union, means any person who is an officer of the union or of a branch or section of the union or who (not being such an officer) is a person elected or appointed in accordance with the rules of the union to be a representative of its members or of some of them, including any person so elected or appointed who is an employee of the same employer as the members, or one or more of the members, whom he is to represent;

"police service" means service—

(a) in England and Wales as a member of a police force or as a special constable;

(b) as a constable within the meaning of the Police (Scotland) Act 1967;

(c) as a member of any constabulary maintained by virtue of any enactment; or

(d) in any other capacity by virtue of which a person has the powers or privileges of a constable;

"position", in relation to an employee, means the following matters taken as a whole, that is to say, his status as an employee, the nature of his work and his terms and conditions of employment;

"Registrar" has the meaning assigned to it by section 8(1) above;

"special register body" means an organisation whose name was immediately before the commencement of sections 2 and 3 above entered in the special register maintained under section 84 of the 1971 Act and which for the time being is a company registered under the Companies Act 1948 or is incorporated by charter or letters patent;

"tort", as respects Scotland, means any wrongful or negligent act giving rise to liability in reparation, and cognate expressions shall be construed accordingly;

"union membership agreement" means an agreement or arrangement which—

    (a) is made by or on behalf of, or otherwise exists between, one or more independent trade unions and one or more employers or employers' associations; and

    (b) relates to employees of an identifiable class; and

    (c) has the effect *in practice of requiring the employees for the time being of the class to which it relates (whether or not there is a condition to that effect in their contract of employment* ro be or become a member of the union or one of the unions which is or are parties to the agreement or arrangement or of another specified independent trade union, *and references in this definition to a trade union include references to a branch or section of a trade union; and a trade union is specified for the purposes, or in relation to, a union membership agreement if it is specified in the agreement or is accepted by the parties to the agreement as being the `equivalent of a union so specified.**

"worker" (subject to the following provisions of this section) means an individual regarded in whichever (if any) of the following capacities is applicable to him, that is to say, as a person who works or normally works or seeks to work—

    (a) under a contract of employment; or

    (b) under any other contract (whether express or

---

*As amended by *The Trade Union and Labour Relations (Amendment) Act, 1976.*

implied, and, if express, whether oral or in writing) whereby he undertakes to do or perform personally any work or services for another party to the contract who is not a professional client of his; or

(c) in employment under or for the purposes of a government department (otherwise than as a member of the naval, military or air forces of the Crown or of any women's service administered by the Defence Council) in so far as any such employment does not fall within paragraph (a) or (b) above,

otherwise than in police service.

(2) Without prejudice to the generality of the definitions in subsection (1) of this section, in this Act—

(a) "worker" includes an individual regarded in his capacity as one who works or normally works or seeks to work as a person providing general medical services, pharmaceutical services, general dental services or general ophthalmic services in accordance with arrangements made by an Area Health Authority or Family Practitioner Committee under section 33, section 38, section 40 or section 41 of the National Health Service Act 1946 or by a Health Board under section 34, section 39, section 40 or section 42 of the National Health Service (Scotland) Act 1947; and

(b) "employer" includes any Area Health Authority, Family Practitioner Committee or Health Board in accordance with whose arrangements a person provides or has provided or normally provides or seeks to provide any such service as aforesaid.

(3) Subject to subsection (4) below, in this Act "successor", in relation to the employer of an employee, means a person who, in consequence of a change occurring (whether by virtue of a sale or other disposition or by operation of law) in the ownership of the undertaking or of part of the undertaking for the purposes of which the employee was employed, has become the owner of that undertaking or of that part of it, as the case may be.

(4) Subsection (3) above shall have effect (subject to the necessary modifications) in relation to a case where—

(a) the person by whom an undertaking or part of an undertaking is owned immediately before a change is one of the persons by whom (whether as partners, trustees or otherwise) it is owned immediately after the change, or

(b) the persons by whom an undertaking or part of an undertaking is owned immediately before a change (whether as partners, trustees or otherwise) include the persons by whom, or include one or more of the persons by whom, it is owned immediately after the change,

as that subsection has effect where the previous owner and the new owner are wholly different persons; and any reference in this Act to a successor of an employer shall be construed accordingly.

(5) For the purposes of this Act any two employers are to be treated as associated if one is a company of which the other (directly or indirectly) has control, or if both are companies of which a third person (directly or indirectly) has control; and in this Act "associated employer" shall be construed accordingly.

(6) For the purposes of this Act it is immaterial whether the law which (apart from this Act) governs any persons' employment is the law of the United Kingdom, or of a part of the United Kingdom, or not.

(7) Except so far as the context otherwise requires, any reference in this Act to any enactment shall be construed as a reference to that enactment as amended or extended by or under any other enactment, including this Act.

Appendix 4

Extracts from *The Employment Protection Act, 1975*

Advisory, Conciliation and Arbitration Service, etc.

1.—(1) There shall be a body to be known as the Advisory, Conciliation and Arbitration Service, in this Act referred to as " the Service ".

(2) The Service shall be charged with the general duty of promoting the improvement of industrial relations, and in particular of encouraging the extension of collective bargaining and the development and, where necessary, reform of collective bargaining machinery.

(3) The provisions (so far as applicable) of Parts I and III of Schedule 1 to this Act shall have effect with respect to the Service.

2.—(1) Where a trade dispute exists or is apprehended the Service may, at the request of one or more parties to the dispute or otherwise, offer the parties to the dispute its assistance with a view to bringing about a settlement.

(2) The assistance offered by the Service may be by way of conciliation or by other means, and may include the appointment of a person other than an officer or servant of the Service to offer assistance to the parties to the dispute with a view to bringing about a settlement.

(3) In exercising its functions under subsection (1) above, the Service shall have regard to the desirability of encouraging the parties to a dispute to use any appropriate agreed procedures for negotiation or the settlement of disputes.

(4) The Service shall designate officers of the Service to perform the functions of conciliation officers under any enactment (including any provision of this Act or any Act passed after this Act) in respect of matters which are or could be the subject of proceedings before an industrial tribunal, and accordingly any reference in any such enactment to a conciliation officer is a reference to an officer designated under this subsection.

3.—(1) Where a trade dispute exists or is apprehended the Service may, at the request of one or more parties to the dispute and with the consent of all the parties to the dispute, refer all or any of the matters to which the dispute relates for settlement to the arbitration of—
- (a) one or more persons appointed by the Service for that purpose (not being an officer or servant of the Service); or
- (b) the Central Arbitration Committee constituted under section 10 below.

(2) In exercising its functions under subsection (1) above, the Service shall consider the likelihood of the dispute being settled by conciliation and, where there exist appropriate agreed procedures for negotiation or the settlement of disputes, shall not refer a matter for settlement to arbitration under that subsection unless those procedures have been used and have failed to result in a settlement or unless, in the opinion of the Service, there is a special reason which justifies arbitration under that subsection as an alternative to those procedures.

(3) Where in any case more than one arbitrator is appointed under subsection (1)(a) above the Service shall appoint one of the arbitrators to act as chairman.

(4) An award by an arbitrator appointed under subsection (1)(a) above may be published if the Service so decides and all the parties consent.

(5) Part I of the Arbitration Act 1950 shall not apply to an arbitration under this section.

(6) In the application of this section to Scotland, references to an arbitrator shall be construed as references to an arbiter.

4.—(1) The Service shall, if it thinks fit, on request or otherwise, provide, without charge, to employers, employers' associations, workers and trade unions such advice as it thinks appropriate on any matter concerned with industrial relations or employment policies, including the following—
- (a) the organisation of workers or employers for the purpose of collective bargaining;
- (b) the recognition of trade unions by employers;
- (c) machinery for the negotiation of terms and conditions of employment, and for joint consultation;
- (d) procedures for avoiding and settling disputes and workers' grievances;
- (e) questions relating to communication between employers and workers;
- (f) facilities for officials of trade unions;
- (g) procedures relating to the termination of employment;
- (h) disciplinary matters;

(i) manpower planning, labour turnover and absenteeism;
(j) recruitment, retention, promotion and vocational training of workers;
(k) payment systems, including job evaluation and equal pay.

(2) The Service may publish general advice on any matter concerned with industrial relations or employment policies, including any of the matters referred to in paragraphs (a) to (k) of subsection (1) above.

5.—(1) The Service may, if it thinks fit, inquire into any question relating to industrial relations generally or to industrial relations in any particular industry or in any particular undertaking or part of an undertaking.

(2) The findings of any inquiry under this section, together with any advice given by the Service in connection with those findings, may be published by the Service if—
- (a) it appears to the Service that publication is desirable for the improvement of industrial relations, either generally or in relation to the specific question inquired into; and,
- (b) after sending a draft of the findings to, and taking into account the views of, all the parties appearing to the Service to be concerned, the Service thinks fit.

6.—(1) The Service may issue Codes of Practice containing such practical guidance as the Service thinks fit for the purpose of promoting the improvement of industrial relations.

(2) Without prejudice to the generality of subsection (1) above, the Service shall, in one or more Codes of Practice, provide practical guidance on the following matters in relation to the application of the following provisions of this Act, that is to say—
- (a) the disclosure of information, in accordance with sections 17 and 18 below, by employers to trade union representatives for the purpose of collective bargaining;
- (b) the time off to be permitted by an employer—
    - (i) to a trade union official in accordance with section 57 below; and
    - (ii) to a trade union member in accordance with section 58 below.

(3) When the Service proposes to issue a Code of Practice, it shall prepare and publish a draft of that Code, shall consider any representations made to it about the draft and may modify the draft accordingly.

(4) If the Service determines to proceed with the draft, it shall transmit the draft to the Secretary of State who shall—
- (a) if he approves of it, lay it before both Houses of Parliament; and

(b) if he does not approve of it, publish details of his reasons for withholding approval.

(5) In the case of a draft Code of Practice containing practical guidance on the matters referred to in paragraph (a) or (b) of subsection (2) above, if the draft is approved by resolution of each House of Parliament the Service shall issue the Code in the form of the draft and the Code shall come into effect on such day as the Secretary of State may by order appoint.

(6) In the case of a draft Code of Practice not containing such practical guidance, if, within the period of forty days beginning with the day on which a copy of the draft is laid before each House of Parliament, or, if such copies are laid on different days, with the later of the two days, either House so resolves, no further proceedings shall be taken thereon, but without prejudice to the laying before Parliament of a new draft.

(7) In reckoning the period of forty days referred to in subsection (6) above, no account shall be taken of any period during which Parliament is dissolved or prorogued or during which both Houses are adjourned for more than four days.

(8) If no such resolution is passed as is referred to in subsection (6) above, the Service shall issue the Code in the form of the draft and the Code shall come into effect on such day as the Secretary of State may by order appoint.

(9) Without prejudice to section 123(3) below, an order under subsection (5) or subsection (8) above may contain such transitional provisions or savings as appear to the Secretary of State to be necessary or expedient in connection with the Code of Practice thereby brought into operation.

(10) The Service may from time to time revise the whole or any part of a Code of Practice issued under this section and issue that revised Code, and subsections (3) to (9) above shall apply (with appropriate modifications) to such a revised Code as they apply to the first issue of a Code.

(11) A failure on the part of any person to observe any provision of a Code of Practice shall not of itself render him liable to any proceedings; but in any proceedings before an industrial tribunal or the Central Arbitration Committee any Code of Practice issued under this section shall be admissible in evidence, and if any provision of such a Code appears to the tribunal or Committee to be relevant to any question arising in the proceedings it shall be taken into account in determining that question.

7.—(1) The Secretary of State shall, after consultation with the Service, appoint an officer to be known as the Certification Officer.

(2) The functions under the following Acts which before the commencement of this section were performed by the Chief Registrar of Friendly Societies or any assistant registrar shall become functions of the Certification Officer, that is to say,—
    (a) the Trade Union Act 1913 ;
    (b) the Trade Union (Amalgamations, etc.) Act 1964 ;
    (c) the 1974 Act.

(3) The provisions (so far as applicable) of Parts I and III of Schedule 1 to this Act shall have effect with respect to the Certification Officer.

(4) The Certification Officer may appoint one or more assistant certification officers and shall appoint an assistant certification officer for Scotland.

(5) The Certification Officer may delegate to an assistant certification officer such functions as he thinks appropriate and in particular may delegate to the assistant certification officer for Scotland such functions as he thinks appropriate in relation to organisations whose principal office is in Scotland.

(6) References in any enactment (except in subsections (4) and (5) above, this subsection, Part I and paragraph 28 of Schedule 1 to this Act and the House of Commons Disqualification Act 1975) to the Certification Officer shall be construed as including, in relation to such functions as have been delegated in accordance with subsection (5) above, references to an assistant certification officer.

Disclosure of information

17.—(1) For the purposes of all the stages of such collective bargaining between an employer and representatives of an independent trade union as is referred to in subsection (2) below, it shall be the duty of the employer, subject to section 18 below, to disclose to those representatives on request all such information relating to his undertaking as is in his possession, or that of any associated employer, and is both—
    (a) information without which the trade union representatives would be to a material extent impeded in carrying on with him such collective bargaining, and
    (b) information which it would be in accordance with good industrial relations practice that he should disclose to them for the purposes of collective bargaining.

(2) The collective bargaining for the purposes of which an employer must disclose information under subsection (1) above is collective bargaining about matters, and in relation to descriptions of workers,—
    (a) in respect of which the trade union is recognised by that employer ; or
    (b) falling within the scope of an operative recommenda-

tion for recognition (within the meaning of section 15 above) relating to the union,
and in this section and sections 19 to 21 below " representative ", in relation to a trade union, means an official or other person authorised by the trade union to carry on such collective bargaining.

(3) Where a request for information is made by trade union representatives under this section, the request shall, if the employer so requests, be in writing or be confirmed in writing.

(4) In determining, for the purposes of subsection (1)(b) above, what would be in accordance with good industrial relations practice, regard shall be had to the relevant provisions of any Code of Practice issued by the Service under section 6 above, but not so as to exclude any other evidence of what that practice is.

(5) Where an employer is required by virtue of this section to disclose any information to trade union representatives, the disclosure of it shall, if they so request, be in writing or be confirmed in writing.

18.—(1) No employer shall, by virtue of section 17 above, be required to disclose—
- (a) any information the disclosure of which would be against the interests of national security, or
- (b) any information which he could not disclose without contravening a prohibition imposed by or under an enactment, or
- (c) any information which has been communicated to the employer in confidence, or which the employer has otherwise obtained in consequence of the confidence reposed in him by another person, or
- (d) any information relating specifically to an individual, unless he has consented to its being disclosed, or
- (e) any information the disclosure of which would cause substantial injury to the employer's undertaking for reasons other than its effect on collective bargaining, or
- (f) any information obtained by the employer for the purpose of bringing, prosecuting or defending any legal proceedings ;

and in formulating the provisions of any Code of Practice relating to the disclosure of information, the Service shall have regard to the provisions of this subsection.

(2) In the performance of his duty under section 17 above an employer shall not be required—
- (a) to produce, or allow inspection of, any document (other than a document prepared for the purpose of conveying or confirming the information) or to make a copy of or extracts from any document, or

(b) to compile or assemble any information where the compilation or assembly would involve an amount of work or expenditure out of reasonable proportion to the value of the information in the conduct of collective bargaining.

21.—(1) On or after presenting a further complaint under section 20 above, the trade union may present to the Committee, in writing, a claim in respect of one or more descriptions of employees (but not workers who are not employees) specified in the claim that their contracts should include the terms and conditions specified in the claim.

(2) The right to present a claim under subsection (1) above shall expire, or, as the case may be, a claim so presented shall be treated as withdrawn, if at any time before the Committee makes an award under this section the employer discloses, or, as the case may be, confirms in writing, to representatives of the trade union the information specified in the declaration under section 19(6)(a) or, as the case may be, section 20(4) above.

(3) If the Committee finds, or has found, the further complaint wholly or partly well-founded, it may, after hearing the parties, make an award that in respect of any description of employees specified in the claim the employer shall, from a specified date, observe either—

(a) the terms and conditions specified in the claim ; or
(b) other terms and conditions which the Committee considers appropriate.

(4) The date specified in an award under subsection (3) above may be a date earlier than that on which the award is made but shall not be earlier than the date specified in accordance with section 19(6)(b) above in the declaration made by the Committee on the original complaint.

(5) An award under subsection (3) above shall be made only in respect of a description of employees, and shall comprise only terms and conditions relating to matters,—

(a) in respect of which the trade union making the claim is recognised by the employer ; or
(b) which fall within the scope of an operative recommendation for recognition (within the meaning of section 15 above) relating to the trade union making the claim.

(6) Any terms and conditions which by an award under this section the employer is required to observe in respect of employees of his shall have effect as part of the contract of employment of any such employee, as from the date specified in the award, except in so far as they are superseded or varied—

(a) by a subsequent award under this section ;

(b) by a collective agreement between the employer and the union for the time being representing that employee; or
(c) by express or implied agreement between the employee and the employer so far as that agreement effects an improvement in any terms and conditions having effect by virtue of the award.

(7) Where—
(a) by virtue of any enactment, other than one contained in this section, providing for minimum remuneration or terms and conditions, a contract of employment is to have effect as modified by an award, order or other instrument under that enactment; and
(b) by virtue of an award under this section any terms and conditions are to have effect as part of that contract,

that contract shall have effect in accordance with that award, order or other instrument or in accordance with the award under this section, whichever is the more favourable, in respect of any terms and conditions of that contract, to the employee.

(8) No award shall be made under this section in respect of any terms and conditions of employment which are fixed by virtue of any enactment.

Appendix 5

Extracts from *The Employment Protection (Consolidation) Act, 1978* (as amended)

Written particulars of terms of employment

Written particulars of terms of employment. 1.—(1) Not later than thirteen weeks after the beginning of an employee's period of employment with an employer, the employer shall give to the employee a written statement in accordance with the following provisions of this section.

(2) An employer shall in a statement under this section—

    (*a*) identify the parties;

    (*b*) specify the date when the employment began;

    (*c*) state whether any employment with a previous employer counts as part of the employee's continuous period of employment, and, if so, specify the date when the continuous period of employment began.

(3) A statement under this section shall contain the following particulars of the terms of employment as at a specified date not more than one week before the statement is given, that is to say—

    (*a*) the scale or rate of remuneration, or the method of calculating remuneration,

    (*b*) the intervals at which remuneration is paid (that is, whether weekly or monthly or by some other period),

    (*c*) any terms and conditions relating to hours of work (including any terms and conditions relating to normal working hours),

    (*d*) any terms and conditions relating to—

        (i) entitlement to holidays, including public holidays, and holiday pay (the particulars given being sufficient to enable the employee's entitlement, including any entitlement to accrued holiday pay on the termination of employment, to be precisely calculated),

        (ii) incapacity for work due to sickness or injury, including any provision for sick pay,

        (iii) pensions and pension schemes,

(e) the length of notice which the employee is obliged to give and entitled to receive to determine his contract of employment, and

(f) the title of the job which the employee is employed to do:

Provided that paragraph (d)(iii) shall not apply to the employees of any body or authority if the employees' pension rights depend on the terms of a pension scheme established under any provision contained in or having effect under an Act of Parliament and the body or authority are required by any such provision to give to new employees information concerning their pension rights, or concerning the determination of questions affecting their pension rights.

(4) Subject to subsection (5), every statement given to an employee under this section shall include a note—

(a) specifying any disciplinary rules applicable to the employee, or referring to a document which is reasonably accessible to the employee and which specifies such rules;

(b) specifying, by description or otherwise—

(i) a person to whom the employee can apply if he is dissatisfied with any disciplinary decision relating to him; and

(ii) a person to whom the employee can apply for the purpose of seeking redress of any grievance relating to his employment,

and the manner in which any such application should be made;

(c) where there are further steps consequent upon any such application, explaining those steps or referring to a document which is reasonably accessible to the employee and which explains them; and

(d) stating whether a contracting-out certificate is in force for the employment in respect of which the statement is given.

(5) The provisions of paragraphs (a) to (c) of subsection (4) shall not apply to rules, disciplinary decisions, grievances or procedures relating to health or safety at work.

(6) The definition of week given by section 153(1) does not apply for the purposes of this section.

Guarantee payments

12.—(1) Where an employee throughout a day during any part of which he would normally be required to work in accordance with his contract of employment is not provided with work by his employer by reason of— *Right to guarantee payment.*

(a) a diminution in the requirements of the employer's business for work of the kind which the employee is employed to do, or

(b) any other occurrence affecting the normal working of the employer's business in relation to work of the kind which the employee is employed to do,

he shall, subject to the following provisions of this Act, be entitled to be paid by his employer a payment, referred to in this Act as a guarantee payment, in respect of that day, and in this section and sections 13 and 16—

(i) such a day is referred to as a " workless day ", and

(ii) " workless period " has a corresponding meaning.

(2) In this section and sections 13 to 17, " day " means the period of twenty-four hours from midnight to midnight, and where a period of employment begun on any day extends over midnight into the following day, or would normally so extend, then—

(a) if the employment before midnight is, or would normally be, of longer duration than that after midnight, that period of employment shall be treated as falling wholly on the first day ; and

(b) in any other case, that period of employment shall be treated as falling wholly on the second day.

General exclusions from right under s. 12.

13.—(1) An employee shall not be entitled to a guarantee payment in respect of a workless day if the failure to provide him with work occurs in consequence of a trade dispute involving any employee of his employer or of an associated employer.

(2) An employee shall not be entitled to a guarantee payment in respect of a workless day if—

(a) his employer has offered to provide alternative work for that day which is suitable in all the circumstances whether or not work which the employee is under his contract employed to perform, and the employee has unreasonably refused that offer ; or

(b) he does not comply with reasonable requirements imposed by his employer with a view to ensuring that his services are available.

Calculation of guarantee payment.

14.—(1) Subject to the limits set by section 15, the amount of a guarantee payment payable to an employee in respect of any day shall be the sum produced by multiplying the number of normal working hours on that day by the guaranteed hourly rate, and, accordingly, no guarantee payment shall be payable to an employee in whose case there are no normal working hours on the day in question.

(2) Subject to subsection (3), the guaranteed hourly rate in relation to an employee shall be the amount of one week's pay

divided by—
- (a) the number of normal working hours in a week for that employee when employed under the contract of employment in force on the day in respect of which the guarantee payment is payable; or
- (b) where the number of such normal working hours differs from week to week or over a longer period, the average number of such hours calculated by dividing by twelve the total number of the employee's normal working hours during the period of twelve weeks ending with the last complete week before the day in respect of which the guarantee payment is payable; or
- (c) in a case falling within paragraph (b) but where the employee has not been employed for a sufficient period to enable the calculation to be made under that paragraph, a number which fairly represents the number of normal working hours in a week having regard to such of the following considerations as are appropriate in the circumstances, that is to say,—
    - (i) the average number of normal working hours in a week which the employee could expect in accordance with the terms of his contract;
    - (ii) the average number of such hours of other employees engaged in relevant comparable employment with the same employer.

(3) If in any case an employee's contract has been varied, or a new contract has been entered into, in connection with a period of short-time working, subsection (2) shall have effect as if for the reference to the day in respect of which the guarantee payment is payable there was substituted a reference to the last day on which the original contract was in force.

Trade union membership and activities

23.—(1) Subject to the following provisions of this section, every employee shall have the right not to have action (short of dismissal) taken against him as an individual by his employer for the purpose of— *Trade union membership and activities.*
- (a) preventing or deterring him from being or seeking to become a member of an independent trade union, or penalising him for doing so; or
- (b) preventing or deterring him from taking part in the activities of an independent trade union at any appropriate time, or penalising him for doing so; or
- (c) compelling him to be or become a member of a trade union which is not independent.

(2) In this section "appropriate time", in relation to an employee taking part in any activities of a trade union, means time which either—
- (a) is outside his working hours, or

(b) is a time within his working hours at which, in accordance with arrangements agreed with, or consent given by his employer, it is permissible for him to take part in those activities;

and in this subsection "working hours", in relation to an employee, means any time when, in accordance with his contract of employment, he is required to be at work.

(3) The provisions of subsection (4) shall have effect in relation to an employee—

(a) of the same class as employees for whom it is the practice in accordance with a union membership agreement to belong to a specified independent trade union or to one of a number of specified independent trade unions; or

(b) not of the same class as described in paragraph (a) but of the same grade or category as such employees as are referred to in that paragraph.

(4) In relation to such an employee the right conferred by subsection (1)(b) in relation to the activities of an independent trade union shall extend to activities on the employer's premises only if that union is a specified union.

(5) For the purposes of this section a trade union—

(a) shall be taken to be specified for the purposes of, or in relation to, a union membership agreement if it is specified in the agreement or is accepted by the parties to the agreement as being the equivalent of a union so specified; and

(b) shall also be treated as so specified if—

(i) the Advisory, Conciliation and Arbitration Service has made a recommendation for recognition of that union covering the employee in question which is operative within the meaning of section 15 of the Employment Protection Act 1975; or

(ii) the union has referred a recognition issue covering that employee to the Advisory, Conciliation and Arbitration Service under section 11 of the said Act of 1975 and the Service has not declined to proceed on the reference under section 12 of that Act, the union has not withdrawn the reference, or from the reference, and the issue has not been settled or reported on under that section.

(6) An employee who genuinely objects on grounds of religious belief to being a member of any trade union whatsoever shall have the right not to have action (short of dismissal) taken

against him by his employer for the purpose of compelling him to belong to a trade union.

(7) In this section, unless the context otherwise requires, references to a trade union include references to a branch or section of a trade union.

25.—(1) On a complaint under section 24 it shall be for the employer to show— Supplementary provisions relating to complaints under s. 24.
   (a) the purpose for which action was taken against the complainant ; and
   (b) that the purpose was not such a purpose as is referred to in section 23(1)(a) to (c) or (6).

(2) In determining on a complaint under section 24, any question as to whether action was taken by the complainant's employer or the purpose for which it was taken, no account shall be taken of any pressure which, by calling, organising, procuring or financing a strike or other industrial action, or threatening to do so, was exercised on the employer to take the action complained of, and that question shall be determined as if no such pressure had been exercised.

Time off work

27.—(1) An employer shall permit an employee of his who is an official of an independent trade union recognised by him to take time off, subject to and in accordance with subsection (2), during the employee's working hours for the purpose of enabling him— Time off for carrying out trade union duties.

   (a) to carry out those duties of his as such an official which are concerned with industrial relations between his employer and any associated employer, and their employees ; or
   (b) to undergo training in aspects of industrial relations which is—
      (i) relevant to the carrying out of those duties ; and
      (ii) approved by the Trades Union Congress or by the independent trade union of which he is an official.

(2) The amount of time off which an employee is to be permitted to take under this section and the purposes for which, the occasions on which and any conditions subject to which time off may be so taken are those that are reasonable in all the circumstances having regard to any relevant provisions of a Code of Practice issued by the Advisory, Conciliation and Arbitration Service under section 6 of the Employment Protection Act 1975.

(3) An employer who permits an employee to take time off under this section for any purpose shall, subject to the following

provisions of this section, pay him for the time taken off for that purpose in accordance with the permission—
> (a) where the employee's remuneration for the work he would ordinarily have been doing during that time does not vary with the amount of work done, as if he had worked at that work for the whole of that time;
> (b) where the employee's remuneration for that work varies with the amount of work done, an amount calculated by reference to the average hourly earnings for that work.

(4) The average hourly earnings referred to in subsection (3)(b) shall be the average hourly earnings of the employee concerned or, if no fair estimate can be made of those earnings, the average hourly earnings for work of that description of persons in comparable employment with the same employer or, if there are no such persons, a figure of average hourly earnings which is reasonable in the circumstances.

(5) Subject to subsection (6), a right to be paid any amount under subsection (3) shall not affect any right of an employee in relation to remuneration under his contract of employment (in this section referred to as " contractual remuneration ").

(6) Any contractual remuneration paid to an employee in respect of a period of time off to which subsection (1) applies shall go towards discharging any liability of the employer under subsection (3) in respect of that period, and conversely any payment of any amount under subsection (3) in respect of a period shall go towards discharging any liability of the employer to pay contractual remuneration in respect of that period.

(7) An employee who is an official of an independent trade union recognised by his employer may present a complaint to an industrial tribunal that his employer has failed to permit him to take time off as required by this section or to pay him the whole or part of any amount so required to be paid.

Time off for trade union activities.

28.—(1) An employer shall permit an employee of his who is a member of an appropriate trade union to take time off, subject to and in accordance with subsection (3), during the employee's working hours for the purpose of taking part in any trade union activity to which this section applies.

(2) In this section " appropriate trade union ", in relation to an employee of any description, means an independent trade union which is recognised by his employer in respect of that description of employee, and the trade union activities to which this section applies are—
> (a) any activities of an appropriate trade union of which the employee is a member; and

(b) any activities, whether or not falling within paragraph (a), in relation to which the employee is acting as a representative of such a union,

excluding activities which themselves consist of industrial action whether or not in contemplation or furtherance of a trade dispute.

(3) The amount of time off which an employee is to be permitted to take under this section and the purposes for which, the occasions on which and any conditions subject to which time off may be so taken are those that are reasonable in all the circumstances having regard to any relevant provisions of a Code of Practice issued by the Advisory, Conciliation and Arbitration Service under section 6 of the Employment Protection Act 1975.

(4) An employee who is a member of an independent trade union recognised by his employer may present a complaint to an industrial tribunal that his employer has failed to permit him to take time off as required by this section.

29.—(1) An employer shall permit an employee of his who is— *Time off for public duties.*

(a) a justice of the peace;
(b) a member of a local authority;
(c) a member of any statutory tribunal;
(d) a member of, in England and Wales, a Regional Health Authority or Area Health Authority or, in Scotland, a Health Board;
(e) a member of, in England and Wales, the managing or governing body of an educational establishment maintained by a local education authority, or, in Scotland, a school or college council or the governing body of a central institution or a college of education; or
(f) a member of, in England and Wales, a water authority or, in Scotland, river purification board,

to take time off, subject to and in accordance with subsection (4), during the employee's working hours for the purposes of performing any of the duties of his office or, as the case may be, his duties as such a member.

(2) In subsection (1)—

(a) " local authority " in relation to England and Wales includes the Common Council of the City of London but otherwise has the same meaning as in the Local Government Act 1972, and in relation to Scotland has the same meaning as in the Local Government (Scotland) Act 1973;
(b) " Regional Health Authority " and " Area Health Authority " have the same meaning as in the National Health Service Act 1977, and " Health Board " has the same meaning as in the National Health Service (Scotland) Act 1972;

(c) " local education authority " means the authority designated by section 192(1) of the Local Government Act 1972, " school or college council " means a body appointed under section 125(1) of the Local Government (Scotland) Act 1973, and " central institution " and " college of education " have the meanings assigned to them by section 145(10) and (14) respectively of the Education (Scotland) Act 1962 ; and

(d) " river purification board " means a board established under section 135 of the Local Government (Scotland) Act 1973.

(3) For the purposes of subsection (1) the duties of a member of a body referred to in paragraphs (b) to (f) of that subsection are : —

(a) attendance at a meeting of the body or any of its committees or sub-committees ;

(b) the doing of any other thing approved by the body, or anything of a class so approved, for the purpose of the discharge of the functions of the body or of any of its committees or sub-committees.

(4) The amount of time off which an employee is to be permitted to take under this section and the occasions on which and any conditions subject to which time off may be so taken are those that are reasonable in all the circumstances having regard, in particular, to the following : —

(a) how much time off is required for the performance of the duties of the office or as a member of the body in question, and how much time off is required for the performance of the particular duty ;

(b) how much time off the employee has already been permitted under this section or sections 27 and 28 ;

(c) the circumstances of the employer's business and the effect of the employee's absence on the running of that business.

(5) The Secretary of State may by order—

(a) modify the provisions of subsection (1) by adding any office or body to, or removing any office or body from, that subsection or by altering the description of any office or body in that subsection ; and

(b) modify the provisions of subsection (3).

(6) An employee may present a complaint to an industrial tribunal that his employer has failed to permit him to take time off as required by this section.

MATERNITY

General provisions

Rights of employee in connection with pregnancy and confinement.

33.—(1) An employee who is absent from work wholly or partly because of pregnancy or confinement shall, subject to the

following provisions of this Act,—
  (a) be entitled to be paid by her employer a sum to be known as maternity pay ; and
  (b) be entitled to return to work.

(2) Schedule 2 shall have effect for the purpose of supplementing the following provisions of this Act in relation to an employee's right to return to work.

(3) An employee shall be entitled to the rights referred to in subsection (1) whether or not a contract of employment subsists during the period of her absence but, subject to subsection (4), she shall not be so entitled unless—
  (a) she continues to be employed by her employer (whether or not she is at work) until immediately before the beginning of the eleventh week before the expected week of confinement ;
  (b) she has at the beginning of that eleventh week been continuously employed for a period of not less than two years ; and
  (c) she informs her employer (in writing if he so requests) at least twenty-one days before her absence begins or, if that is not reasonably practicable, as soon as reasonably practicable,—
    (i) that she will be (or is) absent from work wholly or partly because of pregnancy or confinement, and
    (ii) in the case of the right to return, that she intends to return to work with her employer.

(4) An employee who has been dismissed by her employer for a reason falling within section 60(1)(a) or (b) and has not been re-engaged in accordance with that section, shall be entitled to the rights referred to in subsection (1) of this section notwithstanding that she has thereby ceased to be employed before the beginning of the eleventh week before the expected week of confinement if, but for that dismissal, she would at the beginning of that eleventh week have been continuously employed for a period of not less than two years, but she shall not be entitled to the right to return unless she informs her employer (in writing if he so requests), before or as soon as reasonably practicable after the dismissal takes effect, that she intends to return to work with him.

In this subsection " dismiss " and " dismissal " have the same meaning as they have for the purposes of Part V.

(5) An employee shall not be entitled to either of the rights referred to in subsection (1) unless, if requested to do so by her employer, she produces for his inspection a certificate from a registered medical practitioner or a certified midwife stating the expected week of her confinement.

(6) The Secretary of State may by order vary the periods of two years referred to in subsections (3) and (4), or those periods as varied from time to time under this subsection, but no such order shall be made unless a draft of the order has been laid before Parliament and approved by resolution of each House of Parliament.

Maternity pay

Maternity pay.

34.—(1) Maternity pay shall be paid in respect of a period not exceeding, or periods not exceeding in the aggregate, six weeks during which the employee is absent from work wholly or partly because of pregnancy or confinement (in this section and sections 35 and 36 referred to as the payment period or payment periods).

(2) An employee shall not be entitled to maternity pay for any absence before the beginning of the eleventh week before the expected week of confinement, and her payment period or payment periods shall be the first six weeks of absence starting on or falling after the beginning of that eleventh week.

(3) The Secretary of State may by order vary the periods of six weeks referred to in subsections (1) and (2), or those periods as varied from time to time under this subsection, but no such order shall be made unless a draft of the order has been laid before Parliament and approved by resolution of each House of Parliament.

(4) Where an employee gives her employer the information required by section 33(3)(c) or produces any certificate requested under section 33(5) after the beginning of the payment period or the first of the payments periods, she shall not be entitled to maternity pay for any part of that period until she gives him that information or certificate, but on giving him the information or, as the case may be, producing the certificate, she shall be entitled to be paid in respect of that part of the period or periods which fell before the giving of the information or the production of the certificate.

Calculation of maternity pay.

35.—(1) The amount of maternity pay to which an employee is entitled as respects any week shall be nine-tenths of a week's pay reduced by the amount of maternity allowance payable for the week under Part I of Schedule 4 to the Social Security Act 1975, whether or not the employee in question is entitled to the whole or any part of that allowance.

(2) Maternity pay shall accrue due to an employee from day to day and in calculating the amount of maternity pay payable for any day—

(a) there shall be disregarded Sunday or such other day in each week as may be prescribed in relation to that employee under section 22(10) of the Social Security Act 1975 for the purpose of calculating the daily rate of maternity allowance under that Act ; and

(b) the amount payable for any other day shall be taken as one-sixth of the amount of the maternity pay for the week in which the day falls.

(3) Subject to subsection (4), a right to maternity pay shall not affect any right of an employee in relation to remuneration under any contract of employment (in this section referred to as " contractual remuneration ").

(4) Any contractual remuneration paid to an employee in respect of a day within a payment period shall go towards discharging any liability of the employer to pay maternity pay in respect of that day, and conversely any maternity pay paid in respect of a day shall go towards discharging any liability of the employer to pay contractual remuneration in respect of that day.

Right to return to work

45.—(1) The right to return to work of an employee who has been absent from work wholly or partly because of pregnancy or confinement is, subject to the following provisions of this Act, a right to return to work with her original employer, or, where appropriate, his successor, at any time before the end of the period of twenty-nine weeks beginning with the week in which the date of confinement falls, in the job in which she was employed under the original contract of employment and on terms and conditions not less favourable than those which would have been applicable to her if she had not been so absent.

Right to return to work.

(2) In subsection (1) " terms and conditions not less favourable than those which would have been applicable to her if she had not been so absent " means, as regards seniority, pension rights and other similar rights, that the period or periods of employment prior to the employee's absence shall be regarded as continuous with her employment following that absence.

(3) If an employee is entitled to return to work in accordance with subsection (1), but it is not practicable by reason of redundancy for the employer to permit her so to return to work she shall be entitled, where there is a suitable available vacancy, to be offered alternative employment with her employer (or his successor), or an associated employer, under a new contract of employment complying with subsection (4).

(4) The new contract of employment must be such that—

(a) the work to be done under the contract is of a kind which is both suitable in relation to the employee and appropriate for her to do in the circumstances ; and

(b) the provisions of the new contract as to the capacity and place in which she is to be employed and as to the other terms and conditions of her employment are not substantially less favourable to her than if she had returned to work in accordance with subsection (1).

Termination of Employment

Rights of employer and employee to a minimum period of notice.

49.—(1) The notice required to be given by an employer to terminate the contract of employment of a person who has been continuously employed for four weeks or more—

(a) shall be not less than one week's notice if his period of continuous employment is less than two years;

(b) shall be not less than one week's notice for each year of continuous employment if his period of continuous employment is two years or more but less than twelve years; and

(c) shall be not less than twelve weeks' notice if his period of continuous employment is twelve years or more.

(2) The notice required to be given by an employee who has been continuously employed for four weeks or more to terminate his contract of employment shall be not less than one week.

(3) Any provision for shorter notice in any contract of employment with a person who has been continuously employed for four weeks or more shall have effect subject to the foregoing subsections, but this section shall not be taken to prevent either party from waiving his right to notice on any occasion, or from accepting a payment in lieu of notice.

(4) Any contract of employment of a person who has been continuously employed for twelve weeks or more which is a contract for a term certain of four weeks or less shall have effect as if it were for an indefinite period and, accordingly, subsections (1) and (2) shall apply to the contract.

(5) It is hereby declared that this section does not affect any right of either party to treat the contract as terminable without notice by reason of such conduct by the other party as would have enabled him so to treat it before the passing of this Act.

(6) The definition of week given by section 153(1) does not apply for the purposes of this section.

Meaning of unfair dismissal

Meaning of "dismissal".

55.—(1) In this Part, except as respects a case to which section 56 applies, "dismissal" and "dismiss" shall be construed in accordance with the following provisions of this section.

(2) Subject to subsection (3), an employee shall be treated as dismissed by his employer if, but only if,—

(a) the contract under which he is employed by the employer is terminated by the employer, whether it is so

Employment Protection (Consolidation) Act – extracts

terminated by notice or without notice, or

(b) where under that contract he is employed for a fixed term, that term expires without being renewed under the same contract, or

(c) the employee terminates that contract, with or without notice, in circumstances such that he is entitled to terminate it without notice by reason of the employer's conduct.

(3) Where an employer gives notice to an employee to terminate his contract of employment and, at a time within the period of that notice, the employee gives notice to the employer to terminate the contract of employment on a date earlier than the date on which the employer's notice is due to expire, the employee shall for the purposes of this Part be taken to be dismissed by his employer, and the reasons for the dismissal shall be taken to be the reasons for which the employer's notice is given.

(4) In this Part " the effective date of termination "—

(a) in relation to an employee whose contract of employment is terminated by notice, whether given by his employer or by the employee, means the date on which that notice expires;

(b) in relation to an employee whose contract of employment is terminated without notice, means the date on which the termination takes effect; and

(c) in relation to an employee who is employed under a contract for a fixed term, where that term expires without being renewed under the same contract, means the date on which that term expires.

(5) Where the notice required to be given by an employer by section 49 would, if duly given when notice of termination was given by the employer, or (where no notice was given) when the contract of employment was terminated by the employer, expire on a date later than the effective date of termination as defined by subsection (4), that later date shall be treated as the effective date of termination in relation to the dismissal for the purposes of sections 53(2), 64(1)(a) and 73(3) and paragraph 8(3) of Schedule 14.

56. Where an employee is entitled to return to work and has exercised her right to return in accordance with section 47 but is not permitted to return to work, then she shall be treated for the purposes of this Part as if she had been employed until the notified day of return, and, if she would not otherwise be so treated, as having been continuously employed until that day, and as if she had been dismissed with effect from that day for the reason for which she was not permitted to return. *Failure to permit woman to return to work after confinement treated as dismissal.*

200 Guide to The Employment Act, 1980

General provisions relating to fairness of dismissal.

57.—(1) In determining for the purposes of this Part whether the dismissal of an employee was fair or unfair, it shall be for the employer to show—

(a) what was the reason (or, if there was more than one, the principal reason) for the dismissal, and

(b) that it was a reason falling within subsection (2) or some other substantial reason of a kind such as to justify the dismissal of an employee holding the position which that employee held.

(2) In subsection (1)(b) the reference to a reason falling within this subsection is a reference to a reason which—

(a) related to the capability or qualifications of the employee for performing work of the kind which he was employed by the employer to do, or

(b) related to the conduct of the employee, or

(c) was that the employee was redundant, or

(d) was that the employee could not continue to work in the position which he held without contravention (either on his part or on that of his employer) of a duty or restriction imposed by or under an enactment.

(3) Where the employer has fulfilled the requirements of subsection (1), then, subject to sections 58 to 62, the determination of the question whether the dismissal was fair or unfair, having regard to the reason shown by the employer, shall depend on whether the employer can satisfy the tribunal that in the circumstances (having regard to equity and the substantial merits of the case) he acted reasonably in treating it as a sufficient reason for dismissing the employee.

(4) In this section, in relation to an employee,—

(a) " capability " means capability assessed by reference to skill, aptitude, health or any other physical or mental quality ;

(b) " qualifications " means any degree, diploma or other academic, technical or professional qualification relevant to the position which the employee held.

Dismissal relating to trade union membership.

58.—(1) For the purposes of this Part, the dismissal of an employee by an employer shall be regarded as having been unfair if the reason for it (or, if more than one, the principal reason) was that the employee—

(a) was, or proposed to become, a member of an independent trade union ;

(b) had taken, or proposed to take, part at any appropriate time in the activities of an independent trade union ; or

(c) had refused, or proposed to refuse, to become or remain a member of a trade union which was not an independent trade union.

(2) In subsection (1), "appropriate time" in relation to an employee taking part in the activities of a trade union, means time which either—

(a) is outside his working hours, or

(b) is a time within his working hours at which, in accordance with arrangements agreed with or consent given by his employer, it is permissible for him to take part in those activities;

and in this subsection "working hours", in relation to an employee, means any time when, in accordance with his contract of employment, he is required to be at work.

(3) Dismissal of an employee by an employer shall be regarded as fair for the purposes of this Part if—

(a) it is the practice, in accordance with a union membership agreement, for employees for the time being of the same class as the dismissed employee to belong to a specified independent trade union, or to one of a number of specified independent trade unions; and

(b) the reason for the dismissal was that the employee was not a member of the specified union or one of the specified unions, or had refused or proposed to refuse to become or remain a member of that union or one of those unions;

unless the employee genuinely objects on grounds of religious belief to being a member of any trade union whatsoever, in which case the dismissal shall be regarded as unfair.

(4) For the purposes of subsection (3), a union shall be treated as specified for the purposes of or in relation to a union membership agreement (in a case where it would not otherwise be so treated) if—

(a) the Advisory, Conciliation and Arbitration Service has made a recommendation for recognition covering the employee in question which is operative within the meaning of section 15 of the Employment Protection Act 1975; or

(b) the union has referred a recognition issue (within the meaning of that Act) covering that employee to the Advisory, Conciliation and Arbitration Service under section 11 of that Act and the Service has not declined to proceed on the reference under section 12 of that Act, the union has not withdrawn the reference, or from the reference, and the issue has not been settled or reported on under that section.

(5) Any reason by virtue of which a dismissal is to be regarded

as unfair in consequence of subsection (1) or (3) is in this Part referred to as an inadmissible reason.

(6) In this section, unless the context otherwise requires, references to a trade union include references to a branch or section of a trade union.

Dismissal on ground of redundancy.

59. Where the reason or principal reason for the dismissal of an employee was that he was redundant, but it is shown that the circumstances constituting the redundancy applied equally to one or more other employees in the same undertaking who held positions similar to that held by him and who have not been dismissed by the employer, and either—

(a) that the reason (or, if more than one, the principal reason) for which he was selected for dismissal was an inadmissible reason ; or

(b) that he was selected for dismissal in contravention of a customary arrangement or agreed procedure relating to redundancy and there were no special reasons justifying a departure from that arrangement or procedure in his case,

then, for the purposes of this Part, the dismissal shall be regarded as unfair.

Dismissal on ground of pregnancy.

60.—(1) An employee shall be treated for the purposes of this Part as unfairly dismissed if the reason or principal reason for her dismissal is that she is pregnant or is any other reason connected with her pregnancy, except one of the following reasons—

(a) that at the effective date of termination she is or will have become, because of her pregnancy, incapable of adequately doing the work which she is employed to do ;

(b) that, because of her pregnancy, she cannot or will not be able to continue after that date to do that work without contravention (either by her or her employer) of a duty or restriction imposed by or under any enactment.

(2) An employee shall be treated for the purposes of this Part as unfairly dismissed if her employer dismisses her for a reason mentioned in subsection (1)(a) or (b), but neither he nor any successor of his, where there is a suitable available vacancy, makes her an offer before or on the effective date of termination to engage her under a new contract of employment complying with subsection (3).

(3) The new contract of employment must—

Employment Protection (Consolidation) Act – extracts 203

   (a) take effect immediately on the ending of employment under the previous contract, or, where that employment ends on a Friday, Saturday or Sunday, on or before the next Monday after that Friday, Saturday or Sunday;

   (b) be such that the work to be done under the contract is of a kind which is both suitable in relation to the employee and appropriate for her to do in the circumstances; and

   (c) be such that the provisions of the new contract as to the capacity and place in which she is to be employed and as to the other terms and conditions of her employment are not substantially less favourable to her than the corresponding provisions of the previous contract.

(4) On a complaint of unfair dismissal on the ground of failure to offer to engage an employee as mentioned in subsection (2), it shall be for the employer to show that he or a successor made an offer to engage her in compliance with subsections (2) and (3) or, as the case may be, that there was no suitable available vacancy for her.

(5) Section 55(3) shall not apply in a case where an employer gives notice to an employee to terminate her contract of employment for a reason mentioned in subsection (1)(a) or (b).

61.—(1) Where an employer—   Dismissal of replacement.

   (a) on engaging an employee informs the employee in writing that his employment will be terminated on the return to work of another employee who is, or will be, absent wholly or partly because of pregnancy or confinement; and

   (b) dismisses the first-mentioned employee in order to make it possible to give work to the other employee;

then, for the purposes of section 57(1)(b), but without prejudice to the application of section 57(3), the dismissal shall be regarded as having been for a substantial reason of a kind such as to justify the dismissal of an employee holding the position which that employee held.

(2) Where an employer—

   (a) on engaging an employee informs the employee in writing that his employment will be terminated on the end of a suspension such as is referred to in section 19 of another employee; and

   (b) dismisses the first-mentioned employee in order to make it possible to allow the other employee to resume his original work;

then, for the purposes of section 57(1)(b), but without prejudice to the application of section 57(3), the dismissal shall be regarded as having been for a substantial reason of a kind such as to justify the dismissal of an employee holding the position which that employee held.

62.—(1) The provisions of this section shall have effect in relation to an employee who claims that he has been unfairly dismissed by his employer where at the date of dismissal—

Dismissal in connection with a lock-out, strike or other industrial action.

(a) the employer was conducting or instituting a lock-out, or

(b) the employee was taking part in a strike or other industrial action.

(2) In such a case an industrial tribunal shall not determine whether the dismissal was fair or unfair unless it is shown—

(a) that one or more relevant employees of the same employer have not been dismissed, or

(b) that one or more such employees have been offered re-engagement, and that the employee concerned has not been offered re-engagement.

(3) Where it is shown that the condition referred to in paragraph (b) of subsection (2) is fulfilled, the provisions of sections 57 to 60 shall have effect as if in those sections for any reference to the reason or principal reason for which the employee was dismissed there were substituted a reference to the reason or principal reason for which he has not been offered re-engagement.

(4) In this section—

(a) " date of dismissal " means—

(i) where the employee's contract of employment was terminated by notice, the date on which the employer's notice was given, and

(ii) in any other case, the effective date of termination;

(b) " relevant employees " means—

(i) in relation to a lock-out, employees who were directly interested in the trade dispute in contemplation or furtherance of which the lock-out occurred, and

(ii) in relation to a strike or other industrial action, employees who took part in it; and

(c) any reference to an offer of re-engagement is a reference to an offer (made either by the original employer or by a successor of that employer or an associated employer) to re-engage an employee, either in the job which he held immediately before the date of dismissal or in a different job which would be reasonably suitable in his case.

63. In determining, for the purposes of this Part any question as to the reason, or principal reason, for which an employee was dismissed or any question whether the reason or principal reason for which an employee was dismissed was a reason fulfilling the requirements of section 57(1)(b) or whether the employer acted reasonably in treating it as a sufficient reason for dismissing him,— *Pressure on employer to dismiss unfairly.*
   (a) no account shall be taken of any pressure which, by calling, organising, procuring or financing a strike or other industrial action, or threatening to do so, was exercised on the employer to dismiss the employee, and
   (b) any such question shall be determined as if no such pressure had been exercised.

Exclusion of section 54

64.—(1) Subject to subsection (3), section 54 does not apply to the dismissal of an employee from any employment if the employee— *Qualifying period and upper age limit.*
   (a) was not continuously employed for a period of not less than twenty-six weeks ending with the effective date of termination, or
   (b) on or before the effective date of termination attained the age which, in the undertaking in which he was employed, was the normal retiring age for an employee holding the position which he held, or, if a man, attained the age of sixty-five, or, if a woman, attained the age of sixty.

(2) If an employee is dismissed by reason of any such requirement or recommendation as is referred to in section 19(1), subsection (1)(a) shall have effect in relation to that dismissal as if for the words " twenty-six weeks " there were substituted the words " four weeks ".

(3) Subsection (1) shall not apply to the dismissal of an employee if it is shown that the reason (or, if more than one, the principal reason) for the dismissal was an inadmissible reason.

68.—(1) Where on a complaint under section 67 an industrial tribunal finds that the grounds of the complaint are well-founded, it shall explain to the complainant what orders for reinstatement or re-engagement may be made under section 69 and in what circumstances they may be made, and shall ask him whether he wishes the tribunal to make such an order, and if he does express such a wish the tribunal may make an order under section 69. *Remedies for unfair dismissal.*

(2) If on a complaint under section 67 the tribunal finds that the grounds of the complaint are well-founded and no order is made under section 69, the tribunal shall make an **award of compensation** for unfair dismissal, calculated in accordance with sections 72 to 74, to be paid by the employer to the employee.

Amount of compensation

Compensation for unfair dismissal.

72. Where a tribunal makes an award of compensation for unfair dismissal under section 68(2) or 71(2)(*a*) the award shall consist of a basic award (calculated in accordance with section 73) and a compensatory award (calculated in accordance with section 74).

Calculation of basic award.

73.—(1) The amount of the basic award shall be the amount calculated in accordance with subsections (3) to (6), subject to—

(*a*) subsection (2) of this section (which provides for an award of two weeks' pay in certain redundancy cases);

(*b*) subsection (7) (which provides for the amount of the award to be reduced where the employee contributed to the dismissal);

(*c*) subsection (8) (which provides for a minimum award of two weeks' pay in certain cases);

(*d*) subsection (9) (which provides for the amount of the award to be reduced where the employee received a payment in respect of redundancy); and

(*e*) section 76 (which prohibits compensation being awarded under this Part and under the Sex Discrimination Act 1975 or the Race Relations Act 1976 in respect of the same matter).

(2) The amount of the basic award shall be two weeks' pay where the tribunal finds that the reason or principal reason for the dismissal of the employee was that he was redundant and the employee—

(*a*) by virtue of section 82(5) or (6) is not, or if he were otherwise entitled would not be, entitled to a redundancy payment; or

(*b*) by virtue of the operation of section 84(1) is not treated as dismissed for the purposes of Part VI.

(3) The amount of the basic award shall be calculated by reference to the period, ending with the effective date of termination, during which the employee has been continuously employed, by starting at the end of that period and reckoning backwards the numbers of years of employment falling within that period, and

allowing—
- (a) one and a half weeks' pay for each such year of employment which consists wholly of weeks in which the employee was not below the age of forty-one ;
- (b) one week's pay for each such year of employment which consists wholly of weeks in which the employee was below the age of forty-one and was not below the age of twenty-two ; and
- (c) half a week's pay for each such year of employment which consists wholly of weeks in which the employee was below the age of twenty-two and was not below the age of eighteen.

(4) Where, in reckoning the number of years of employment in accordance with subsection (3), twenty years of employment have been reckoned no account shall be taken of any year of employment earlier than those twenty years.

(5) Where in the case of an employee the effective date of termination is after the specified anniversary the amount of the basic award calculated in accordance with subsections (3) and (4) shall be reduced by the appropriate fraction.

(6) In subsection (5) " the specified anniversary " in relation to a man means the sixty-fourth anniversary of the day of his birth, and in relation to a woman means the fifty-ninth anniversary of the day of her birth, and " the appropriate fraction " means the fraction of which—
- (a) the numerator is the number of whole months reckoned from the specified anniversary in the period beginning with that anniversary and ending with the effective date of termination ; and
- (b) the denominator is twelve.

(7) Where the tribunal finds that the dismissal was to any extent caused or contributed to by any action of the complainant it shall, except in a case where the dismissal was by reason of redundancy, reduce the amount of the basic award by such proportion as it considers just and equitable having regard to that finding.

(8) Where the amount calculated in accordance with subsections (3) to (7) is less than the amount of two weeks' pay, the amount of the basic award shall be two weeks' pay.

(9) The amount of the basic award shall be reduced or, as the case may be, be further reduced, by the amount of any redundancy payment awarded by the tribunal under Part VI in respect of the same dismissal or of any payment made by the employer to the employee on the ground that the dismissal was by reason of redundancy, whether in pursuance of Part VI or otherwise.

74.—(1) Subject to sections 75 and 76, the amount of the compensatory award shall be such amount as the tribunal considers just and equitable in all the circumstances having regard

Calculation of compensatory award.

to the loss sustained by the complainant in consequence of the dismissal in so far as that loss is attributable to action taken by the employer.

(2) The said loss shall be taken to include—
  (a) any expenses reasonably incurred by the complainant in consequence of the dismissal, and
  (b) subject to subsection (3), loss of any benefit which he might reasonably be expected to have had but for the dismissal.

(3) The said loss, in respect of any loss of any entitlement or potential entitlement to, or expectation of, a payment on account of dismissal by reason of redundancy, whether in pursuance of Part VI or otherwise, shall include only the loss referable to the amount, if any, by which the amount of that payment would have exceeded the amount of a basic award (apart from any reduction under section 73(7) or (9)) in respect of the same dismissal.

(4) In ascertaining the said loss the tribunal shall apply the same rule concerning the duty of a person to mitigate his loss as applies to damages recoverable under the common law of England and Wales or of Scotland, as the case may be.

(5) In determining, for the purposes of subsection (1), how far any loss sustained by the complainant was attributable to action taken by the employer no account shall be taken of any pressure which, by calling, organising, procuring or financing a strike or other industrial action, or threatening to do so, was exercised on the employer to dismiss the employee, and that question shall be determined as if no such pressure had been exercised.

(6) Where the tribunal finds that the dismissal was to any extent caused or contributed to by any action of the complainant it shall reduce the amount of the compensatory award by such proportion as it considers just and equitable having regard to that finding.

(7) If the amount of any payment made by the employer to the employee on the ground that the dismissal was by reason of redundancy, whether in pursuance of Part VI or otherwise, exceeds the amount of the basic award which would be payable but for section 73(9) that excess shall go to reduce the amount of the compensatory award.

Limit on compensation.
75.—(1) The amount of compensation awarded to a person under section 71(1) or of a compensatory award to a person calculated in accordance with section 74 shall not exceed £5,200.

(2) The Secretary of State may by order increase the said limit of £5,200 or that limit as from time to time increased under this subsection, but no such order shall be made unless a draft of the order has been laid before Parliament and approved by a resolution of each House of Parliament.

(3) It is hereby declared for the avoidance of doubt that the limit imposed by this section applies to the amount which the industrial tribunal would, apart from this section, otherwise award in respect of the subject matter of the complaint after taking into account any payment made by the respondent to the complainant in respect of that matter and any reduction in the amount of the award required by any enactment or rule of law.

REDUNDANCY PAYMENTS
Right to redundancy payment

81.—(1) Where an employee who has been continuously employed for the requisite period— *(General provisions as to right to redundancy payment.)*
- (a) is dismissed by his employer by reason of redundancy, or
- (b) is laid off or kept on short-time to the extent specified in subsection (1) of section 88 and complies with the requirements of that section,

then, subject to the following provisions of this Act, the employer shall be liable to pay to him a sum (in this Act referred to as a " redundancy payment ") calculated in accordance with Schedules 4, 13 and 14.

(2) For the purposes of this Act an employee who is dismissed shall be taken to be dismissed by reason of redundancy if the dismissal is attributable wholly or mainly to—
- (a) the fact that his employer has ceased, or intends to cease, to carry on the business for the purposes of which the employee was employed by him, or has ceased, or intends to cease, to carry on that business in the place where the employee was so employed, or
- (b) the fact that the requirements of that business for employees to carry out work of a particular kind, or for employees to carry out work of a particular kind in the place where he was so employed, have ceased or diminished or are expected to cease or diminish.

For the purposes of this subsection, the business of the employer together with the business or businesses of his associated employers shall be treated as one unless either of the conditions specified in this subsection would be satisfied without so treating those businesses.

(3) In subsection (2), " cease " means cease either permanently or temporarily and from whatsoever cause, and " diminish " has a corresponding meaning.

(4) For the purposes of subsection (1), the requisite period is the period of two years ending with the relevant date, excluding any week which began before the employee attained the age of eighteen.

210 Guide to The Employment Act, 1980

General exclusions from right to redundancy payment.

82.—(1) An employee shall not be entitled to a redundancy payment if immediately before the relevant date the employee—

(a) if a man, has attained the age of sixty-five, or

(b) if a woman, has attained the age of sixty.

(2) Except as provided by section 92, an employee shall not be entitled to a redundancy payment by reason of dismissal where his employer, being entitled to terminate his contract of employment without notice by reason of the employee's conduct, terminates it either—

 (a) without notice, or

 (b) by giving shorter notice than that which, in the absence of such conduct, the employer would be required to give to terminate the contract, or

 (c) by giving notice (not being such shorter notice as is mentioned in paragraph (b)) which includes, or is accompanied by, a statement in writing that the employer would, by reason of the employee's conduct, be entitled to terminate the contract without notice.

(3) If an employer makes an employee an offer (whether in writing or not) before the ending of his employment under the previous contract to renew his contract of employment, or to re-engage him under a new contract of employment, so that the renewal or re-engagement would take effect either immediately on the ending of his employment under the previous contract or after an interval of not more than four weeks thereafter, the provisions of subsections (5) and (6) shall have effect.

(4) For the purposes of the application of subsection (3) to a contract under which the employment ends on a Friday, Saturday or Sunday—

 (a) the renewal or re-engagement shall be treated as taking effect immediately on the ending of the employment under the previous contract if it takes effect on or before the next Monday after that Friday, Saturday or Sunday ; and

 (b) the interval of four weeks shall be calculated as if the employment had ended on that Monday.

(5) If an employer makes an employee such an offer as is referred to in subsection (3) and either—

 (a) the provisions of the contract as renewed, or of the new contract, as to the capacity and place in which he would be employed, and as to the other terms and conditions of his employment, would not differ from the corresponding provisions of the previous contract ; or

 (b) the first-mentioned provisions would differ (wholly or in

Employment Protection (Consolidation) Act – extracts

part) from those corresponding provisions, but the offer constitutes an offer of suitable employment in relation to the employee;

and in either case the employee unreasonably refuses that offer, he shall not be entitled to a redundancy payment by reason of his dismissal.

(6) If an employee's contract of employment is renewed, or he is re-engaged under a new contract of employment, in pursuance of such an offer as is referred to in subsection (3), and the provisions of the contract as renewed, or of the new contract, as to the capacity and place in which he is employed, and as to the other terms and conditions of his employment, differ (wholly or in part) from the corresponding provisions of the previous contract but the employment is suitable in relation to the employee, and during the trial period referred to in section 84 the employee unreasonably terminates the contract, or unreasonably gives notice to terminate it and the contract is thereafter, in consequence, terminated, he shall not be entitled to a redundancy payment by reason of his dismissal from employment under the previous contract.

(7) Any reference in this section to re-engagement by the employer shall be construed as including a reference to re-engagement by the employer or by any associated employer, and any reference in this section to an offer made by the employer shall be construed as including a reference to an offer made by an associated employer.

83.—(1) In this Part, except as respects a case to which section 86 applies, "dismiss" and "dismissal" shall, subject to sections 84, 85 and 93, be construed in accordance with subsection (2). *Dismissal by employer.*

(2) An employee shall be treated as dismissed by his employer if, but only if,—

   (a) the contract under which he is employed by the employer is terminated by the employer, whether it is so terminated by notice or without notice, or

   (b) where under that contract he is employed for a fixed term, that term expires without being renewed under the same contract, or

   (c) the employee terminates that contract with or without notice, in circumstances (not falling within section 92(4)) such that he is entitled to terminate it without notice by reason of the employer's conduct.

84.—(1) If an employee's contract of employment is renewed, or he is re-engaged under a new contract of employment in pursuance of an offer (whether in writing or not) made by his *Renewal of contract or re-engagement.*

employer before the ending of his employment under the previous contract, and the renewal or re-engagement takes effect either immediately on the ending of that employment or after an interval of not more than four weeks thereafter, then, subject to subsections (3) to (6), the employee shall not be regarded as having been dismissed by his employer by reason of the ending of his employment under the previous contract.

(2) For the purposes of the application of subsection (1) to a contract under which the employment ends on a Friday, Saturday or Sunday—

- (a) the renewal or re-engagement shall be treated as taking effect immediately on the ending of the employment if it takes effect on or before the Monday after that Friday, Saturday or Sunday, and
- (b) the interval of four weeks referred to in that subsection shall be calculated as if the employment had ended on that Monday.

(3) If, in a case to which subsection (1) applies, the provisions of the contract as renewed, or of the new contract, as to the capacity and place in which the employee is employed, and as to the other terms and conditions of his employment, differ (wholly or in part) from the corresponding provisions of the previous contract, there shall be a trial period in relation to the contract as renewed, or the new contract (whether or not there has been a previous trial period under this section).

(4) The trial period shall begin with the ending of the employee's employment under the previous contract and end with the expiration of the period of four weeks beginning with the date on which the employee starts work under the contract as renewed, or the new contract, or such longer period as may be agreed in accordance with the next following subsection for the purpose of retraining the employee for employment under that contract.

(5) Any such agreement shall—
- (a) be made between the employer and the employee or his representative before the employee starts work under the contract as renewed or, as the case may be, the new contract;
- (b) be in writing;
- (c) specify the date of the end of the trial period; and
- (d) specify the terms and conditions of employment which will apply in the employee's case after the end of that period.

(6) If during the trial period—
- (a) the employee, for whatever reason, terminates the contract, or gives notice to terminate it and the contract

is thereafter, in consequence, terminated; or
(b) the employer, for a reason connected with or arising out of the change to the renewed, or new, employment, terminates the contract, or gives notice to terminate it and the contract is thereafter, in consequence, terminated,

then, unless the employee's contract of employment is again renewed, or he is again re-engaged under a new contract of employment, in circumstances such that subsection (1) again applies, he shall be treated as having been dismissed on the date on which his employment under the previous contract or, if there has been more than one trial period, the original contract ended for the reason for which he was then dismissed or would have been dismissed had the offer (or original offer) of renewed, or new, employment not been made, or, as the case may be, for the reason which resulted in that offer being made.

(7) Any reference in this section to re-engagement by the employer shall be construed as including a reference to re-engagement by the employer or by any associated employer, and any reference in this section to an offer made by the employer shall be construed as including a reference to an offer made by an associated employer.

85.—(1) The provisions of this section shall have effect where— *Employee anticipating expiry of employer's notice.*
   (a) an employer gives notice to an employee to terminate his contract of employment, and
   (b) at a time within the obligatory period of that notice, the employee gives notice in writing to the employer to terminate the contract of employment on a date earlier than the date on which the employer's notice is due to expire.

(2) Subject to the following provisions of this section, in the circumstances specified in subsection (1) the employee shall, for the purposes of this Part, be taken to be dismissed by his employer.

(3) If, before the employee's notice is due to expire, the employer gives him notice in writing—
   (a) requiring him to withdraw his notice terminating the contract of employment as mentioned in subsection (1)(b) and to continue in the employment until the date on which the employer's notice expires, and
   (b) stating that, unless he does so, the employer will contest any liability to pay to him a redundancy payment in respect of the termination of his contract of employment,

but the employee does not comply with the requirements of that notice, the employee shall not be entitled to a redundancy payment by virtue of subsection (2) except as provided by subsection (4).

(4) Where, in the circumstances specified in subsection (1), the employer has given notice to the employee under subsection (3), and on a reference to a tribunal it appears to the tribunal, having regard both to the reasons for which the employee seeks to leave the employment and those for which the employer requires him to continue in it, to be just and equitable that the employee should receive the whole or part of any redundancy payment to which he would have been entitled apart from subsection (3), the tribunal may determine that the employer shall be liable to pay to the employee—

    (a) the whole of the redundancy payment to which the employee would have been so entitled, or

    (b) such part of that redundancy payment as the tribunal thinks fit.

(5) In this section—

    (a) if the actual period of the employer's notice (that is to say, the period beginning at the time when the notice is given and ending at the time when it expires) is equal to the minimum period which (whether by virtue of any enactment or otherwise) is required to be given by the employer to terminate the contract of employment, " the obligatory period ", in relation to that notice, means the actual period of the notice;

    (b) in any other case, " the obligatory period ", in relation to an employer's notice, means that period which, being equal to the minimum period referred to in paragraph (a), expires at the time when the employer's notice expires.

Failure to permit woman to return to work after confinement treated as dismissal.

86. Where an employee is entitled to return to work and has exercised her right to return in accordance with section 47 but is not permitted to return to work, then she shall be treated for the purposes of the provisions of this Part as if she had been employed until the notified day of return, and, if she would not otherwise be so treated, as having been continuously employed until that day, and as if she had been dismissed with effect from that day for the reason for which she was not permitted to return.

Lay-off and short-time.

87.—(1) Where an employee is employed under a contract on such terms and conditions that his remuneration thereunder depends on his being provided by the employer with work of the kind which he is employed to do, he shall, for the purposes of this Part, be taken to be laid off for any week in respect of which, by reason that the employer does not provide such work for him, he is not entitled to any remuneration under the contract.

(2) Where by reason of a diminution in the work provided for an employee by his employer (being work of a kind which under his contract the employee is employed to do) the employee's remuneration for any week is less than half a week's pay, he shall for the purposes of this Part be taken to be kept on short-time for that week.

88.—(1) An employee shall not be entitled to a redundancy payment by reason of being laid off or kept on short-time unless he gives notice in writing to his employer indicating (in whatsoever terms) his intention to claim a redundancy payment in respect of lay-off or short-time (in this Act referred to as a "notice of intention to claim") and, before the service of that notice, either— *Right to redundancy payment by reason of lay-off or short-time.*

    (a) he has been laid off or kept on short-time for four or more consecutive weeks of which the last before the service of the notice ended on the date of service thereof or ended not more than four weeks before that date, or

    (b) he has been laid off or kept on short-time for a series of six or more weeks (of which not more than three were consecutive) within a period of thirteen weeks, where the last week of the series before the service of the notice ended on the date of service thereof or ended not more than four weeks before that date.

(2) Where an employee has given notice of intention to claim,—

    (a) he shall not be entitled to a redundancy payment in pursuance of that notice unless he terminates his contract of employment by a week's notice which (whether given before or after or at the same time as the notice of intention to claim) is given before the end of the period allowed for the purposes of this paragraph (as specified in subsection (5) of section 89), and

    (b) he shall not be entitled to a redundancy payment in pursuance of the notice of intention to claim if he is dismissed by his employer (but without prejudice to any right to a redundancy payment by reason of the dismissal):

Provided that, if the employee is required by his contract of employment to give more than a week's notice to terminate the contract, the reference in paragraph (a) to a week's notice shall be construed as a reference to the minimum notice which he is so required to give.

(3) Subject to subsection (4), an employee shall not be entitled to a redundancy payment in pursuance of a notice of intention to claim if, on the date of service of that notice, it was reasonably to be expected that the employee (if he con-

tinued to be employed by the same employer) would, not later than four weeks after that date, enter upon a period of employment of not less than thirteen weeks during which he would not be laid off or kept on short-time for any week.

(4) Subsection (3) shall not apply unless, within seven days after the service of the notice of intention to claim, the employer gives to the employee notice in writing that he will contest any liability to pay to him a redundancy payment in pursuance of the notice of intention to claim.

PART VI
Supplementary provisions relating to redundancy payments in respect of lay-off or short-time.

89.—(1) If, in a case where an employee gives notice of intention to claim and the employer gives notice under section 88(4) (in this section referred to as a " counter-notice "), the employee continues or has continued, during the next four weeks after the date of service of the notice of intention to claim, to be employed by the same employer, and he is or has been laid off or kept on short-time for each of those weeks, it shall be conclusively presumed that the condition specified in subsection (3) of section 88 was not fulfilled.

(2) For the purposes of both subsection (1) of section 88 and subsection (1) of this section, it is immaterial whether a series of weeks (whether it is four weeks, or four or more weeks, or six or. more weeks) consists wholly of weeks for which the employee is laid off or wholly of weeks for which he is kept on short-time or partly of the one and partly of the other.

(3) For the purposes mentioned in subsection (2), no account shall be taken of any week for which an employee is laid off or kept on short-time where the lay-off or short-time is wholly or mainly attributable to a strike or a lock-out (within the meaning of paragraph 24 of Schedule 13) whether the strike or lock-out is in the trade or industry in which the employee is employed or not and whether it is in Great Britain or elsewhere.

(4) Where the employer gives a counter-notice within seven days after the service of a notice of intention to claim, and does not withdraw the counter-notice by a subsequent notice in writing, the employee shall not be entitled to a redundancy payment in pursuance of the notice of intention to claim except in accordance with a decision of an industrial tribunal.

(5) The period allowed for the purposes of subsection (2)(a) of section 88 is as follows, that is to say,—
(a) if the employer does not give a counter-notice within seven days after the service of the notice of intention to claim, that period is three weeks after the end of those seven days ;
(b) if the employer gives a counter-notice within those seven days, but withdraws it by a subsequent notice

in writing, that period is three weeks after the service of the notice of withdrawal;

(c) if the employer gives a counter-notice within those seven days and does not so withdraw it, and a question as to the right of the employee to a redundancy payment in pursuance of the notice of intention to claim is referred to a tribunal, that period is three weeks after the tribunal has notified to the employee its decision on that reference.

(6) For the purposes of paragraph (c) of subsection (5) no account shall be taken of any appeal against the decision of the tribunal, or of any requirement to the tribunal to state a case for the opinion of the High Court or the Court of Session, or of any proceedings or decision in consequence of such an appeal or requirement.

90.—(1) Subject to the following provisions of this section, for the purposes of the provisions of this Act so far as they relate to redundancy payments, " the relevant date ", in relation to the dismissal of an employee— *The relevant date.*

- (a) where his contract of employment is terminated by notice, whether given by his employer or by the employee, means the date on which that notice expires;
- (b) where his contract of employment is terminated without notice, means the date on which the termination takes effect;
- (c) where he is employed under a contract for a fixed term and that term expires as mentioned in subsection (2)(b) of section 83, means the date on which that term expires;
- (d) where he is treated, by virtue of subsection (6) of section 84, as having been dismissed on the termination of his employment under a previous contract, means—

    (i) for the purposes of section 101, the date which is the relevant date as defined by paragraph (a), (b) or (c) in relation to the renewed, or new, contract, or, where there has been more than one trial period under section 84, the last such contract; and

    (ii) for the purposes of any other provision, the date which is the relevant date as defined by paragraph (a), (b) or (c) in relation to the previous contract, or, where there has been more than one trial period under section 84, the original contract; and

- (e) where he is taken to be dismissed by virtue of section 85(2), means the date on which the employee's notice to terminate his contract of employment expires.

(2) "The relevant date", in relation to a notice of intention to claim or a right to a redundancy payment in pursuance of such a notice,—

    (a) in a case falling within paragraph (a) of subsection (1) of section 8, means the date on which the last of the four or more consecutive weeks before the service of the notice came to an end, and

    (b) in a case falling within paragraph (b) of that subsection, means the date on which the last of the series of six or more weeks before the service of the notice came to an end.

(3) Where the notice required to be given by an employer to terminate a contract of employment by section 49(1) would, if duly given when notice of termination was given by the employer, or (where no notice was given) when the contract of employment was terminated by the employer, expire on a date later than the relevant date as defined by subsection (1), then for the purposes of section 81(4) and paragraph 1 of Schedule 4 and paragraph 8(4) of Schedule 14, that later date shall be treated as the relevant date in relation to the dismissal.

Change of ownership of business.

94.—(1) The provisions of this section shall have effect where—

    (a) a change occurs (whether by virtue of a sale or other disposition or by operation of law) in the ownership of a business for the purposes of which a person is employed, or of a part of such a business, and

    (b) in connection with that change the person by whom the employee is employed immediately before the change occurs (in this section referred to as "the previous owner") terminates the employee's contract of employment, whether by notice or without notice.

(2) If, by agreement with the employee, the person who immediately after the change occurs is the owner of the business, or of the part of the business in question, as the case may be (in this section referred to as "the new owner"), renews the employee's contract of employment (with the substitution of the new owner for the previous owner) or re-engages him under a new contract of employment, sections 84 and 90 shall have effect as if the renewal or re-engagement had been a renewal or re-engagement by the previous owner (without any substitution of the new owner for the previous owner).

(3) If the new owner offers to renew the employee's contract of employment (with the substitution of the new owner for the previous owner) or to re-engage him under a new contract of employment, subsections (3) to (6) of section 82 shall have effect, subject to subsection (4), in relation to that offer as they would have had effect in relation to the like offer made by the previous owner.

142.—(1) Section 54 does not apply to dismissal from employment under a contract for a fixed term of two years or more, where the dismissal consists only of the expiry of that term without its being renewed, if before the term so expires the employee has agreed in writing to exclude any claim in respect of rights under that section in relation to that contract. *Contracts for a fixed term.*

(2) An employee employed under a contract of employment for a fixed term of two years or more entered into after 5th December 1965 shall not be entitled to a redundancy payment in respect of the expiry of that term without its being renewed (whether by the employer or by an associated employer of his), if before the term so expires he has agreed in writing to exclude any right to a redundancy payment in that event.

(3) Such an agreement as is mentioned in subsection (1) or (2) may be contained either in the contract itself or in a separate agreement.

(4) Where an agreement under subsection (2) is made during the currency of a fixed term, and that term is renewed, the agreement under that subsection shall not be construed as applying to the term as renewed, but without prejudice to the making of a further agreement under that subsection in relation to the term so renewed.

Appendix 6

Extracts from *The Companies Act, 1980*

This latest Companies Act includes a number of substantive reforms of company law. Two sections are of particular interest and these are reproduced below. Section 46 requires directors to have regard in the performance of their duties to the interests of employees as well as the interests of the company's shareholders. Section 47 regulates contracts of employment for directors. Employment for a period in excess of five years will only be permitted with the prior approval of the shareholders in general meeting.

Duty in relation to employees

46.—(1) The matters to which the directors of a company are to have regard in the performance of their functions shall include the interests of the company's employees in general as well as the interests of its members.

(2) Accordingly, the duty imposed by subsection (1) above on the directors of a company is owed by them to the company (and the company alone) and is enforceable in the same way as any other fiduciary duty owed to a company by its directors.

Particular transactions giving rise to a conflict of interest

47.—(1) Subject to subsection (6) below, a company shall not incorporate in any agreement a term to which this section applies unless the term is first approved by a resolution of the company in general meeting and, in the case of a director of a holding company, by a resolution of that company in general meeting.

(2) This section applies to any term by which a director's employment with the company of which he is the director or,

where he is the director of a holding company, his employment within the group is to continue, or may be continued, otherwise than at the instance of the company (whether under the original agreement or under a new agreement entered into in pursuance of the original agreement), for a period exceeding five years during which the employment—

    (a) cannot be terminated by the company by notice ; or

    (b) can be so terminated only in specified circumstances.

(3) In any case where—

    (a) a person is or is to be employed with a company under an agreement which cannot be terminated by the company by notice or can be so terminated only in specified circumstances ; and

    (b) more than six months before the expiration of the period for which he is or is to be so employed, the company enters into a further agreement (otherwise than in pursuance of a right conferred by or by virtue of the original agreement on the other party thereto) under which he is to be employed with the company or, where he is a director of a holding company, within the group,

subsection (2) above shall apply as if to the period for which he is to be employed under that further agreement there were added a further period equal to the unexpired period of the original agreement.

(4) A resolution of a company approving a term to which this section applies shall not be passed at a general meeting of the company unless a written memorandum setting out the proposed agreement incorporating the term is available for inspection, by members of the company both—

    (a) at the registered office of the company for not less than the period of 15 days ending with the date of the meeting ; and

    (b) at the meeting itself.

(5) A term incorporated in an agreement in contravention of this section shall to the extent that it contravenes this section be void ; and that agreement and in a case where subsection (3) above applies the original agreement shall be deemed to contain a term entitling the company to terminate it at any time by the giving of reasonable notice.

(6) No approval is required to be given under this section by any body corporate unless it is a company within the meaning of the 1948 Act or registered under Part VIII of that Act or if it is, for the purposes of section 150 of that Act, a wholly owned subsidiary of any body corporate, wherever incorporated.

(7) In this section—
- (a) " employment " includes employment under a contract for services ; and
- (b) " group ", in relation to a director of a holding company, means the group which consists of that company and its subsidiaries.

Appendix 7

Extracts from ACAS Code of Practice: *Disciplinary Practice and Procedures in Employment*

©Crown Copyright 1977. Reprinted by kind permission of HMSO.

Rules

It is unlikely that any set of disciplinary rules can cover all circumstances that may arise : moreover the rules required will vary according to particular circumstances such as the type of work, working conditions and size of establishment. When drawing up rules the aim should be to specify clearly and concisely those necessary for the efficient and safe performance of work and for the maintenance of satisfactory relations within the workforce and between employees and management. Rules should not be so general as to be meaningless.

Rules should be readily available and management should make every effort to ensure that employees know and understand them. This may be best achieved by giving every employee a copy of the rules and by explaining them orally. In the case of new employees this should form part of an induction programme.

Employees should be made aware of the likely consequences of breaking rules and in particular they should be given a clear indication of the type of conduct which may warrant summary dismissal.

Essential features of disciplinary procedures

Disciplinary procedures should not be viewed primarily as a means of imposing sanctions. They should also be designed to emphasise and encourage improvements in individual conduct.

Disciplinary procedures should :
(a) Be in writing.

(b) Specify to whom they apply.
(c) Provide for matters to be dealt with quickly.
(d) Indicate the disciplinary actions which may be taken.
(e) Specify the levels of management which have the authority to take the various forms of disciplinary action, ensuring that immediate superiors do not normally have the power to dismiss without reference to senior management.
(f) Provide for individuals to be informed of the complaints against them and to be given an opportunity to state their case before decisions are reached.
(g) Give individuals the right to be accompanied by a trade union representative or by a fellow employee of their choice.
(h) Ensure that, except for gross misconduct, no employees are dismissed for a first breach of discipline.
(i) Ensure that disciplinary action is not taken until the case has been carefully investigated.
(j) Ensure that individuals are given an explanation for any penalty imposed.
(k) Provide a right of appeal and specify the procedure to be followed.

The procedure in operation

When a disciplinary matter arises, the supervisor or manager should first establish the facts promptly before recollections fade, taking into account the statements of any available witnesses. In serious cases consideration should be given to a brief period of suspension while the case is investigated and this suspension should be with pay. Before a decision is made or penalty imposed the individual should be interviewed and given the opportunity to state his or her case and should be advised of any rights under the procedure, including the right to be accompanied.

Often supervisors will give informal oral warnings for the purpose of improving conduct when employees commit minor infringements of the established standards of conduct. However, where the facts of a case appear to call for disciplinary action, other than summary dismissal, the following procedure should normally be observed:

(a) In the case of minor offences the individual should be given a formal oral warning or if the issue is more serious, there should be a written warning setting out the nature of the offence and the likely consequences of further offences. In either case the individual should be advised that the warning constitutes the first formal stage of the procedure.
(b) Further misconduct might warrant a final written warning which should contain a statement that any recurrence would lead to suspension or dismissal or some other penalty, as the case may be.
(c) The final step might be disciplinary transfer, or disciplinary suspension without pay (but only if these are allowed for by an express or implied condition of the contract of employment), or

dismissal, according to the nature of the misconduct. Special consideration should be given before imposing disciplinary suspension without pay and it should not normally be for a prolonged period.

Except in the event of an oral warning, details of any disciplinary action should be given in writing to the employee and if desired, to his or her representative. At the same time the employee should be told of any right of appeal, how to make it and to whom.

When determining the disciplinary action to be taken the supervisor or manager should bear in mind the need to satisfy the test of reasonableness in all the circumstances, So far as possible, account should be taken of the employee's record and any other relevant factors.

Special consideration should be given to the way in which disciplinary procedures are to operate in exceptional cases. For example:
(a) **Employees to whom the full procedure is not immediately available.** Special provisions may have to be made for the handling of disciplinary matters among nightshift workers, workers in isolated locations or depots or others who may pose particular problems for example because no one is present with the necessary authority to take disciplinary action or no trade union representative is immediately available.
(b) **Trade union officials.** Disciplinary action against a trade union official can lead to a serious dispute if it is seen as an attack on the union's functions. Although normal disciplinary standards should apply to their conduct as employees, no disciplinary action beyond an oral warning should be taken until the circumstances of the case have been discussed with a senior trade union representative or full-time official.
(c) **Criminal offences outside employment.** These should not be treated as automatic reasons for dismissal regardless of whether the offence has any relevance to the duties of the individual as an employee. The main considerations should be whether the offence is one that makes the individual unsuitable for his or her type of work or unacceptable to other employees. Employees should not be dismissed solely because a charge against them is pending or because they are absent through having been remanded in custody.

Appeals

Grievance procedures are sometimes used for dealing with disciplinary appeals though it is normally more appropriate to keep the two kinds of procedure separate since the disciplinary issues are in general best resolved within the organisation and need to be dealt with more speedily than others. The external stages of a grievance procedure may however, be the appropriate machinery for dealing with appeals against disciplinary action where a final decision within the organisation is contested or where the matter becomes a collective issue between management and a trade union.

Independent arbitration is sometimes an appropriate means of resolving disciplinary issues. Where the parties concerned agree, it may constitute the final stage of procedure.

Records

Records should be kept, detailing the nature of any breach of disciplinary rules, the action taken and the reasons for it, whether an appeal was lodged, its outcome and any subsequent developments. These records should be carefully safeguarded and kept confidential.

Except in agreed special circumstances breaches of disciplinary rules should be disregarded after a specified period of satisfactory conduct.

Further action

Rules and procedures should be reviewed periodically in the light of any developments in employment legislation or industrial relations practice and, if necessary, revised in order to ensure their continuing relevance and effectiveness. Any amendments and additional rules imposing new obligations should be introduced only after reasonable notice has been given to all employees and, where appropriate, their representatives have been informed.

Appendix 8

Extracts from ACAS Code of Practice: *Disclosure of Information to Trade Unions for Collective Bargaining Purposes*

©Crown Copyright 1977. Reprinted by kind permission of HMSO.

Providing information

The absence of relevant information about an employer's undertaking may to a material extent impede trade unions in collective bargaining; particularly if the information would influence the formulation, presentation or pursuance of a claim, or the conclusion of an agreement. The provision of relevant information in such circumstances would be in accordance with good industrial relations practice.

To determine what information will be relevant negotiators should take account of the subject-matter of the negotiations and the issues raised during them; the level at which negotiations take place (department, plant, division, or company level); the size of the company; and the type of business the company is engaged in.

Collective bargaining within an undertaking can range from negotiations on specific matters arising daily at the work place affecting particular sections of the workforce, to extensive periodic negotiations on terms and conditions of employment affecting the whole workforce in multiplant companies. The relevant information and the depth, detail and form in which it could be presented to negotiators will vary accordingly. Consequently, it is not possible to compile a list of items that should be disclosed in all circumstances. Some examples of information relating to the undertaking which could be relevant in certain collective bargaining situations are given below:

(i) **Pay and benefits:** principles and structure of payment systems; job evaluation systems and grading criteria; earnings and hours analysed according to work-group, grade, plant, sex, out-workers and homeworkers, department or division, giving, where appropriate, distributions and make-up of pay showing any additions to basic rate or salary; total pay bill; details of fringe benefits and non-wage labour costs.

(ii) **Conditions of service:** policies on recruitment, redeployment, redundancy, training, equal opportunity, and promotion; appraisal systems; health, welfare and safety matters.

(iii) **Manpower:** numbers employed analysed according to grade, department, location, age and sex; labour turnover; absenteeism; overtime and short-time; manning standards; planned changes in work methods, materials, equipment or organisation; available manpower plans; investment plans.

(iv) **Performance:** productivity and efficiency data; savings from increased productivity and output; return on capital invested; sales and state of order book.

(v) **Financial:** cost structures; gross and net profits; sources of earnings; assets; liabilities; allocation of profits; details of government financial assistance; transfer prices; loans to parent or subsidiary companies and interest charged.

These examples are not intended to represent a check list of information that should be provided for all negotiations. Nor are they meant to be an exhaustive list of types of information as other items may be relevant in particular negotiations.

Restrictions on the duty to disclose

Trade unions and employers should be aware of the restrictions on the general duty to disclose information for collective bargaining.

Some examples of information which if disclosed in particular circumstances might cause substantial injury are: cost information on individual products; detailed analysis of proposed investment, marketing or pricing policies; and price quotas or the make-up of tender prices. Information which has to be made available publicly, for example under the Companies Acts, would not fall into this category.

Substantial injury may occur if, for example, certain customers would be lost to competitors, or suppliers would refuse to supply necessary materials, or the ability to raise funds to finance the company would be seriously impaired as a result of disclosing certain information. The burden of establishing a claim that disclosure of certain information would cause substantial injury lies with the employer.

Trade union responsibilities

Trade unions should identify and request the information they require for collective bargaining in advance of negotiations whenever practicable. Misunderstandings can be avoided, costs reduced, and time saved, if requests state as precisely as possible all the information required, and the reasons why the information is considered relevant. Requests should conform to an agreed procedure. A reasonable period of time should be allowed for employers to consider a request and to reply.

Trade unions should keep employers informed of the names of the representatives authorised to carry on collective bargaining on their behalf.

Where two or more trade unions are recognised by an employer for collective bargaining purposes they should co-ordinate their requests for information whenever possible.

Trade unions should review existing training programmes or establish new ones to ensure negotiators are equipped to understand and use information effectively.

Employers' responsibilities

Employers should aim to be as open and helpful as possible in meeting trade union requests for information. Where a request is refused, the reasons for the refusal should be explained as far as possible to the trade union representatives concerned and be capable of being substantiated should the matter be taken to the Central Arbitration Committee.

Information agreed as relevant to collective bargaining should be made available as soon as possible once a request for the information has been made by an authorised trade union representative. Employers should present information in a form and style which recipients can reasonably be expected to understand.

Joint arrangements for disclosure of information

Employers and trade unions should endeavour to arrive at a joint understanding on how the provisions on the disclosure of information can be implemented most effectively. They should consider what information is likely to be required, what is available, and what could reasonably be made available. Consideration should also be given to the form in which the information will be presented, when it should be presented and to whom. In particular, the parties should endeavour to reach an understanding on what information could most appropriately be provided on a regular basis.

Procedures for resolving possible disputes concerning any issues associated with the disclosure of information should be agreed. Where possible such procedures should normally be related to any existing arrangements within the undertaking or industry and the complaint, conciliation and arbitration procedure described in the Act.

Appendix 9

Extracts from ACAS Code of Practice: *Time Off for Trade Union Duties and Activities*

©Crown Copyright 1977. Reprinted by kind permission of HMSO.

General considerations for time off arrangements

The general purpose of the statutory provisions on time off for trade union duties and activities is to aid and improve the conduct of industrial relations. These provisions apply to all employers without exception as to size or type of business or service. But trade unions should be aware of the wide variety of circumstances and the different operational requirements which will have to be taken into account in any arrangements for dealing with time off. For example, some employers face particular exigencies of production, services and safety in process industries. Others operate in the special circumstances of the small firm In enterprises large and small the workforce may be fragmented. Proper regard will therefore have to be paid to particular operational requirements and obligations of different industries and services.

Union officials and members may face particular problems of effective representation and communication, and employers in their turn should be aware of these. They may arise, for example, from the differing hours or shifts worked by members in a single negotiating area; from employment part-time; from the scattered or isolated locations of workplaces and, particularly in the case of some married women, from domestic commitments which limit the possibilities of active participation in their union outside the workplace and outside the hours of normal day working.

To take account of this wide variety of circumstances and problems, employers and unions should reach agreement on arrangements for handling time off in ways appropriate to their own situations. Subsequent advice in the Code should be read in the light of this primary point of guidance which ACAS considers fundamental to the proper operation of time off facilities. The absence of a formal agreement dealing specifically with time off for trade union duties and activities should not of itself preclude the granting of release.

Employers and unions, at the appropriate level, will need to review jointly their current time off provisions bearing in mind the statutory requirements, this Code of Practice and the particular workplace circumstances. Where existing arrangements meet these requirements and are working to the satisfaction of both parties they need not be changed. In some situations time off arrangements will have to be revised and it may be helpful to set out any such revised arrangements in formal agreements.

Arrangements for the handling of time off for union duties, industrial relations training and union activities should accord with agreed procedures for negotiation, consultation, grievance handling and dispute settlement. Agreements on time off and on other facilities for union representation should be consistent with wider agreements which should deal with such matters of workplace representation as constituencies, number of representatives and the form of any joint credentials.

Trade union officials' duties concerned with industrial relations

In addition to his or her work as an employee a trade union official may have important duties concerned with industrial relations. An official's duties are those duties pertaining to his or her role in the jointly agreed procedures or customary arrangements for consultation, collective bargaining and grievance handling, where such matters concern the employer and any associated employer and their employees. To perform these duties properly an official should be permitted to take reasonable paid time off during working hours for such purposes as

(a) collective bargaining with the appropriate level of management;
(b) informing constituents about negotiations or consultations with management;
(c) meetings with other lay officials or with full-time union officers on matters which are concerned with industrial relations between his or her employer and any associated employer and their employees;
(d) interviews with and on behalf of constituents on grievance and discipline matters concerning them and their employer;

Codes of Practice   233

(e) appearing on behalf of constituents before an outside official body, such as an industrial tribunal, which is dealing with an industrial relations matter concerning the employer; and

(f) explanations to new employees whom he or she will represent of the role of the union in the workplace industrial relations structure.

Training of officials in aspects of industrial relations

To carry out their duties effectively officials need to possess skills and knowledge. In addition to the practical experience obtained from holding office, officials should undertake training in relevant subjects when necessary.

Training should be relevant to the industrial relations duties of an official. It should be approved by the TUC or the official's union. An official's industrial relations duties will vary according to the collective bargaining arrangements at the place of work, the structure of the union and the role of the official. Accordingly there is no universally applicable syllabus for training.

An official who has duties concerned with industrial relations should be permitted to take reasonable paid time off work for initial basic training and such training should be arranged as soon as possible after the official is elected or appointed.

An official should be permitted to take reasonable paid time off work for further training relevant to the carrying out of his or her duties concerned with industrial relations where he or she has special responsibilities or where such training is necessary to meet circumstances such as changes in the structure or topics of negotiation at the place of employment or leglisative changes affecting industrial relations.

When the trade union has identified a need for basic or further training and wishes an official to receive training it should inform management what training it has approved for the purpose and, if the employer asks for it, supply a copy of the syllabus or prospectus indicating the contents of the training course or programme

The number of officials receiving training form any one place of employment at any one time should be that which is reasonable in the circumstances, bearing in mind such factors as the operational requirements of the employer and the availability of relevant courses.

Trade unions should normally give at least a few weeks notice of their nominations for training.

Unions and management should endeavour to reach agreement on the appropriate numbers and arrangements and should refer any problem which may arise to the relevant procedure.

Trade union activities

To operate effectively and democratically trade unions need the active participation of members in certain union activities. A member should therefore be permitted to take reasonable time off during working hours for union activities such as taking part, as a representative, in meetings of official policy-making bodies of the union such as the executive committee or annual conference, or representing the union on external bodies such as the committees of industrial training boards.

Members should be permitted to take reasonable time off during working hours for such purposes as voting at the workplace in union elections. Also there may be occasions when it is reasonable for unions to hold meetings of members during working hours because of the urgency of the matter to be discussed or where to do so would not adversely affect production or services. Employers may also have an interest in ensuring that meetings are representative.

Conditions relating to time off

For time off arrangements to work satisfactorily the trade union should ensure that its officials are fully aware of their role, responsibilities and functions. The union should inform management, in writing, as soon as possible after officials are appointed or have resigned and should ensure that officials receive any appropriate written credentials promptly. Management at all levels should be familiar with agreements and arrangements relating to time off.

Management should make available to officials the facilities necessary for them to perform their duties efficiently and to communicate effectively with members, fellow lay officials and full-time officers. Such facilities may include accommodation for meetings, access to a telephone, notice boards and, where the volume of the official's work justifies it, the use of office facilities.

Management is responsible for maintaining production and service to customers, and for making the operational arrangements for time off. Union officials should bear in mind management's problems in discharging these responsibilities. The union official who seeks time off should ensure that the appropriate management representative is informed as far in advance as is reasonable in the circumstances. The official should indicate the nature of the business for which time off is required, the intended location and the expected period of absence. Management and the union should seek to agree arrangements, where necessary, for other employees to cover the work of officials or members taking time off.

Where it is necessary for the union to hold meetings of members during working hours it should seek to agree the arrangements with management as far in advance as is practicable. Where such meetings necessarily involve a large proportion of employees at the workplace at any one time, management and unions should agree on a convenient time which minimises the effects on production or service— for example, towards the end of the shift or the working week or just before or after a meal break.

When a number of members needs time off at any one time there should be agreement to leave at work such members as are essential for safety or operational reasons—for example, to keep premises open to the public or to provide necessary manning in a continuous process firm.

Management may want time off work for union duties or activities to be deferred because, for example, problems of safety or of maintenance of production or service would ensue if time off were taken at a particular time. The grounds for postponement should be made clear and parties should endeavour to agree on an alternative time for the union duty or activity. In considering postponement parties should weigh the urgency of the matter for which time off is required against the seriousness of any problems arising.

The union official and union member should not unduly or unnecessarily prolong the time they are absent from work on union duties or activities.

A dispute or grievance in relation to time off work for union duties or activities should be referred to the relevant procedure.

Industrial action

Management and unions have a responsibility to use agreed procedures to resolve problems constructively and avoid industrial action. Time off should be provided for this purpose. Satisfactory time off arrangements are particularly needed where communication and co-operation between management and unions are in danger of breaking down. Where industrial action has not occurred employers and unions should avoid hastily altering these arrangements since to do so may damage relationships.

A distinction should be made between situations where an official is engaged in industrial action along with his or her constituents and those where the official is not—for example, where only some of the constituents are taking unofficial action. Where an official is not taking part in industrial action but represents members involved, normal arrangements for time off with pay for the official should apply.

There is no obligation on employers to permit time off for union activities which themselves consist of industrial action but where a group of members not taking part in such action is directly affected by other people's industrial action these members and their officials may need to seek the agreement of management to time off for an emergency meeting.

Appendix 10

'TUC disputes, principles and procedures' — a summary

In 1976 the TUC published a booklet entitled *TUC Disputes, Principles and Procedures**. This incorporated the Bridlington Principles, adopted at the 1939 TUC Congress.

These Principles are a series of recommendations designed to minimise disputes between unions over membership disputes. They lay down the procedures by which the TUC deals with complaints by one organisation against another and considers disputes between unions. They were supplemented by recommendations adopted 30 years later at the Special Congress held at Croydon which gave the General Council powers to take action not only in respect of differences over membership, covered by the Bridlington Principles, but also in respect of inter-union differences over recognition, demarcation, wages and conditions of employment.

The Principles only constitute a Code of conduct. They are not intended to be *legally* binding, but the Code is accepted as *morally* binding by all TUC-affiliated organisations. In particular, 'poaching' of members from other TUC affiliates is banned.

The Principles are accompanied by notes which have the same status as the Principles themselves and it is these notes which were altered following the approval of the 1979 Congress, to include guidance on mergers with non-affiliated unions.

*The booklet (revised version 1979) is obtainable from the TUC, Great Russell Street, London WC1B 3LS. Tel: 01-636 4030.

Appendix 11

New employment forms

Form 1 Notice of intended absence due to pregnancy and intention to return

Employee's name:
Department/Section:
Location:
Date of commencement of employment:

I am expecting a baby on . . . (*date*). I have discussed my position with . . . of the Personnel Office, and he has explained to me what my legal rights are with regard to my job under the Employment Protection (Consolidation) Act. In particular it has been explained to me that provided I have the necessary service I am entitled to maternity pay and to come back to work within 29 weeks after the baby is born. I also understand that if I resign my job earlier than 11 weeks before the baby is due, I shall lose both of these rights, and that if I say now that I do not want to come back to work, I cannot change my mind later.

    I wish to make the following decisions with regard to my job:
* I give notice of resignation with effect from:
* I expect my confinement to begin during the week beginning:
* I do/do not intend to return to work after the birth of my baby. Provisional date of intended return:
* I shall give you written confirmation of my intention to return to work at least twenty-one days before I wish to exercise my right to return.

* I have made the following arrangements for the baby to be looked after while I am at work:
* I intend to cease working for the company on ... (*date*) until my return to work and apply for maternity leave for that period.
  I attach a certificate from a qualified medical practitioner/midwife of the expected date of my confinement.
  I have made an appointment at the   clinic on   for the purpose of receiving my ante-natal care and therefore request paid time off for this appointment and such time off work (with pay) as shall be deemed necessary by my doctor/midwife/health visitor for the purpose of receiving antenatal care.

*Delete as appropriate

Signed: Date:

Form 2   Employer's request for confirmation of intended return to work

XYZ Co. Ltd
To:

YOUR APPLICATION TO RETURN TO WORK

(To be sent to the employee not earlier than seven weeks after the certified expected date of confinement)

Further to your "Notice of intended absence due to pregnancy and intention to return", dated ... we are now writing to ask you to confirm, in writing, that you still intend to return to work. We remind you that you will not be entitled to return unless you confirm your intention to return, in writing, within fourteen days of receiving this request.

We further remind you of your obligation to notify us in writing at least twenty-one days in advance of your intended date of return.

Please also remember that your entitlement to return will expire, 29 weeks after the date of your confinement. But you may postpone your return for a further four weeks, if you can prove a medical reason for necessary delay.

Please use the tear-off section at the bottom of this form for your reply. We enclose S.A.E.

--- --- --- --- --- --- --- --- --- --- --- --- --- --- --- --- --- --- ---

To the Personnel Manager   Date:
XYZ Co. Ltd

Name of employee:

Address:

Telephone No.:

Previous post:

Date of leaving:

Date of birth of baby:

I hereby give notice that I intend to exercise my right of return to work in my former job on . . . *(put in the date of intended return, giving at least 21 days' notice).**

I understand that I may postpone my return for not more than 4 weeks from this date on medical grounds but that otherwise if I do not return to work on the date I have given I shall lose my entitlement to return.

Signed:

**The latest date you can exercise your right to return is 29 weeks from the beginning of the week in which your baby was born.*

Appendix 12

Help! — where to get advice

As an employer or in your capacity as a manager or executive, you may get advice on industrial relations and dismissal matters from your company lawyer (who may himself be an employee or in private practice). Or you may go to ACAS.

Suppose, though, that *you* need help in your position as an employee? Perhaps you believe that your position is rocky or that you need legal advice or representation. How, when and where is it available? And how can you keep its cost to a minimum?

Equally, decent employers and their representatives frequently refer aggrieved employees to the appropriate legal advisers. 'If you think you have a case, then by all means take advice. . . .' To whom should you send them and what help can they get?

The best way to find a lawyer is by recommendation. Once you have found a good lawyer whom you trust, stick to him. Remember that you back horses for courses and lawyers for jobs — some are specialists in one area, some in another.

If you need to choose a firm and you have a number of recommendations — or none at all — you may be happier with a medium-sized one. The very large outfits provide excellent service through specialised and expert departments but like all vast organisations tend to be rather more impersonal. On the other hand, if you go to a very small firm, then if the principal is away, there may be no one else suitable to handle your affairs.

Free legal advice may be obtained from a number of sources. For instance:

1. *Trade unions and professional associations* — if you are a member of either it may provide you with help.

2   *Citizen's Advice Bureaux* — give basic and free legal guidance through local offices throughout Britain. They may also recommend particular solicitors in your area able to deal with employment problems.

3   *Local law centres* — concentrate on immigration, housing, employment and social security problems. Service is free. Law centres handle cases in a similar way to private solicitors.

4   *Legal advice centres* — only give advice or general guidance — but will not provide you with legal representation.

5   *Legal aid and advice scheme* — names of solicitors prepared to do work under the scheme can be found at the local library on the Legal Aid Solicitors List. You may get £25 worth* of initial advice free — if you need legal representation, your disposable income and capital will be assessed before your solicitor can proceed further.

6   *Members of Parliament* — if your local MP happens to be a lawyer or to have friends in the profession, you may get some advice from or via him. But he is unlikely to intervene in a purely legal matter, especially if a case is *sub judice* — on its way to trial. But he can often 'lean' on behalf of constituents who are being badly treated.

   A polite letter from your MP may often help. Approaching your MP costs nothing — write to him at the House of Commons, London SW1. Or see him at one of his 'surgeries' — details of which are normally in the local paper or available from his local political HQ.

---

*This limit is likely to be raised to £40 by September 1980.

Appendix 13

Code of Practice on Picketing

Section A
Introduction

Section B
Picketing and the civil law

Section C
Picketing and the criminal law

Section D
Role of the police

Section E
Limiting numbers of pickets

Section F
Organisation of picketing

Section G
Essential supplies and services

Annex
Secondary action and picketing

Section A

INTRODUCTION

1   The Code is intended to provide practical guidance on picketing in trade disputes for those who may be contemplating, organising or taking part in a picket and for those who as employers or workers or members of the general public may be affected by it.

2   There is no legal "right to picket" as such but peaceful picketing has long been recognised as being lawful. However, the law imposes certain limits on how and where lawful picketing can be undertaken so as to ensure that there is proper protection for those who may be affected by picketing, including those who want to go to work normally.

3   It is a *civil* wrong, actionable in the civil courts, to persuade someone to break his contract of employment or to secure the breaking of a commercial contract. But the law exempts from this liability those acting in contemplation or furtherance of a trade dispute, including pickets, provided that they are picketing only at their own place of work.* The *criminal* law, however, applies to pickets just as it applies to everyone else: they have no exemption from the provisions of the criminal law (eg as to obstruction and public order).

4.   The Code outlines the law on picketing (although it is of course for the courts and industrial tribunals to interpret and apply the law in particular cases). Sections B and C outline the provisions of the civil and criminal law respectively and Section D describes the role of the police in enforcing the law. The Code – in Sections E, F and G – also gives guidance on good practice in the conduct of picketing.

5   The Code itself imposes no legal obligations and failure to observe it does not by itself render

---

* Subject additionally in cases of secondary action to the limitations described in paragraph 9 below.

anyone liable to proceedings. But Section 3(8) of the Employment Act 1980 provides that any provisions of the Code are to be admissible in evidence and taken into account in proceedings before any court or industrial tribunal or the Central Arbitration Committee where they consider them relevant.

Section B
PICKETING AND THE CIVIL LAW

6   Section 15 of the Trade Union and Labour Relations Act 1974 (as amended by the Employment Act 1980) provides the basic rules for lawful industrial picketing:
   (i)   it may only be undertaken in contemplation or furtherance of a trade dispute;
   (ii)   it may only be carried out by a person *attending at or near his own place of work;* a trade union official in addition to attending at or near his own place of work may also attend at or near the place of work of a member of his trade union whom he is accompanying on the picket line and whom he represents;
   (iii)   its only purpose must be peacefully obtaining or communicating information or peacefully persuading a person to work or not to work.

7   Picketing commonly involves persuading employees to break their contracts of employment by not going into work and, by disrupting the business of the employer who is being picketed, interfering with his commercial contracts with other employers. If pickets follow the rules outlined in paragraph 6 they are protected by Section 13 of the Trade Union and Labour Relations Act 1974 (as amended)* from being sued in the civil courts for these civil wrongs. These rules are explained more fully in paragraphs 10 to 19 below.

---

* Unless otherwise stated by the Trade Union and Labour Relations (Amendment) Act 1976.

8   These rules apply in the normal cases where employees picket at their own place of work in support of a dispute with their own employer. Cases may arise, however, where employees picket at their own place of work in support of a dispute between another employer and his employees, for example, where employees at one place are involved in a strike in support of a dispute elsewhere and have mounted a picket line at their own place of work in the course of that strike.

9   In such cases the picketing, in order to be protected, must further satisfy the requirements of lawful secondary action contained in Section 17 of the Employment Act 1980. (These are described in detail in the Annex.) In practice this means that these pickets will have to target their picketing precisely on the supply of goods or services between their employer and the employer in dispute. If they impose or threaten an indiscriminate blockade on their employer's premises, they will be liable to be sued in the civil courts.

In contemplation or furtherance of a trade dispute

10   Picketing is lawful only if it is carried out in contemplation or furtherance of a trade dispute. A trade dispute is defined in Section 29 of the Trade Union and Labour Relations Act 1974 (as amended). It covers all the matters which normally occasion disputes between employers and workers such as terms and conditions of employment, the allocation of work, matters of discipline, trade union recognition and membership or non-membership of a trade union.

Attendance at or near his own place of work

11   It is lawful for a person to induce a breach of contract in the course of picketing only if he pickets at or near his own place of work.

12   "At or near his own place of work" is not defined in statute. In general, however, except for those covered by paragraphs 13 and 14 below,

lawful picketing normally involves attendance at an entrance to or exit from the factory, site or office at which the picket works. It does not enable a picket to attend lawfully at an entrance to or exit from any place of work which is not his own, even if those who work there are employed by the same employer or covered by the same collective bargaining arrangements. The law does not protect anyone who pickets without permission on or inside any part of premises which are private property. Pickets who trespass may be sued in the civil courts.

13   Section 15 of the 1974 Act (as amended by the Employment Act 1980) distinguishes two specific groups of employees:

- those (eg mobile workers) who work at more than one place; and
- those for whom it is impracticable to picket at their own place of work because of its location.

It declares that it is lawful for such workers to picket those premises of their employer from which they work or from which their work is administered. In the case of lorry drivers, for example, this will usually mean in practice those premises of their employer from which their vehicles operate.

14   Special provisions also govern people who are not in employment and who have lost their jobs for reasons connected with the dispute which has occasioned the picketing. This might arise, for example, where the dismissal of a group of employees has led directly to a strike, or where in the course of a dispute an employer has terminated his employees' contracts of employment because those employees refuse to work normally. In such cases Section 15 declares that it is lawful for a worker to picket *at his former place of work*. This does not apply, however, to any workers who have subsequently found a job at another place of work. Such workers may only picket lawfully at their new place of work in the course of a dispute with their new employer or in the course of lawful secondary action.

Trade union officials

15   For the reasons described in Section F it is often helpful to the orderly organisation and conduct of picketing for a trade union official to be present on a picket line where his members are picketing. Section 15 of the 1974 Act (as amended by the Employment Act 1980) therefore makes it lawful for a trade union official to picket at any place of work provided that:

(i)   he is accompanying members of his trade union who are picketing lawfully at or near their own place of work; and

(ii)   he personally represents those members within their trade union.

If these conditions are satisfied then a trade union official has the same legal protection as other pickets who picket lawfully at or near their own place of work.

16   Under Section 15 of the 1974 Act (as amended by the Employment Act 1980) an official* – whether a lay official or an employee of the union – is regarded for this purpose as representing only those members of his union whom he has been specifically appointed or elected to represent. An official cannot, therefore, claim that he represents a group of members simply because they belong to his trade union. He must represent and be responsible for them in the normal course of his trade union duties. For example, it is lawful for an official (such as a shop steward) who represents members at a particular place of work to be present on a picket line where those members are picketing lawfully; for a branch official to be present only where members of his branch are lawfully picketing; for a regional official to be present only where members of his region are lawfully picketing; for a national official who represents a particular trade group or section within the union, to be present wherever members of that trade group or section are lawfully picketing; and for a national official such as a General Secretary or

---

* as defined in Section 30 of the Trade Union and Labour Relations Act 1974 (as amended by the Employment Protection Act 1975).

President who represents the whole union to be present wherever any members of his union are picketing lawfully.

17 Trade union officials may, of course, picket lawfully at their own place of work, whether or not their members are also picketing. However, to be entitled to picket at a place of work other than their own, they must satisfy the conditions laid down in Section 15 of the Trade Union and Labour Relations Act 1974 (as amended by the Employment Act 1980) and described in paragraphs 15 and 16 above.

Lawful purposes of picketing

18 The only purposes of picketing declared lawful by section 15 are:
- peacefully obtaining and communicating information; and
- peacefully persuading a person to work or not to work.

Pickets may, therefore, seek to explain their case to those entering or leaving the picketed premises and to ask them not to enter or leave the premises where the dispute is taking place. This may be done verbally or it may involve the distribution of leaflets or the carrying of banners or placards putting the pickets' case. Pickets have, however, no powers to require other people to stop or to compel them to listen or to do what they have asked them to do. A person who decides to cross a picket line must be allowed to do so.

19 Picketing which is accompanied by, for example, violent, threatening or obstructive behaviour goes beyond peaceful persuasion and is therefore unlawful. As explained in Section C, a picket who threatens or intimidates someone, or obstructs an entrance to a workplace, or causes a breach of the peace commits a criminal offence. But in addition pickets who commit such criminal offences, may forfeit their immunity under the civil law and may be liable to be sued for inducing or threatening to induce a breach of contract.

Seeking redress

20 An employer or an employee whose

contracts are interfered with by picketing which does not comply with the rules described in paragraphs 10–19 above has a civil law remedy. He may start an action for damages against those responsible and also ask the court to make an order* stopping the unlawful picketing.

21   An order will normally be sought against the person on whose instructions or advice the picketing is taking place, but it will usually apply not only to him but to any others acting on his behalf or on his instructions. Thus an organiser of picketing cannot avoid liability by, for example, changing the members of the picket line each day. Moreover, if a person knows that such an order has been made against someone and yet aids and abets him in breaking it, he may be in contempt of court himself and liable to be punished by the court.

Section C

PICKETING AND THE CRIMINAL LAW

22   If a picket commits a criminal offence he is just as liable to be prosecuted as any other member of the public who breaks the law. The immunity provided under the civil law does not protect him in any way.

23   The criminal law protects the right of every person to go about his lawful daily business free from interference by others. No one is under any obligation to stop when a picket asks him to do so or, if he does stop, to comply with the picket's request, for example, not to go into work. Everyone has the right, if he wishes to do so, to cross a picket line in order to go into his place of work or to deliver or collect goods. A picket may exercise peaceful persuasion, but if he goes beyond that and tries by means other than peaceful persuasion to deter another person from exercising those rights he may commit a criminal offence.

---

* An injunction in England and Wales and an interdict in Scotland

24 Among other matters it is a criminal offence for pickets (as for others)

- to use threatening or abusive language or behaviour directed against any person, whether a worker seeking to cross a picket line, an employer, an ordinary member of the public or the police;
- to use or threaten violence to a person or to his family;
- to intimidate a person by threatening words or behaviour which cause him to fear harm or damage if he fails to comply with the pickets' demands;
- to obstruct the highway or the entrance to premises or to seek physically to bar the passage of vehicles or persons by lying down in the road, linking arms across or circling in the road, or jostling or physically restraining those entering or leaving the premises;
- to be in possession of an offensive weapon;
- intentionally or recklessly to damage property;
- to engage in violent, disorderly or unruly behaviour or to take any action which is likely to lead to a breach of the peace;
- to obstruct a police officer in the execution of his duty.

25 A picket has no right under the law to require a vehicle to stop or to be stopped. The law allows him only to ask a driver to stop by words or signals. A picket may not physically obstruct a vehicle if the driver decides to drive on or, indeed, in any other circumstances. A driver must – as on all other occasions – exercise due care and attention when approaching or driving past a picket line, and may not drive in such a manner as to give rise to a reasonably foreseeable risk of injury.

Section D

ROLE OF THE POLICE

26 It is not the function of the police to take

a view of the merits of a particular trade dispute. They have a general duty to uphold the law and keep the peace, whether on the picket line or elsewhere. The law gives the police discretion to take whatever measures may reasonably be considered necessary to ensure that picketing remains peaceful and orderly.

27   The police have *no* responsibility for enforcing the *civil* law. An employer cannot require the police to help in identifying the pickets against whom he wishes to seek an order from the civil court. Nor is it the job of the police to enforce the terms of an order. Enforcement of an order on the application of a plaintiff is a matter for the court and its officers. The police may, however, decide to assist the officers of the court if they think there may be a breach of the peace.

28   As regards the *criminal* law the police have considerable discretionary powers to limit the number of pickets at any one place where they have reasonable cause to fear disorder.* The law does not impose a specific limit on the number of people who may picket at any one place; nor does this Code affect in any way the discretion of the police to limit the number of people on a particular picket line. It is for the police to decide, taking into account all the circumstances, whether the number of pickets at any particular place is likely to lead to a breach of the peace. If a picket does not leave the picket line when asked to do so by the police, he is liable to be arrested for obstruction either of the highway or of a police officer in the execution of his duty if the obstruction is such as to cause, or be likely to cause, a breach of the peace.

Section E

LIMITING NUMBERS OF PICKETS

29   The main cause of violence and disorder on the picket line is excessive numbers. Wherever

---

* In Piddington v. Bates (1960) the High Court upheld the decision of a police constable in the circumstances of that case to limit the number of pickets to two.

large numbers of people with strong feelings are involved there is a danger that the situation will get out of control and that those concerned will run the risk of arrest and prosecution.

30   This is particularly so whenever people seek by sheer weight of numbers to stop others going into work or delivering or collecting goods. In such cases, what is intended is not peaceful persuasion, but obstruction, if not intimidation. Such a situation is often described as "mass picketing". In fact, it is not picketing in its lawful sense of an attempt at peaceful persuasion and may well result in a breach of the peace or other criminal offences. Moreover, anyone seeking to demonstrate support for those in dispute should keep well away from any picket line so as not to create the risk of a breach of the peace or other criminal offence being committed on that picket line.

31   Large numbers on a picket line are also likely to give rise to fear and resentment amongst those seeking to cross that picket line even where no criminal offence is committed. They exacerbate disputes and sour relations not only between management and employees but between the pickets and their fellow employees. Accordingly pickets and their organisers should ensure that in general the number of pickets does not exceed six at any entrance to a workplace; frequently a smaller number will be appropriate.

Section F

ORGANISATION OF PICKETING

Functions of the picket organiser

32   An experienced person, preferably a trade union official who represents those picketing, should always be in charge of the picket line. He should have a letter of authority from his union which he can show to police officers or to people who want to cross the picket line. Even when he is not on the picket line himself he should be available to give the pickets advice if a problem arises.

33 An organiser of pickets should maintain close contact with the police. Advance consultation with the police is always in the best interests of all concerned. In particular the organiser and the pickets should seek directions from the police on the number of people who should be present on the picket line at any one time and on where they should stand in order to avoid obstructing the highway.

34 The other main functions of the picket organiser should be:
- to ensure that pickets understand the law and the provisions of this Code and that the picketing is conducted peacefully and lawfully;
- to be responsible for distributing badges or armbands, which authorised pickets should wear so that they are clearly identified;
- to ensure that employees from other places of work do not join the picket line and that any offers of support on the picket line from outsiders are refused;
- to remain in close contact with his own union office, and with the offices of other unions if they are involved in the picketing;
- to ensure that such special arrangements as may be necessary for essential supplies or maintenance (see paragraph 38) are understood and observed by the pickets.

Consultation with other trade unions

35 Where several unions are involved in a dispute, they should consult each other about the organisation of any picketing. It is important that they should agree how the picketing is to be carried out, how many pickets there should be from each union and who should have overall responsibility for organising them.

Right to cross picket lines

36 Everyone has the right to decide for himself whether he will cross a picket line. Disciplinary action should not be taken or threatened by a union against a member on the ground that he has crossed a picket line which it had not authorised or which was not at the member's place of work. Under Section 4 of the Employment Act 1980 exclusion or expulsion from a union in a closed shop on such grounds may be held to be unreasonable.

Section G

ESSENTIAL SUPPLIES AND SERVICES

37 Pickets should take very great care to ensure that their activities do not cause distress, hardship or inconvenience to members of the public who are not involved in the dispute. Pickets should take particular care to ensure that the movement of essential goods and supplies, the carrying out of essential maintenance of plant and equipment and the provision of services essential to the life of the community are not impeded, still less prevented. Arrangements to ensure this should be agreed in advance between the unions and employers concerned.

38 The following list of essential supplies and services is provided as an illustration but it is not intended to be comprehensive:
- supplies for the production, packaging, marketing and/or distribution of medical and pharmaceutical products;
- supplies essential to health and welfare institutions, eg hospitals, old peoples' homes;
- heating fuel for schools, residential institutions and private residential accommodation;
- other supplies for which there is a crucial need during a crisis in the interests of public health and safety (eg chlorine, lime and other agents for water purification; industrial and medical gases; sand and salt for road gritting purposes);
- supplies of goods and services necessary to the maintenance of plant and machinery;
- livestock;
- supplies for the production, packaging, marketing and/or distribution of food and animal feeding stuffs;
- the operation of essential services, such as police, fire, ambulance, medical and nursing services, air safety, coastguard and air sea rescue services and services provided by voluntary bodies (eg Red Cross and St. John's ambulances, meals on wheels, hospital car service) and mortuaries, burial and cremation services.

Annex

SECONDARY ACTION AND PICKETING

1 This Annex amplifies the description of lawful secondary action in paragraph 9 of Section B (Picketing and the Civil Law).

2 It is lawful for employees who are in dispute with their own employer to picket peacefully at their own place of work. As the Code explains such pickets have immunity from civil actions if in the course of picketing they interfere with contracts.

3 Anyone who contemplates picketing at his own place of work in furtherance of a dispute between another employer and his workers is subject to separate and more restrictive provisions. In such cases picketing must satisfy the requirements of Section 17 of the Employment Act 1980 (as set out in paragraphs 4 and 5 below).

4 If such pickets interfere only with contracts of employment then they are protected by the statutory immunity. If, however, they also interfere with commercial contracts (by means, for example, of inducing breaches of contracts of employment), their activities will be immune from civil proceedings only if:

(a) their employer is a supplier to, or customer of, the employer in dispute under a contract to provide goods or services; and

(b) the principal purpose of the picketing is directly to prevent or disrupt the supply of goods or services during the dispute between their employer and the employer in dispute; and

(c) the picketing is likely to achieve that purpose.

5 Employees of an associated employer* of the

---

* Two employers are associated if one is a company of which the other has control or both are companies of which a third has control (Section 30 (5) of the Trade Union and Labour Relations Act 1974).

employer in dispute and of suppliers and customers of that associated employer may also picket lawfully at their own place of work if:

> *(a)* their principal purpose is to disrupt the supply of goods and services between the associated employer and his supplier or customer; and
>
> *(b)* those goods or services are in substitution for goods or services which but for the dispute would have been supplied to or by the employer in dispute; and
>
> *(c)* the secondary action is likely to achieve the purpose in *(a)* above.

6   In practice this means that any picketing by employees who are not in dispute with their own employer must be very specifically targeted

- in the case of customers and suppliers of the employer in dispute, on the business being carried out during the dispute between the customer or supplier and the employer in dispute; or
- in the case of the associated employer, on work which has been transferred from the employer in dispute because of the dispute.

There is no immunity for interfering with commercial contracts by indiscriminate picketing at customers and suppliers or at associated employers of the employer in dispute.

Appendix 14

Code of Practice on the Closed Shop

Section A
Introduction

Section B
Legal rights of individuals

Section C
Closed shop agreements and arrangements
- (a) Before a closed shop is considered
- (b) Scope and content of agreements
- (c) Secret ballots
- (d) Operation of new or existing agreements
- (e) Review of closed shop agreements and arrangements

Section D
Union treatment of members and applicants

Section E
The closed shop and the freedom of the press

Annex
Definition of a union membership agreement

Section A

INTRODUCTION

1   The purpose of the Code is to provide practical guidance on questions which arise out of the formulation and operation of closed shop agreements* — that is collective agreements that have the effect of requiring employees to be, or remain, members of one or more unions.

2   The Code applies to all employment and to all closed shops whether these are written agreements or informal arrangements which have grown up between employer and union. It applies to closed shops already in existence as well as those which might be proposed for the future.

3   Changes in existing practices and written agreements required to meet the standards set by the Code should be adopted in the light of the Code's general approach — and that of the 1980 Employment Act, which it complements. This is that any agreement or practice on union membership should protect basic individual rights; should enjoy the overwhelming support of those affected; and should be flexibly and tolerantly applied.

4   Section B of the Code outlines the provisions of the law on the closed shop as it now stands, (although it is of course for the courts and industrial tribunals to interpret and apply the law in particular cases); Sections C, D and E provide practical guidance concerning the operation of closed shops and related matters.

5   The Code itself imposes no legal obligations and failure to observe it does not by itself render anyone liable to proceedings. But Section 3(8) of the Employment Act provides that any provisions of the Code are to be admissible in evidence and taken into account in proceedings before any court or industrial tribunal or the Central Arbitration Committee where they consider them relevant.

---

* Closed shop agreements in the Code are union membership agreements as defined by Section 30 of the Trade Union and Labour Relations Act 1974 as amended in 1976. That definition covers both agreements and arrangements requiring employees to become or remain union members. (See Annex for the full definition and how it is to be applied for the purpose of Section 7 of the Employment Act 1980.)

Section B

LEGAL RIGHTS OF INDIVIDUALS

6 The statutory rights of individuals in relation to the closed shop are now contained in the Employment Act 1980.

Unfair dismissal or action short of dismissal

7 It is unfair in the circumstances listed below to dismiss an employee for not complying with a requirement to be or become a member of a union. An employee so dismissed has a right of complaint against the employer to an industrial tribunal.*

8 Similarly in these circumstances an employee has a right of complaint to an industrial tribunal if, in a closed shop, action short of dismissal is taken against him by his employer in order to compel him to be or become a union member.

9 The circumstances in which these rights apply are where:

(a) the employee genuinely objects on grounds of conscience or other deeply held personal conviction to being a member of any trade union whatsoever, or of a particular trade union; or

(b) the employee belonged to the class of employee covered by the closed shop agreement before it took effect, and has not been a member of a union specified in the agreement since; or

(c) the closed shop agreement came into effect for the first time on or after 15 August 1980 and has not been approved by a secret ballot of all employees affected showing that at least 80% of those entitled to vote supported the agreement.**

---

* The normal service qualification necessary to make a complaint of unfair dismissal – one year's service – does not apply in the circumstances described in paragraph 9.
** Where a union membership agreement takes effect on or after 15 August and is subsequently approved by the necessary majority in a secret ballot, an individual may resign his membership of a union. An individual who resigns his membership of a union and whose resignation has effect by the day of the ballot will be protected as in paragraph 9(b) above.

10 A complaint of unfair dismissal, or action short of dismissal, may be made to an industrial tribunal within a period of three months* after the action complained of. If the dismissed employee's complaint is upheld the tribunal may award compensation. Alternatively or in addition it may make an order requiring the employer to reinstate or re-engage the individual. In a case of action short of dismissal the tribunal may make a declaration that the complaint is well-founded and may award compensation.

Joinder

11 An employer who faces a complaint of unfair dismissal or action short of dismissal and who claims that his action resulted from pressure put on him by a union or other person calling or threatening to take industrial action because of the complainant's non-membership of the appropriate union, may require the union or other person whom he alleges exerted that pressure to be joined,** ie brought into the proceedings, as a party to the proceedings. If the tribunal finds the dismissal unfair and the employer's claim well-founded it may make an order requiring that union or other person to pay the employer any contribution which it considers to be just and equitable up to the full amount of any compensation it has awarded.

12 Similar provisions apply where an employer who faces an unfair dismissal complaint claims that he has dismissed the employee concerned because of a requirement in a contract with another employer that employees doing certain work should be members of a union. If the employer has asked the employer who is the other party to the contract to waive that requirement in respect of the employee concerned but the other party has refused and the tribunal finds the employer's claim well-founded, it may make an order requiring the other party to indemnify the employer for the compensation awarded. If the other party claims that he refused to waive the requirement of union membership in this case because of pressure exerted on him by a union or other person calling or threatening to take

---

* A tribunal may consent to examine a complaint presented outside this period if it considers that it was not reasonably practicable for it to be presented within the period.
** sisted in Scotland.

industrial action, he may require the person he claims exercised the pressure also to be joined as a party.

Unreasonable exclusion or expulsion from a union

13   The Employment Act 1980 provides individuals with new statutory rights in relation to their unions. Any person who is employed or is seeking employment in a job where it is the practice, in accordance with a closed shop agreement, to require membership of a specified trade union or one of a number of unions, has the right not to have an application for membership of the union unreasonably refused and the right not to be unreasonably expelled from that union.

14   An individual may present a complaint to an industrial tribunal against a trade union that he has been unreasonably excluded or expelled from that union, within a period of six months* of the refusal or expulsion. Where the tribunal finds the complaint well-founded it will make a declaration that his exclusion or expulsion was unreasonable.

15   Where such a declaration has been made by the tribunal, or by the Employment Appeal Tribunal on appeal, the person who made the complaint may make an application for compensation from the union concerned for any loss he has suffered. Such an application may not be made before the end of the period of four weeks following the date of declaration or after the end of the period of six months following the date of the declaration.

16   If, following the tribunal's declaration, the complainant has been admitted or re-admitted to the union by the time he applies for compensation, the application shall be to the industrial tribunal which may award compensation to be paid by the union up to a statutory maximum.

17   If, following the declaration, the complainant has not been admitted or re-admitted to the union, the application shall be to the Employment

---

* A tribunal may consent to examine a complaint presented outside this period if it considers that it was not reasonably practicable for it to be presented within the period.

Common law rights

18   The provisions of the Act do not in any way detract from existing rights under the common law. At common law a person may complain to the courts either that action taken against him by a trade union is contrary to its own rules or that in expelling or otherwise disciplining him the union did not act in accordance with the requirements of natural justice.

Section C

CLOSED SHOP AGREEMENTS AND ARRANGEMENTS

(a)   BEFORE A CLOSED SHOP IS CONSIDERED

19   Before there is any question of negotiating on proposals for a closed shop, employers and trade unions should take account of the following factors.

Employers

20   Closed shop agreements, like other collective agreements, require the participation of both parties. Employers are under no obligation to agree to a closed shop.

21   Employers' associations may be able to advise on the implications of a closed shop agreement for industrial relations in the industry or locality generally. They should be consulted by their members at an early stage.

22   Employers should expect a union to show a very high level of membership before agreeing to consider the introduction of a closed shop.

23   Employers should acquaint themselves with the legislation (see Section B above). In particular they should be aware of the provisions of the legislation on closed shop ballots.

24   The employer should have special regard to

the interests of particular groups of staff who as members of professional associations are subject to their own code of ethics or conduct. Because the obligations imposed by such a code may be incompatible with the full range of union activities including, for example, participation in industrial action endangering health or safety, the employees concerned might well reasonably object to joining a union whose rules do not respect such obligations.

25   The employer should also carefully consider the effects of a closed shop on his future employment policy and on industrial relations.

Unions

26   Before seeking a closed shop a union should be recognised and should already have recruited voluntarily a very high proportion of the employees concerned.

27   A union should be sure that its members who would be affected themselves favour a closed shop. High union membership among those to be covered by the proposed closed shop agreement is not in itself a sufficient indication of their views on this question and indeed some employees might decide to leave their union if a closed shop was in prospect.*

28   A union should not start negotiations for a closed shop agreement which excludes other unions with a membership interest in the area concerned before the matter has been resolved with the other unions. If affiliated to the TUC, the union should have regard to the relevant TUC guidance on this matter.

29   If proposals for a new closed shop agreement become a matter of dispute between employer and union, the issue should be dealt with where appropriate in accordance with the disputes procedure to which the firm and the union are parties. The conciliation services of the Advisory, Conciliation and Arbitration Service will be available.

(b)   SCOPE AND CONTENT OF AGREEMENTS

30   Any new closed shop agreements should be

---

* See paragraph 9(b) above on the legal rights of the individual.

clearly drafted. The agreement should:

(i) indicate clearly the class of employees to be covered. This can be done by reference, for example, to the grade or location or bargaining unit concerned. An agreement should not necessarily cover all employees at a location or in a grade. Some examples of groups which might well be excluded are professional, managerial, personnel or part-time employees. All exclusions or exemptions should be clearly stated in the agreement;

(ii) make clear that existing employees who are not members when the agreement comes into effect and those who can show that they have genuine objections on grounds of conscience or other deeply-held personal conviction to union membership, will not be required to be union members;

(iii) specify a reasonable period within which employees should join the union;

(iv) make clear that, where an individual has been excluded or expelled by his union, no other action, whether by the union or the employer, will be taken against him before any appeal or complaint regarding the exclusion or expulsion has been determined;

(v) provide that an employee will not be dismissed if expelled from his union for refusal to take part in industrial action;

(vi) set out clearly how complaints or disputes arising from it are to be resolved. It should provide appropriate procedures which give the individual concerned an adequate right to be heard and enable any question about non-membership of a union to be fairly tested. Such procedures can usefully provide for independent conciliation or arbitration;

(vii) provide for periodic reviews (see paragraphs 42–46 below) and the procedure for termination.

31 It is open to the parties to agree that an alternative to union membership would be the payment to a charity by individual non-unionists of a sum equivalent to the union membership subscription. However, such an agreement cannot limit the statutory rights of individuals described in paragraph 9.

32 Where other unions have a known interest in the area to be covered by the agreement, it may specify as appropriate membership of unions other than those actually party to it. Where unions affiliated to the TUC find themselves in a dispute which has not been settled locally or within the industry they should refer the issue to the TUC.

(c) SECRET BALLOTS

33 Under the Employment Act 1980 (see paragraph 9(c) above) a secret ballot should be held of those to be included within the scope of any proposed new closed shop.

34 Employers and unions should seek agreement on the following aspects of the conduct of such a ballot:

(i) *The proposed union membership agreement*
The terms of the proposed agreement should be worked out before it is put to the test of a ballot of those to be affected by it.

(ii) *The definition of the electorate*
The electorate should be all the members of the class of employee to be covered by the proposed closed shop including those who are not union members.

(iii) *Informing the electorate*
Steps should be taken to ensure that each employee affected is aware of the intention to hold a ballot and of the terms of the agreement and any other relevant information a reasonable time before the date of the ballot. Suitable arrangements should be made to inform those members of the electorate who might otherwise not have access to such information due to sickness or absence from work or for other reasons.

(iv) *The framing of the question*
The ballot form should be clear and simple. The question asked should be limited to the single issue of whether or not membership of the union(s) party to the proposed agreement or otherwise specified in it (see paragraph 32 above) should be a requirement for employees in the class of employment it would cover.
If several questions are asked or other issues raised in the ballot this may confuse the outcome.

(v) *Method of balloting*
The ballot should be conducted in such a way

as to ensure that, so far as reasonably practicable, all those entitled to vote have an opportunity of voting and of doing so in secret. Either a workplace or a postal ballot may meet these requirements. In the case of a workplace ballot arrangements should be made for those absent from work for any reason at the date(s) of the ballot to register their vote.

(vi) *Holding the ballot*
Before the ballot can be held, decisions will be needed on such matters as the method of distributing the ballot forms and arranging for their return and counting, the time to be allowed for voting, and the persons charged with conducting the ballot. The ballot should be secret and greater confidence will result if it is independently conducted.

(vii) *Other matters*
Agreement should also be reached in advance on such matters as procedure for handling disputes about eligibility, spoilt votes and any other issues, and the safe keeping of ballot papers until an agreed destruction date.

35   The Employment Act 1980 lays down a *minimum* level of support for a new closed shop — that is 80% of those entitled to vote — if this is to furnish employers with a defence against possible future unfair dismissal claims or complaints of action short of dismissal. While 80% is the minimum of support necessary under the Employment Act to provide a defence against claims of unfair dismissal in a new closed shop, this does not prevent an employer from deciding that there should be a higher percentage in favour before he agrees to such a radical change in his employees' terms and conditions of employment. Employers should agree with the union on the figure appropriate in their case before the ballot and make this known to those entitled to vote.

36   Disagreements on arrangements for secret ballots should be dealt with, if necessary, by the normal disputes machinery to which the firm and the union are parties. The conciliation services of ACAS will be available.

(d) OPERATION OF NEW OR EXISTING AGREEMENTS

Those in scope of or parties to agreements

37 Closed shop agreements should be applied flexibly and tolerantly and with due regard to the interests of the individuals as well as unions and employers.

38 Before any potential new employee is recruited he should be informed of any requirement to become a union member and any relevant arrangements which apply to the operation of the closed shop.

39 Employers and unions should not contemplate any disciplinary action before procedures for resolving disputes and grievances which arise under the agreement are exhausted.

40 Employers and unions should take no action against an employee who has been expelled or excluded from a union until any appeal under union appeal procedures has been determined and any industrial tribunal proceedings concerning the exclusion or expulsion have been completed.

Those not in scope of or parties to agreements

41 Employers and unions who have negotiated a closed shop, and employees in scope of it, should not impose unreasonable requirements on those who are not parties or in scope of the agreement. There should be no attempt, by formal or informal means, to impose a requirement of union membership on the employees of contractors, suppliers and customers of an employer.*

(e) REVIEW OF CLOSED SHOP AGREEMENTS AND ARRANGEMENTS

42 All closed shop agreements, whether new or existing, or whether covering a firm or industry should be subject to periodic review.

43 Reviews should take place every few years,

---

* The Employment Act 1980 includes special provisions for joinder in unfair dismissal cases in this situation. See paragraph 12 above.

Code on the Closed Shop 269

and more frequently if changes of the following types occur:

- where there is evidence that the support of the employees for the closed shop has declined;
- where there has been a change in the parties to the agreement;
- where there is evidence that the agreement, or parts of it, are not working satisfactorily;
- when there is a change in the law affecting the closed shop, such as the Employment Act 1980.

44 If in the course of the review the parties decide that they wish to continue the agreement (or informal arrangements) they should consider what changes should be renegotiated to bring it into line with the requirements of paragraph 30 above. If, however, the agreement is thought no longer to serve the purpose for which it was intended or there is evidence of insufficient support among those covered by the agreement, the parties should agree to allow it to lapse. And either party, having given any period of notice specified in an agreement, can terminate it.

45 Where, as a result of this review the employer and union favour continuing the agreement or arrangement, they should ensure that it has continued support among the current employees to whom it applies. Where no secret ballot has previously been held – or where one has not been held for a long time – it would be appropriate to use one to test opinion. In that event the guidance in paragraphs 33–36 above will be relevant.

46 Closed shop agreements which require people to belong to a trade union before they can be employed (the pre-entry closed shop) may particularly infringe the freedom of individuals to work. No new agreements of this type should be contemplated and where they currently exist the need for their continuation should be carefully reviewed.

Section D

UNION TREATMENT OF MEMBERS AND APPLICANTS

47   Union decisions on exclusion or expulsion from membership in a closed shop should be taken only after all rules and procedures have been fully complied with.

Union rules and procedures

48   In handling admissions to membership, unions should adopt and apply clear and fair rules covering:

- who is qualified for membership;
- who has power to consider and decide upon applications;
- what reasons will justify rejecting an application;
- the appeals procedure open to a rejected applicant;
- the power to admit applicants where an appeal is upheld.

49   When determining whom they might accept into membership the factors to which unions may have regard include the following:

- whether the person applying for membership of a union or section of it has the appropriate qualifications for the type of work done by members of the union or section concerned;
- whether, because of the nature of the work concerned, for example acting, the number of applicants or potential applicants has long been and is likely to continue to be so great as to pose a serious threat of undermining negotiated terms and conditions of employment;
- whether the TUC's principles and procedures governing relations between unions or any findings of a TUC Dispute Committee are relevant.

50   In handling membership discipline, unions should adopt and apply clear and fair rules covering:

- the offences for which the union is entitled to take disciplinary action and the penalties applicable for each of these offences;
- the procedure for hearing and determining complaints in which offences against the rules are alleged;
- a right to appeal against the imposition of any penalty;
- the procedure for the hearing of appeals against any penalty by a higher authority comprised of persons other than those who imposed the penalty;
- the principle that a recommendation for expulsion should not be made effective so long as a member is genuinely pursuing his appeal.

51 Union procedures on exclusion or expulsion should comply with the rules of natural justice. These include giving the individual member fair notice of the complaint against him, a reasonable opportunity of being heard, a fair hearing and an impartial decision.

52 Unions affiliated to the Trades Union Congress should bear in mind its guidance on these matters, and inform individuals of the appeals procedure the TUC provides for those expelled or excluded from membership of a union.

53 In general voluntary procedures are to be preferred to legal action and all parties should be prepared to use them. However, since an individual may face considerable economic loss or adverse social consequences as a result of exclusion or expulsion from a union it would be unreasonable to expect him to defer his application to a tribunal.* Unions should therefore not consider taking action likely to lead to an individual losing his job until its own procedures have been fully used and any decision of an external body has been received. Any decision of the Independent Review Committee of the TUC should be fully taken into account.

Industrial action

54 Disciplinary action should not be taken or threatened by a union against a member on the

---

* Complaints of unreasonable exclusion or expulsion to a tribunal are subject to a time limit of six months. (See paragraph 14 above).

grounds of refusal to take part in industrial action called for by the union —

(a) because industrial action would involve a breach of a statutory duty or the criminal law, would contravene the member's professional or other code of ethics, would constitute a serious risk to public safety, health or property; or

(b) because the action was in breach of a procedure agreement; or

(c) because the action had not been affirmed in a secret ballot.

55   Furthermore, disciplinary action should not be taken or threatened by a union against a member on the ground that he has crossed a picket line which it had not authorised or which was not at the member's place of work.

Section E

THE CLOSED SHOP AND THE FREEDOM OF THE PRESS

56   The freedom of the press to collect and publish information and to publish comment and criticism is an essential part of our democratic society. All concerned have a duty to ensure that industrial relations are conducted so as not to infringe or jeopardise this principle.

57   Journalists, wherever employed, should enjoy the same rights as other employees to join trade unions and participate in their activities. However, the actions of unions must not be such as to conflict with the principle of press freedom. In particular any requirement on journalists to join a union creates the possibility of such a conflict.

58   Individual journalists may genuinely feel that membership of a trade union is incompatible with their need to be free from any serious risk of interference with their freedom to report or comment. This should be respected by employers and unions.

59   A journalist should not be disciplined by a trade union for anything he has researched or written for publication in accordance with generally accepted professional standards.

60   Editors should be free to decide whether to become or remain a member of any trade union.

61   Within the agreed basic policy of the publication:

(i)   Editors have final responsibility for the content of their publications. An editor should not be subjected to improper pressure – that is, any action or threat calculated to induce him to distort news, comment or criticism, or contrary to his judgement, to publish or to suppress or to modify news, comment or criticisms.

(ii)   The editor should be free to decide whether or not to publish any material submitted to him from any source. He should exercise this right responsibly with due regard for the interests of the readers of the publication and the employment or opportunities of employment of professional journalists.

Annex

THE DEFINITION OF A UNION MEMBERSHIP AGREEMENT

Section 30 of the Trade Union and Labour Relations Act 1974 (as amended in 1976) says

> "union membership agreement" means an agreement or arrangement which —
>
> > *(a)* is made by or on behalf of, or otherwise exists between, one or more independent trade unions and one or more employers or employers' associations; and
> > *(b)* relates to employees of an identifiable class; and
> > *(c)* has the effect in practice of requiring the employees for the time being of the class to which it relates (whether or not there is a condition to that effect in their contract of employment) to be or become a member of the union or one of the unions which is or are parties to the agreement or arrangement or of another specified independent trade union;
>
> and references in this definition to a trade union include references to a branch or section of a trade union; and a trade union is specified for the purposes of, or in relation to, a union membership agreement if it is specified in the agreement or is accepted by the parties to the agreement as being the equivalent of a union so specified."

Section 58 (3E) of the Employment Protection (Consolidation) Act 1978 (contained in Section 7 of the Employment Act 1980) has the effect that for the purpose of determining

> *(a)* whether a person has been a member of the class of employees to which the agreement relates since before it took effect,* or
> *(b)* whether or not the employee belongs to the relevant class of employees entitled to vote in a ballot on a new closed shop,**

any attempt by the parties to the agreement to define the class by reference to employees' membership or non-membership of a union, or objection to membership, shall be disregarded by tribunals.

---

* See paragraph 9(b). ** See paragraph 9(c).

IN CASE OF TRIBUNAL CLAIM – BREAK GLASS
JANNER'S EMPLOYMENT ACT 1980
toki

Index

In this index reference to 'The Act' means The Employment Act, 1980. *The letter-by-letter system has been adopted.*

General index

ACAS:
  Act's specific provisions, as to advice from 111-14
  address of, 112
  and recognition procedure, 63-6
  conciliation and arbitration discussed, 115-17
Advice, where to get, 241-2
Arbitration discussed, 115-17
Assistance, where to get, 241-2

Ballots, *see* Secret ballots
Bullock Report, 56, 69-70

Citizens Advice Bureaux, advice from, 242
Closed Shops, xiii, 80-2
  draft code of practice on, 258-75
    Act, requirements of the, 258
    agreements, 264-71
    individuals, legal right of, 261-4
    membership agreement defined, 274-5
    press, safeguards for freedom of, 273-4
    purpose and policy, 258-9
    representations over, closing date for, 259
    trade union procedures and membership, 271-3
  future for, 83-5
  membership agreements, 80-2
  new rules for, 83-5
Codes of Practice, 57-8, 128
  disciplinary practice and procedures, 221-4
  information, disclosure of, to trade unions, 227-230
  time off, 231-36
  see also Closed shop; Disputes; Picketing
Collective bargaining, 69-71
  and Code of Practice, 227-230
Compendium of Employment Law (Janner), xiv
Conciliation discussed, 115-17
Contracts, fixed term, 26-7

Damages for wrongful dismissal, 11
  strict liability, burden of proof as to, 24-5
Discipline, Code of Practice and, 223-6
Discrimination, race, religious or sex, 42-4
Dismissal:
  amendment to rules, 3
  borderline cases, 9
  'constructive', 8-9, 18-19

contract of employment, 5-6
'dismissed', meaning of, 7
examples of fair and unfair, 7-8
  rules not to apply, 20-23
  what constitutes, 10-13
finality of, 9
fixed-term contracts, 26-7
free riders, 88-90
grounds for, good reason for, 12
length of service, 12
misconduct, 14-15
moral considerations, 8
notice, must be reasonable, 11
of non-union members, 100-4
redundancies, 30-3
Redundancy Fund and, 8
remedies for unfair, 7
retirement age, bar for wrongful, 12
retrenchment of business and, 7
summary, 14-15
unfair, Act's provisions as to, 128
written reasons for, 28-9
wrongful, explained, 6, 10-13
  remedies for, 16-17
  see also Maternity rights
Disputes, principles and procedures concerning, 237

EEC Directives, 118-19
Employer's Guide to the Law on Health and Safety at Work (Janner), xiv
Employment Act, 1980:
  a martyr's charter?, xii, 120-2
  application of, to England, Scotland and Wales, 134
  'basic award' explained, 129
  closed shops, xiii, 80-5, 258-75
  collective bargaining, 69-71
  effect of an industrial relations law, 55-6
  fair wages provisions, 67-8
  future proposals for further legislation, 4
  general summary of, 127-34
  guarantee pay, 132
  indemnity from trade unions, xi-xiii
  information, disclosure of, 69-71
  management, need to understand, xi
  maternity rights, effect of, on, 3, 130-2
  Northern Ireland excluded, 134
  picketing, effect of on, xii, 91-7, 133
  political impact of, xi
  press freedom, 134
  recognition procedure under, 63-6
  secret ballots, 72-4, 127
  small undertakings, 129
  union activities, how affected by, 3
  union membership, 132-3
  work participation, 69-71
  see also Codes of Practice; Dismissal; Maternity rights; Trade unions
  (for verbatim reproduction of sections and schedules, see Index of Statutes).
Employment Appeal Tribunals, *see* Tribunals
Employment forms, 238-240
Employment Forms (Janner), xiv

Fair dismissal, *see under* Dismissal
Fair Wages Resolution (1946), 67
Fixed-term contracts, 26-7
Forms, employment, 238-240
Free riders, 88-90

Guarantee pay, 132

Help, where to get, 241-2

Industrial relations, *see under* Trade unions
Information, disclosure of, 69-71, 99, 227-230
In Place of Strife (White Paper 1969), 93

Law Centres, advice from, 242

Legal aid and advice, 242
Liability, strict, 24–5
Local Law Centres, advice from, 242

Maternity rights, 3, 34–7
  Act's provisions as to, 130–2
  forms, employment, 238–240
  notices required, 38–9
Membership Agreements, 80–7, 133

Negligence, 24
Notice, giving of reasonable, 11

Parliament, advice from members of, 242
Pay:
  fair, 67–8
  guarantee, 40–1
Picketing, xii
  Act's provisions as to, 133
  draft code of practice on, 243–57
    Act, requirements of the, 243
    civil law context, 246–50
    criminal law context, 250–2
    lines, organisation of, 253–4
    numbers of pickets, limiting, 252–3
    purpose, 244
    representations over, closing date for, 244
    secondary action, 255–7
    services and supplies, treatment of essential, 254–5
  law of, and in practice, 91–3
  new rules for, 94–6
Product liability, 25
Proof, discussed, 24–5
Public duties, time off for, 78–9

Redundancies, 30–3
Relf, Robert, 121
Rules and regulations, 57–8

Secondary picketing, 91–3, 132–3, 255–7

Secret ballots, 72–4, 127–8
Sexes, discrimination between the, 42–4
Short weeks, 40
Social Fund, EEC's, 119
Spy in the cab, 118
Steer, Bernie, 120–1
Strikes, *see* Picketing
Study, outlines of aims of this, xi–xv

Tachographs, 118
Time Off Work Code, 77–8, 231–36
Trade unions:
  collective bargaining, 69–71
  conscience and, xiii
  court actions, 108–110
  dismissal of non-members, 103–4
  election procedures, 75–9
    see also Secret ballots
  exclusion or expulsion unreasonable, from, 128
  free riding, 88–90
  how Parliament acts, 57–8
  immunities of, 98–9
  indemnity from, xi–xii, 105–7, 130
  'independent', meaning of, 59–60
  industrial relations, guide to law on, 54–6
  information, disclosure of, 69–71
  'Judge-made law', 52–3
  lawyers representing, 108–110
  legal advice from, 239
  legal aspects, outline of, 49–51
  recognition of, 61–2
    procedures establishing, 63–6
  secret ballots, 72–4
  time off work, 75–9
  unreasonable exclusion, etc., from, 100–4
  worker participation, 56, 69–71
Treaty of Rome, 118–19
Tribunals, claims for wrongful dismissal, 6, 13, 103

UMAs, 80-7, 133
Unfair dismissal, *see under*
  Dismissa¹
Union Membership Agreements,
  80-7, 133

Wages, *see* Pay
Work, time off, 75-9
Workless days, 40
Work participation, 69-71

Index of cases

Bonsor *v.* Musicians' Union, 102
British Steel Corporation *v.*
  Granada Television, 99
Express Newspapers *v.* McShane,
  94
Grunwick Processing Laboratories
  v. ACAS, 63
Heaton *v.* T & GWU, 98
Leary *v.* National Union of
  Vehicle Builders, 102
National Union of Gold, Silver
  and Allied Trades *v.* Albry
  Brothers Ltd, 62
National Union of Tailors and
  Garment Workers *v.*
  Charles Ltd, 61
Radford *v.* NATSOPA, 102
Ridge *v.* Baldwin, 102
Stevenson *v.* United Road Transport Union, 102
Taff Vale Case 1901, 110
Transport and General Workers'
  Union *v.* Andrew Dyer, 61
Western Excavating (ECC) Ltd *v.*
  Sharp, 19

Index of Statutes

Verbatim reproduction of sections
  is denoted in bold

Arbitration Act 1950, 177
Companies Act 1948, 166, 175,
  222 s. 150, 220
Companies Act 1980:
  s. 46, **220**
  s. 47, **220-2**
Conspiracy and Protection of
  Property Act 1875, 171
Education (Scotland) Act 1962:
  s.145, 192
Employer's Liability (Defective
  Equipment) Act 1969, 24,
  105
Employment Act 1980, *see also*
  Main Subject Index.
  s.1, secret ballots, payments in
    respect of, 127, **137**
  s.2, secret ballots on employer's
    premises,127-8, **138-40**
  s.3, codes of practice, authority
    to issue, 128, **140-1**
  s.4, trade union, any reasonable
    exclusion or expulsion
    from 128, **141-2**
  s.5, compensation provisions,
    128, **142-4**
  s.6, dismissal, fairness of or
    otherwise, 128, **144**
  s.7, trade union, dismissal and
    membership of, 129, **144-5**
  s.8, exclusion of rights, 129,
    145-6
  s.9, unfair dismissal, calculation
    basis of basic award for,
    129, **146-7**
  s.10, contribution in respect of
    compensation, 147-9
    indemnity aspects, 130, **148-9**
  s.11, notice to employer as to
    maternity, 130-31, **149-50**
  s.12, right to return following
    maternity, certain
    exclusions, 131-2, **150-1**
  s.13, ante-natal care, time off
    for, 132, **151-4**
  s.14, guarantee payments, 132,
    154
  s.15, trade union membership
    and activities, legislative
    amendments to, 132-3,
    154-6
  s.16, picketing, 133, **156**

Index 281

s.17, secondary action, 133–4, **157–8**
s.18, trade union membership, acts to compel, 134, **158–9**
s.19, enactments ceasing to have effect, 134, **159**
s.20, definitions, **159**
s.21, as to commencement etc., **159–60**
sch.1, consequential amendments to other Acts, **161–3**
sch. 2, repeals, 127, **164–5**
Employment Protection Act 1975, 31, 34–7, 40, 51, 54, 108, 134
  ss.1 and 2, **178**
  s. 3, **179**
  s. 4, **179–82**
  s. 5, **180**
  s. 6, **180–1**, 183, 191, 193
  s. 7, **181–2**
  ss. 11 and 12, 190, 201
  s. 15, 183, 184, 190, 201
  s. 17, **182–3**
  s. 18, 180, 182, **183–4**
  ss. 19 and 20, 183, 184
  s. 21, 181, **184–5**
  ss. 57 and 58, 180
  s. 123, 181
  sch. 1, 178, 182
Employment Protection (Consolidation) Act 1978, 4, 54
  s. 1, **186–7**
  s. 8, 218
  s. 12, **187–8**
  s. 13, **188**
  s. 14, **188–9**
  ss. 15, 16 and 17, 188
  s. 19, 203, 205
  s. 23, **189–91**
  s. 24, 191
  s. 25, **191**
  s. 27, **191–2**, 194
  s. 28, **192–3**, 194
  s. 29, **193–4**
  s. 33, **194–6**
  s. 34, **196**
  s. 35, **196–7**
  s. 36, 196
  s. 45, **197–8**
  s. 47, 199, 214
  s. 49, **198**, 218
  s. 53, 199
  s. 54, 205
  s. 55, **198–9**, 203
  s. 56, **199**
  s. 57, **200**, 203, 204, 205
  s. 58, **200–2**, 204
  s. 59, 202, 204
  s. 60, 195, 200, **202–3**, 204
  s. 61, 200, **203–4**
  s. 62, **204–5**
  s. 64, 199, **205**
  s. 67, 205, 206
  s. 68, **205–6**
  s. 69, 205, 206
  s. 71, 206, 208
  s. 72, **206**
  s. 73, 197, **206–7**, 208
  s. 74, 206, **207–8**
  s. 75, 207, **208–9**
  s. 76, 206, 207
  s. 81, **209**, 218
  s. 82, 206, **210–11**, 218
  s. 83, **211**, 217
  s. 84, 206, **211–13**, 217, 218
  s. 85, 211, **213–14**, 217
  s. 86, 211, **214**
  s. 87, **214–15**
  s. 88, 209, **215–16**
  s. 89, 215, **216–17**
  s. 90, **217–18**
  s. 92, 210
  s. 93, 211
  s. 94, **218**
  s. 101, 217
  s. 142, **219**
  s. 153, 187, 198
  sch. 2, 195
  sch. 4, 209, 218
  sch. 13, 209, 216
  sch. 14, 199, 209

Equal Pay Act 1970, 42, 113
Friendly and Industrial Provident Societies Act 1968, 59
Friendly Societies Act, 1896, 167

Health and Safety at Work etc.
　　Act 1974, 24–5, 51, 101
　　ss. 28 and 30, 59–60
House of Commons Disqualification Act 1975, 182
Industrial and Provident Societies Act 1965, 166–7
Industrial Relations Act 1971, xi, 25, 54, 174
　　s. 84, 175
Landlord and Tenant Act 1954, 10
Local Government Act 1972, 193
　　s. 192, 194
Local Government (Scotland) Act 1973, 193
　　s. 125, 194
　　s. 135, 194
National Health Service Act 1946:
　　ss. 33, 38, 40 and 41, 176
National Health Service (Scotland) Act 1947:
　　ss. 34, 39, 40 and 42, 176
Police (Scotland) Act 1967, 174
Race Discrimination Act 1975, 113
Race Relations Act 1976, 206
Redundancy Payments Act 1965, 9
Sex Discrimination Act 1975, 42–4, 113, 206
Social Security Act 1975:
　　s. 22, 197
　　sch. 4, 196
Terms and Conditions of Employment Act 1959, 67
Trade Union Act 1913, 182
Trade Union (Amalgamations etc.) Act 1964, 182
Trade Union and Labour Relations Act 1974, 54–5, 84, 94, 133–4, 182
　　s. 2, **166–7**, 170
　　s. 4, 167
　　s. 5, **167–8**
　　s. 8, 175
　　s. 13, **168–9**
　　s. 14, 166, **169–70**
　　ss. 15–17, **170**
　　s. 19, 167
　　s. 28, **170–3**
　　s. 29, 173
　　s. 30, **173–7**
Trade Union and Labour Relations (Amendment) Act 1976, 170, 172, 175